Public Private Partnerships

Public Private Partnerships

The Worldwide Revolution in Infrastructure
Provision and Project Finance

Darrin Grimsey

*Partner, Ernst & Young, Melbourne and Fellow of the Australian
Centre for Public Infrastructure at the University of Melbourne,
Australia*

Mervyn K. Lewis

*Professor of Banking and Finance, University of South Australia,
Australia and Fellow of the Academy of Social Sciences in
Australia*

Edward Elgar
Cheltenham, UK • Northampton, MA, USA

© Darrin Grimsey and Mervyn K. Lewis 2004

Published by
Edward Elgar Publishing Limited
Glensanda House
Montpellier Parade
Cheltenham
Glos GL50 1UA
UK

Edward Elgar Publishing, Inc.
William Pratt House
9 Dewey Court
Northampton
Massachusetts 01060
USA

Paperback edition 2007
Reprinted 2007

A catalogue record for this book
is available from the British Library

Library of Congress Cataloguing in Publication Data

Grimsey, Darrin, 1966–
    Public private partnerships : the worldwide revolution in infrastructure provision
    and project finance / by Darrin Grimsey, Mervyn K. Lewis.
        p. cm.
    Includes bibliographical references and index.
        1. Infrastructure (Economics) – Management. 2. Project finance –
    Management. 3. Economic development projects – Finance. 4. Public–private
    sector cooperation. 5. Risk management. I. Title: Infrastructure provision and
    project finance. II. Lewis, Mervyn. III. Title.

    HC79.C3G755 2004
    363.6'068'1–dc22   2004053037

ISBN 978 1 84064 711 2 (cased)
        978 1 84720 226 0 (paperback)

Typeset by Cambrian Typesetters, Frimley, Surrey
Printed in Great Britain by Biddles Ltd, King's Lynn, Norfolk

Contents

Figures

Tables

Foreword

This volume is the result of a collaboration that crossed a number of divides. First, one author is an engineer by training, the other is an economist. (Both, however, have finished up working in the finance area.) Second, one is a practitioner who has worked on PPPs in both the UK and Australia, while the other is an academic. Third, one is British, the other is Australian (although each has spent a lot of time in both countries). Fourth, and most significantly, an almost unbridgeable divide has been spanned, for one is the son-in-law of the other.

The collaboration is evident in a number of respects, most notably in the practitioner-based knowledge brought to bear in the book. Some of the case studies directly reflect this 'hands-on' experience. Another way it shows up is in terms of the literature covered. Broadly speaking, the literature on public private partnerships falls into three groups. First, there is an engineering dimension, reflecting practitioner material. Second, there is the academic literature which stems from economics, finance and public policy. Third, there are voluminous government and independent reports and guidance documents prepared by specialized units and audit offices. We have tried to thread our way through all three, but have found the latter source to be especially valuable, if only because one of us had a hand in the preparation of a set of guidance documents and was, for a time, seconded to the State Government of Victoria, Australia to advise the Treasurer on PPPs. That fund of knowledge and material has found its way indirectly into the analysis at a number of points.

It is also perhaps worth mentioning that 36 of the engineering and economics articles that we have referred to and used in our study have been collected together by us (Grimsey and Lewis, 2004b) in what can be seen in many ways as a companion volume to this one.

There are a number of people to thank. The worldwide network of PricewaterhouseCoopers provided information about developments in the PPP markets around the globe. Raphael Arndt helped us with one of the case studies. Ron McIver of the University of South Australia gave us valuable feedback on Chapter 6. The InterLibrary Loans section of the University of South Australia, in their usual fast and efficient manner, tracked down many difficult-to-find references. On the production side, Janelle McHale and Belinda Spagnoletti prepared some of the figures and tables, and helped with some of the text. The greatest burden, however, fell on Kay Lewis who typed

almost all of the text with remarkable speed and accuracy (although under-
standably, not always with good humour). Our publishers provided great
support.

Glossary

Accountability. The ability of the public (state and citizens) to hold to account those exercising public authority over standards and the use of public funds in delivery of services.

Annual debt service cover ratio (ADSCR). This measures the pre-finance post-tax cashflow for the previous year in relation to the amount of loan interest and principal payable for that period.

Bidder. A respondent to a request for Expressions of Interest or an invitation to submit a bid in response to a Project Brief. Typically, a bidder will be a consortium of parties with one lead party responsible for the provision of all contracted services on behalf of the consortium.

Build, own, operate (BOO). The developer is responsible for design, funding, construction, operation and maintenance of the facility during the concession period, with no provision for transfer of ownership to the government. At the end of the concession period, the original agreement may be re-negotiated, a new agreement may be negotiated, or the facility may be purchased by the government.

Build, own, operate, transfer (BOOT). An arrangement whereby a facility is designed, financed, operated and maintained by a concession company. Ownership rests with the concessionaire until the end of the concession period, at which point ownership and operating rights are transferred to the government (normally without charge).

Build, operate, transfer (BOT). An agreement where a facility is designed, financed, operated and maintained by the concessionaire for the period of the concession. Legal ownership of the facility may or may not rest with the concession company.

Bundling. This refers to the integration in a PPP of functions such as design, construction, financing, operations and maintenance of the facility, often in the form of a special purpose vehicle.

Business case. The business case provides an overview of a partnership approach, a preliminary view on how the project will be delivered, an analysis of the various impacts of the project, and an indication of the likely level of market interest, before significant resources are spent on its development.

Capital asset pricing model (CAPM). A model of the market for different financial assets which suggests that asset prices will adjust to ensure that the return on an asset precisely compensates investors for the risk of that asset when held with a perfectly diversified portfolio.

Concession. Concession-based approaches are the oldest form of public private partnership, and a variety of arrangements are based on the concept of a fixed-term concession, using various combinations of private sector resources to design, construct, finance, renovate, operate and maintain facilities. Ownership of the facility may remain with government or be transferred to the government on completion of the construction or at the end of the concession period.

Contracting out. An 'outsourcing' arrangement in which a public agency contracts with an external supplier for the provision of goods and/or services.

Conventional procurement. A conventional (traditional) public procurement contract is one in which a public agency secures the finance directly and pays the contractor as works progress.

Core activities. Those operational elements, involving making key decisions (setting service strategy) and/or the delivery of services, that may remain with government.

Default. The failure of a party to perform a contractual requirement or obligation, including failures to meet deadlines, to perform to a specified standard, to meet a loan repayment or to meet its obligations in relation to a materialized risk.

Design, build, finance (DBF). A form of PPP that involves the procurement of an asset using private finance, without private sector operation and provision of the associated services.

Design, build, finance and operate (DBFO). The main form of contract in the PFI whereby the service provider is responsible for the design, construction, financing and operation of an asset. Operation refers to the provision of some or all of the services related to the asset's use.

Design, build, operate (DBO). A form of PPP, in which the public sector provides finance for a capital investment project but the providers of the projects retain the design and construction, and deliver some or all of the operational elements.

Discount rate. The rate used to calculate the present value of future cash flows, usually determined on the basis of the cost of capital used to fund the investment from which the cash flow is expected.

Discounted cash flow. A general term for analysis which discounts a stream of future cash flows in order to calculate a net present value.

Expected value. The weighted average of possible values of a variable, where the weights are the probabilities of cost estimates.

Internal rate of return (IRR). That discount rate which would give a project a present value of zero.

Joint venture (JV). A distinct legal form of PPP arrangement involving public and private bodies assuming some form of equity stake in a PPP.

Key performance indicators (KPIs). Measures developed under a performance management regime to indicate how well specified performance targets are being realized.

Loan life cover ratio (LLCR). This is a measure at a given date of the NPV of the project pre-finance post-tax cashflows from that date until retirement of the senior loans relative to the loan outstanding on that particular date.

National Audit Office (NAO). The UK's National Audit Office scrutinizes public spending on behalf of Parliament. Totally independent, it audits the accounts of all government departments and agencies as well as a wide range of other public bodies, and reports to Parliament on the economy, efficiency and effectiveness with which government bodies have used public money.

National Health Service (NHS). The UK's National Health Service established in 1948 to provide medical services largely financed by general taxation.

NHS Trust. The organizational structure adopted in the UK to manage individual hospitals.

Net present value (NPV). The discounted value of a stream of either future costs or benefits, with NPV used to describe the difference between the present value of a stream of costs and a stream of benefits.

Office of Government Commerce (OGC). Established in April 2000, the OGC works with UK government departments to achieve best value for money in their commercial activities. Its responsibilities include central government procurement policy and the development of procurement partnerships with the private sector.

Optimism bias. The demonstrated systematic tendency for appraisers to be over-optimistic about key project parameters, including capital costs, operating costs, works duration and benefits delivery.

Output specification. The output specification sets out the range of services that government is seeking to procure and the performance levels required for each of those services.

Partnerships UK. Partnerships UK is the successor to the Treasury Taskforce. It works with the government in the development of PPP policy and contract standardization, helps with project evaluation and implementation, and supports PPPs in difficulty. It also works closely with 4Ps (a Local Government agency set up to help Local Authorities develop and deliver PPPs) in local authority projects.

Partnerships Victoria. Partnerships Victoria is a policy in the State of Victoria, Australia giving effect to a commitment to optimize the level of infrastructure spending through responsible use of the resources of both the public and private sectors. Value for money and the public interest are keynotes of the policy.

Private Finance Initiative (PFI). A UK programme encompassing arrangements whereby a consortium of private sector partners come together to provide an asset-based public service under contract to a public body.

Private party. The private sector entity with which the government contracts in a PPP. Traditionally the private party has been a special purpose vehicle created specifically for the purposes of the project.

Probity. Uprightness, honesty, proper and ethical conduct and propriety in dealings. Used by government to mean 'good process'.

Procurement. The component of the commissioning process that deals specifically with purchasing a service from a provider. This occurs once decisions have been taken over what outcomes or outputs are to be secured and involves the negotiation of contracts.

Project Brief. The Project Brief details government's objectives, service delivery requirements, policy and commercial matters, material background information and the processes for lodging and evaluating submissions.

Project finance. A way of financing capital projects that depends for its security on the expected cash flow of the project itself rather than guarantees from the borrower or third parties.

Project life cover ratio (PLCR). This is a measure at a given date of the NPV of the projected pre-finance post-tax cashflows from that date until the end of the project relative to the loan outstanding on that particular date.

Public interest test. An assessment of the impact of the project on effectiveness, accountability and transparency, affected individuals and communities, equity, consumer rights, public access, security and privacy.

Public private partnership (PPP). A risk-sharing relationship based on a shared aspiration between the public sector and one or more partners from the private and/or voluntary sectors to deliver a publicly agreed outcome and/or public service.

Public sector. Refers to public agencies and enterprises that are state financed, owned and controlled.

Public sector comparator (PSC). A hypothetical constructed benchmark to assess the value-for-money of conventionally financed procurement in comparison with a privately financed scheme for delivering a publicly funded service.

Risk. A situation involves risk if the randomness facing an economic entity can be expressed in terms of specific numerical probabilities (objective or subjective).

Risk allocation. The allocation of responsibility for dealing with the consequences of each risk to one of the parties to the contract, or agreeing to deal with the risk through a specified mechanism which may involve sharing the risk.

Sensitivity analysis. Analysis of the effects on an appraisal of varying the projected values of important variables.

Shadow toll. A payment for road usage made by the government, rather than road users, based on vehicles using a kilometre of the project road, in accordance with a tolling structure. Now supplemented or replaced in the UK by availability and performance measures.

Special purpose vehicle (SPV). An organization that can be established as a distinct legal entity to bring together the companies involved in a PPP in order to manage the project and share the risks and rewards.

Systematic risk. Risk that is correlated with movements in the economic cycle and therefore cannot be diversified away.

Uncertainty. There is uncertainty where an economic entity cannot assign actual probabilities to the alternative possible occurrences.

Unitary payment. Payment for services delivered by an SPV under a PFI- or PPP-type arrangement.

Value-for-money. The optimum combination of whole-of-life cycle costs, risks, completion time and quality in order to meet public requirements.

Whole-of-life cycle. Costs associated with the ongoing repair and maintenance of a facility for the term of a facility's economic life.

1. The nature of partnerships

INTRODUCTION

In 1998, the British Inland Revenue service completed the process of relocating 2000 staff from 11 buildings in the Manchester area to a single site, and moved into new fully serviced offices in the city centre of Manchester. The building is ventilated (i.e. no air conditioning), has lighting that switches itself off when people leave, contains gas-fired heating with individual thermostatically controlled radiators, double glazing, building materials made from sustainable sources and building management systems that monitor the use of resources. It was also constructed under the UK government's Private Finance Initiative (PFI) as a result of a 20-year design-build-finance-operate (DBFO) contract awarded to a private sector body as a partnership arrangement.[1]

The idea of designing a building to be environmentally efficient is not new. What is new is the realization that partnership arrangements such as the PFI are particularly good vehicles for bringing about this objective because they emphasize value for money over the life of the building, not just the cheapest cost, and encourage a focus on whole-of-life cycle costing implications. Rather than there being separate design, construction, financing, operations and maintenance arrangements as occurs with traditional public procurement, these functions are combined under one contractor. This integration ('bundling') within a long-term partnership framework provides financial motivation for the project company to think beyond the design stage and build in energy-reducing and waste-minimizing features that may cost more initially but result later in lower operating and running costs, and so deliver cost effectiveness over time.

Such 'green' public private partnerships are a recent manifestation of the public private partnership (PPP)[2] agenda that has revolutionized the provision of public infrastructure-based services over the last decade (although we will show that private sector involvement in infrastructure provision is no new thing). Another new development is that of social housing schemes, which involve partnerships between public sector bodies, private entities and non-profit organizations. More familiar examples of PPPs come from toll roads, light rail systems, bridges, tunnels, waste water treatment facilities, hospitals, courts, museums, schools and private prisons.

This last example is a reminder that not all PPPs have been a success. For example, the Victorian Government in Australia took back its Deer Park women's prison following poor performance of the private operator. By contrast, some other privately operated prisons like that in Bridgend, South Wales have been a considerable success. Nevertheless, despite the fact that there are over 180 private correctional facilities operating internationally, they remain one of the most widely discussed and controversial forms of partnership arrangement.[3] The same can be said of some other applications, such as PPPs in the British National Health Service (NHS). One of the major objectives of this volume is to analyse what makes for a successful partnership and develop a framework that will assist in bringing this result about. But, first, we need to be clear what is meant by a PPP.

THE NATURE OF A PPP

Table 1.1 surveys the recent experience with PPPs in Europe. The projects covered include wastewater treatment works, public use motorways, toll roads, power plants, telecommunications infrastructure, tunnels, school buildings, airport facilities, toll bridges, government offices, prisons, light rail systems, railways, parking stations, subways, museum buildings, harbours, pipelines, road upgrading and maintenance, health services and waste management.

These examples probably make clear what we have in mind by a PPP. Nevertheless, since any relationship involving some combination of the private, voluntary and public sectors is prone to be labelled a 'partnership', it may be useful to define what is a partnership in this context. For our purpose, PPPs can be defined as arrangements whereby private parties participate in, or provide support for, the provision of infrastructure, and a PPP project results in a contract for a private entity to deliver public infrastructure-based services.

The mechanics of the arrangements can take many forms and may incorporate some or all of the following features (Pierson and McBride, 1996):

- the public sector entity transfers land, property or facilities controlled by it to the private sector entity (with or without payment in return) usually for the term of the arrangement;
- the private sector entity builds, extends or renovates a facility;
- the public sector entity specifies the operating services of the facility;
- services are provided by the private sector entity using the facility for a defined period of time (usually with restrictions on operations standards and pricing); and
- the private sector entity agrees to transfer the facility to the public sector (with or without payment) at the end of the arrangement.

Table 1.1   Public private partnerships in Europe

Country	Experience with PPPs
Bulgaria	The Sofia Water and Wastewater Concession Project is the major municipal infrastructure concession in Bulgaria and one of the first water concessions to be financed on a limited recourse basis in Eastern Europe via a special purpose vehicle. International Water is the majority shareholder and private sector operator. This 15-year project reached financial close in October 2000.
Croatia	The government's policy is favourable to the use of BOT schemes for transport (Istrian toll road), energy (Lukovo Sugarje power project) and water (wastewater treatment plant for Zagreb). New legislation is designed to facilitate concessions.
Czech Republic	Joint ventures have taken place between public institutions and private entities in the energy sector, telecommunications and water and wastewater treatment, mainly as a result of privatization. Toll roads have been rejected with two BOT projects not realized. A task force was created in 2000 to develop PPPs, in order to complete the road network.
Finland	The Helsinki–Lahti motorway, conceived in 1995 and begun in 1997, is the first and largest PPP in Finland, involving equity from the UK, Sweden and local entities. A pilot PPP project was to build a sixth-form college specializing in IT.
France	France has a long-established tradition of public–private cooperation (especially in sectors such as water) using the concession structure. PPPs are not permitted in the social infrastructure area. The tunnel Prado–Carrenage in Marseille was toll-financed. Three major road projects have been launched under PPPs since 2000 (Millau Viaduct, A19 and A28) and cross border projects such as the Perpignon–Figueras high speed link and the Lyon–Turin high speed link have involved recourse to PPPs.
Germany	Germany has no formal PPP programme, although it has in the past involved private sector contractors in road projects (e.g. the Warnow tunnel), some of which did involve risk transfer to the private sector under a

Table 1.1   continued

Country	Experience with PPPs
	concession framework. A BOT law has been passed, although specific taxation issues complicate the procurement process.
Greece	Those projects completed include Spata Airport and the Athens ring road. The government launched a PPP programme in 2000, as well as setting up a central PPP Unit. Nevertheless, some legal issues remain to be resolved.
Hungary	Some transport projects have been developed by PPPs (e.g. M5 BOT project), but others have not been realized or transferred to the National Highway Agency (e.g. M1). The *Szechenyi* Plan seeks to expand PPPs, but there is no government authority specially assigned to deal with PPPs.
Ireland	In 1999, a pilot PPP road programme including three roads and a light rail system was initiated. The M4 PPP Toll Motorway Project, agreements for which were signed in March 2003, is part of a group of 11 projects to be finalized over the 2004–2007 period. Toll bridges, government offices and prisons have been designed, built, financed and operated by the private sector. There is a strong commitment to a formal PPP programme. A clear legislative framework is in place, a dedicated PPP unit has been set up and central committees facilitate PPPs.
Italy	The Merloni Bill in 1994 and 1998 set the framework for using private sector contractors and later a special PPP taskforce, UFP, was created and its powers reinforced in 2001. There have been projects in the water and power sectors in particular which involve the private sector, on a concession-style basis. However, new PPP projects are discouraged, perhaps due to the administrative complexity associated with the civil code.
Netherlands	*Kennis-centrum PPPs* was set up in 1999 and a major pilot project (the high speed rail) was started. Projects underway since then include road, railway, harbours and

Country	Experience with PPPs
	water projects, i.e. *Zuiderzeelijn/Randstad Circle Line* (magnetic levitation technique), 2nd *Maasvlakte* (enlargement harbour Rotterdam) and the *Delfland* wastewater treatment project.
Poland	The A4 Katowice–Krakow is the first toll highway in Poland. The government is anxious to facilitate PPPs and two bridges identified as PPP projects. The legal, accounting and taxation systems hinder the implementation of PPPs.
Portugal	Under the *SCUT* programme, three toll roads have reached financial close and one syndicated. Around a dozen other road projects are being implemented, six of which involve shadow tolls. Motorways, railways, airports, water, parking, subways, local transportation and museums involving PPPs are under consideration, although union resistance and constraints on issuing project bonds hinder implementation.
Romania	Concession-based financing techniques are favoured. In 2000, the French utility company Vivendi was awarded a 25-year concession to provide water and pipeline rehabilitation services to Bucharest, in the form of a new treatment system and modernizing the existing water system. Commercialization of road maintenance activities is being investigated, and PPPs are being promoted for infrastructure development as part of Romania's preparations for accession to the EU.
Slovenia	An EBRD-assisted project is investigating private investment in the maintenance of the national road network. Development of a private finance concession-based highway maintenance scheme is a planned pilot for PPPs.
Spain	The government has a road programme using the shadow toll structure. Private sector involvement is sought in three new rail lines and other initiatives. PPP projects are also planned in the health and waste management sector. However, the legal framework is not supportive, and there is no law to cover concessions.

Table 1.1   continued

Country	Experience with PPPs
United Kingdom	The British government launched its PPP development policy in 1992 under the 'Private Finance Initiative'. Since then, the technique has been applied systematically to virtually every area of significant government capital spending in the UK. Partnerships UK was established in 2000 to promote PPP/PFI concepts. It also works on local authority projects.

Sources: D & P (2001), American Chamber of Commerce (2002), United Nations (2002), von Hirschhausen (2002), European Investment Bank (2004).

However, there are no hard and fast rules, as we shall see.

It may also be worth saying what a PPP is not. A common misconception about PPP projects is that they are principally about private sector financing of public infrastructure. This is not strictly correct. Financing is only one element. The essence of a PPP is that the public sector does not buy an asset; it is purchasing a stream of services under specified terms and conditions. This feature is the key to the viability (or not) of the transaction since it provides the right economic incentives.

Our central proposition is that the PPP is a strongly incentive-compatible contracting arrangement. The cost effectiveness of a PPP relative to traditional procurement (and we will provide evidence on this point in later chapters) is a result of upfront engineering of the design solution and the financing structure combined with downstream management of project delivery and the revenue stream. All of this is a consequence of the incentives built in to the services payment mechanism and the risk transfer in the PPP model.

The PPP model that closely approximates what we have in mind is that developed in the UK, Australia, Canada and South Africa (Allen, 2001; Commission on Public Private Partnerships, 2001; Partnerships Victoria, 2001), the basic elements of which are as follows:

- The public sector defines the services it requires over a long-term period (typically 15–30 years) by reference to an output specification and closely specified performance criteria, without being too prescriptive about the means of delivery.
- No payments are made until the asset is delivered and working, and subsequent payments are subject to reduction if service performance standards are not met.

- Design risk, in terms of the decision on the type of assets needed to deliver the services to the required standard, is left to the private sector entity and the assets are effectively owned and operated by the private sector.
- The public sector provides no funding during the construction phase, and the risk of cost overruns, delays, etc. rests with the private sector.
- The public sector has to devolve control to the private sector over the assets and resources needed to deliver the service to such an extent that the private sector bears the risks and receives the rewards of effective ownership.

Others would suggest that this emphasis on asset-based infrastructure is too narrowly based, and would define PPPs much more broadly. Table 1.2 gives some details of PPPs in the United States. PPPs have covered transport (e.g. toll roads) and private prisons and detention facilities, but have also dealt with education policy priority setting, welfare provision, health and medical services, and a range of community activities and services from schooling to urban regeneration and environmental policy. This broader framework encompasses both 'policy-level' partnerships and 'project-level' partnerships. Policy-level partnerships coordinate public sector and private sector inputs into decision-making about the design and formulation of policy initiatives. In the case of transportation, for example, policy-level partnerships evaluate the various models of transport, general rules for operation, investment and the resolution of disputes. Project-level partnerships, by contrast, focus on specific sites or situations, such as the development of a new urban transit terminal, with the aim of drawing private capital and management into the project. Policy-level and project-level partnerships have always gone hand-in-hand in the United States, but this has not always been the case elsewhere. American writers, such as Linder (1999), define PPPs as 'a rubric for describing cooperative ventures between the state and private business' (p. 35).

The reconciliation between these two views of PPPs turns in part also on how we define 'infrastructure'. Many of the apparent differences disappear once we allow for the variety of forms that infrastructure can take, in particular the distinction between 'economic' and 'social', and 'hard' and 'soft'. Infrastructure is examined in Chapter 2. For the present we may note that when PPPs began in the UK (and Australia), they were largely applied to 'economic' areas like motorways, bridges, tunnels, and so on. Then they were used for government office accommodation, hospitals, schools, prisons, and so on. Now social housing, urban regeneration, and waste management are being targeted (HM Treasury, 2003b). Experiments are underway with new integrated ways of delivering health care. There are partnerships for heritage sites, estates and facilities management, and a 'green' agenda has been overlaid, as we saw earlier. This evolution shows the adaptability of the concept.

Table 1.2   Public private partnerships in the United States

Field	Experience with PPPs
Transport	Policy-level partnerships develop a set of rules for investment and operation in various transport modes such as urban transit, railroads, highways, and inland waterways. Examples are the Federal highway assistance program, urban mass transit assistance program and initiatives under the Intermodel Surface Transportation Act (ISTEA). Project-level partnerships focus on specific projects or situations. For example, in 1988–89, California and Virginia initiated toll-financed concessions for the design, finance, development, building and operation of public-use toll roads, with the states' role limited to right-of-way, and regulation of toll rates and/or profits. Examples are the Dulles Toll Road Extension in Virginia under a BOO concession, and State Routes 91 and 125 in California under BTO schemes.
Technology	Technology partnerships generally take two forms. The first involves government funding of private industrial R & D. Examples are the Small Business Innovation Research Program (SBIR) begun in 1982 and expanded in 1992, the Advanced Technology Program (ATP) to commercialize new scientific discoveries implemented in 1990, and Sematech involving a semiconductor industry consortium founded in 1987, but changed to the second type of partnership in 1997. In the second type of technology partnership, there is direct collaboration between government and industry scientists. Examples are the Cooperative Research and Development Agreements (CRADAs) involving formal agreements between national laboratories and private firms in the 1990s, the Partnership for a New Generation of Vehicles (PNGV) begun in 1993 to develop an environmentally friendly car, and the Manufacturing Extension Partnership (MEP) offices to establish partnerships between businesses and government agencies.

Field	Experience with PPPs
Water	A number of cities have formed partnerships to operate and maintain wastewater treatment systems. Examples are the Milwaukee Metropolitan Sewerage District involving a 10-year operations and maintenance (O & M) contract; City of Indianapolis, Wastewater Treatment Plants and Collection System, involving a 10-year O & M contract; Buffalo Water Treatment System with a 5-year O & M contract as well as customer billing and collection services.
Prisons	As of September 2001, there were 151 private correctional facilities in 32 states with the capacity to house 119, 023 prisoners or detainees. Some of the private prisons have emerged as a result of contracts with the state in which they are located. More usually, a private corporation builds a facility in a particular state and then negotiates contracts either with that state or with another state, county or federal body to house or reserve places for prisoners from that jurisdiction, with payment on a per diem basis.
Health	In Medicare and Medicaid, the government has always relied on private firms to actually deliver medical care, although the form of the partnership has changed with the advent of managed care. Organizations providing managed care (both commercial health maintenance organizations and provider-sponsored health plans) compete for Medicaid business. Government offers contracts to the best health plans. In turn, the health plans hire and regulate medical providers. Beneficiaries choose between several competing plans. Each client has a primary care provider to both deliver care and act as gatekeeper to the rest of the health care system. Regulation occurs via contracts with the health plans, which set the terms, and conditions under which health plans can participate.
Welfare	A variety of welfare programmes are provided with the involvement of private sector entities. For example, 'small cards' are used for the electronic benefits transfer (EBT) of food stamps benefits,

Table 1.2   continued

Field	Experience with PPPs
	maternal and child health services, and other government assistance. Private contractors are used to develop and implement these electronic systems. Many non-profit organizations are used to deliver child welfare services including investigation, foster homes, and therapeutic services. Most employment and training services are contracted to vocational schools and community colleges (e.g. Jobs Corps). Since the Personal Responsibility and Work Opportunity Reconciliation Act (PRWORA) of 1996, state or local welfare agencies can contract out their entire welfare programme, including intake, eligibility, and service provision. This has allowed companies (e.g. EDS, IBM) to enter the welfare market.
Urban regeneration	Urban redevelopment partnerships were established in the 1950s between local government and business lenders, and operated at a policy level to plan for downtown redevelopment. At a project level, private sector developers and local government were involved in joint ventures for the construction of government offices, housing and sporting facilities. Since the 1980s, development corporations have worked with individual property developers on specific projects. Examples are Battery Park City, the redevelopment of Times Square, Boston Housing Partnership, Cleveland Tomorrow, Rebuild LA, Dev Co New Jersey.

TYPES OF PPPS

PPPs can take many different forms, the most usual being BOT/BOO arrangements, joint ventures (JV), leasing, contracting out or management contracts, and various forms of public–private cooperation. Some examples are:

- *BOT (Build Operate Transfer)*. These are contracts where the private sector takes primary responsibility for funding (financing), designing, building and operating the project. Control and formal ownership of the project is then transferred back to the public sector. A classic example of a BOT arrangement is the third Dartford Crossing of the River Thames linking two stretches of the M25 motorway circling London, operated (with virtually guaranteed toll income) by the vehicle company for up to 20 years, with the facility reverting to the UK government (probably well ahead of schedule). In Australia, projects such as the Sydney Harbour Tunnel and the City Link (linked motorways) project in Melbourne are also BOT arrangements.

- *BOO (Build Own Operate)*. In these arrangements, the control and the ownership of the projects remain in private hands. With a BOO project, the private sector entity finances, builds, owns and operates an infrastructure facility effectively in perpetuity. An example comes from the water treatment plants serving parts of South Australia. These facilities, financed, designed, built and operated by a private sector firm, process raw water, provided by the public sector entity, into filtered water which is then returned to the public sector utility for delivery to consumers.
- *Leasing*. Here part of the risk is transferred to the private sector. In France, most PPPs are performed under *concession* contracts (essentially BOT-type contracts) or *affermage* (lease) contracts (which cover design and building, or operation, but do not embrace project financing). Several of the ex-French colonies in Africa (Francophone African countries) have adopted the *affermage* system in which a municipality has a water facility constructed and then contracts with a private firm to operate and maintain the facility (Rondinelli, 2002).
- *Joint ventures* (JV) take place when the private and public sectors jointly finance, own and operate a facility. As examples there are urban regeneration schemes in the United States in which local government authorities purchase and clear blighted areas for private developers or themselves to invest in new construction, such as a new city hall or a government office as part of downtown redevelopments (Beauregard, 1998). A more controversial example is the Japanese 'third sector' approach introduced in the mid-1980s, bringing together the public (the 'first sector') and the private sector (the 'second sector') to form project-based companies. In 1995, there were 7580 such entities, where the capital share contributed by the local government exceeded 25 per cent, engaged in urban developments, leisure/resort developments, transport, telecommunications and other regional activities. Many have faced severe financial difficulties with the burst of the 'bubble economy' (Kagami, 2002).
- *Operations or management contracts*. In these, the private sector is only partially involved, for example it provides a service or manages the operation. Service or management contracts allow the private sector to provide infrastructure-related services for specified periods of time.

Examples are the management of state-owned agro-businesses in Senegal, Cote d'Ivoire and Cameroon, water and electricity in Guinea-Bissau, and mining operations in Latin America and Africa (Rondinelli, 2002). Of six PPPs in Canada involving wastewater treatment facilities, two are DBFO (Design, Build, Finance and Operate) contracts, one is an OM & M (Operate, Maintain and Manage) contract and the other three are O & M (Operate and Maintain) contracts. The O & M contracts range from 5 to 10 years in length.

- *Cooperative arrangements* that occur between governments and private entities are more informal than many of the equity partnerships and concession-type franchise arrangements for social housing projects. In many localities, fiscal incentives or guarantees are given to attract private capital into low-cost housing associations for social housing projects. In the United States, technology partnerships embrace different degrees of public–private cooperation. In Korea and many other countries, independent power producers and self-generators (in Australia they include households with solar panels) can sell power into the national grid. In Costa Rica, the government creates and maintains national parks, while private organizations develop the eco-tourist programmes and finance some of the tourist promotion campaigns (Rondinelli, 2002).

These examples constitute some of the more common types of partnership. In addition, in terms of the 'alphabet soup' of acronyms, there are also BLT (Build, Lease, Transfer), BLTM (Build, Lease, Transfer, Maintain), BTO (Build, Transfer, Operate), BOOR (Build, Own, Operate, Remove), BOOT (Build, Own, Operate, Transfer), LROT (Lease, Renovate, Operate, Transfer), DBFO (Design, Build, Finance, Operate), DCMF (Design, Construct, Manage, Finance) and DBFOM (Design, Build, Finance, Operate, Manage). Policy-level partnerships operate at another level again.

GENERAL CHARACTERISTICS OF PPPS

Quite clearly, then, there are many different types of PPPs and the models applied differ from country to country. In fact, the PPP concept is evolving in different ways in each country in which the arrangements are being implemented. Some countries have a central body dealing with PPPs (e.g. the Netherlands), some do so for particular applications (e.g. the UK), while others leave it to individual states or municipalities (Australia, United States). Chile is experimenting with a different system for auctioning franchises (the least-present-value-of-revenue or LPVR system). France has an administrative framework governing PPP-type private concessions (*delegation de service public*) different from than that which operates under English law.

Given this diversity, what are the common threads? What are the distinguishing features of a PPP? In short, what are the characteristics which might entitle us to say that any arrangement is part of the PPP family? The following would seem to be the most important elements.

- *Participants*. A PPP fairly obviously involves two (or more) parties, and at least one of them has to be a public body. Each, however, needs to be a principal, capable of negotiating and contracting on its own behalf. All parties must make an organizational commitment to the partnership.
- *Relationship*. Partnerships need to be enduring and relational. Governments buy goods and services, they give grants, and they impose fines and taxes. None of these transactions implies any real continuity of behaviour. Even if a public sector body were to use the same supplier year after year, this pattern would not be regarded as a partnership. A government department ordering sandwiches each day for lunch from the same catering firm does not create a partnership. (Kelly, 2000, p. 10).
- *Resourcing*. Each of the participants must bring something of value to the partnership. PPPs seek to draw on the best available skills, knowledge and resources, whether they are in the public or the private sector, and deliver value for money in the provision of public infrastructure services. For this to happen, each partner must transfer resources (money, property, authority, reputation) to the arrangement.
- *Sharing*. PPPs involve a sharing of responsibility and risk for outcomes (whether financial, economic, environmental or social) in a collaborative framework. This mutual responsibility contrasts with relationships between the public and private sectors in which the public body retains control over policy decisions after getting the advice of private sector entities. It also contrasts with relations between the public and private sectors that are primarily contractual in nature and involve essentially command relationships. In these cases, the private sector bodies are not partners in any real sense. There has to be a mutual interest and unified commitment.
- *Continuity*. Underpinning the partnership will be a framework contract, which sets out the 'rules of the game' and provides the partners with some certainty. Its existence enables the parties involved to make decisions without having to start from scratch each time and develop from first principles the rules that govern these interactions. While the PPP contract provides the basic architecture of the arrangement, it is necessarily 'incomplete' and does not (and cannot) specify all

components and allow for all outcomes. There must be shared values, a common understanding of priorities and policy objectives, and a good measure of trust.

SPECIFIC CHARACTERISTICS

Having identified some of the general distinguishing features of what we mean by a partnership, we now need to be more explicit about what kinds of partnerships we have in mind and their characteristics. These are:

- *Type*. While some partnerships are created for the purpose of policy formulation, priority setting and coordinating organizations from the various sectors (e.g. crime prevention strategies, educational action), our primary (but not exclusive) concern is with asset-based services and long-term service provision contracts related to social and economic infrastructure. There are important differences between partnerships that are predominantly economic in their orientation as opposed to those concerned with welfare, educational and other policies, in part because of the need to marshall financial resources (Peters, 1998).
- *Focus on services*. The emphasis is on services received by government, not government procurement of economic or social infrastructure. Government pays for services provided by the private party, which are delivered through privately owned or rented infrastructure as part of the service package.
- *Whole-of-life cycle costing*. With a PPP contract there is the opportunity for a complete integration – under one party – of upfront design and construction costs with ongoing service delivery, operational, maintenance and refurbishment costs.
- *Innovation*. A PPP approach focuses on output specifications, and provides enhanced opportunities and incentives for bidders to fashion innovative solutions to meet those requirements.
- *Risk allocation*. Risk retained by government in owning and operating infrastructure typically carries substantial, often unvalued, cost. Transferring some of the risk to a private party, which can manage it at less cost, can substantially lower the overall cost to government.

QUESTIONS ABOUT PPPS

The growth of PPPs in so many countries raises a number of issues which form the basis of this volume. The first and most obvious question is: from where did PPPs and the idea of private financing and operation of infrastructure come? At one level, the answer is very simple. The idea is not a new one. Toll roads and toll bridges have been around since antiquity. In Britain and the United States in the eighteenth and nineteenth centuries, over 2500 companies were chartered and incorporated to develop private turnpikes. They in turn came under competitive pressures from the next private infrastructure development – the railways. PPP-type arrangements have been used in France to privately finance public infrastructure since the seventeenth century, when the French concession model was pioneered. In the second half of the nineteenth century, France extensively used concessions to finance its infrastructure development. Railways, water, electricity and tramways were all designed, constructed, financed and operated by private enterprises and banks. Thus the question really is one of what has caused a regrowth of PPPs in recent decades, which we trace to changing attitudes to public services delivery, dissatisfaction with conventional procurement and construction methods, and the development of the project financing model.

However, changing attitudes to infrastructure have also played a part, prompting a second question: what is the role of the private sector in infrastructure? The answer is almost axiomatic in the United States where PPPs must be viewed against the historical background of 'privatism' that has dominated thinking in the US since the early nineteenth century (Beauregard, 1998). Privatism is the presumption that economic activity should be left to the market; 'a belief that private institutions are intrinsically superior to public institutions for the delivery of goods and services' and 'a confidence that market efficiency is the appropriate criterion of social performance in virtually all spheres of community activity' (Barnekov *et al.*, 1989).

In Europe, no such equivalent tradition exists. In the United States, the role of government has been described as one of creating coalitions among diverse interests in a fragmented and pluralist system. In Europe, government is seen as a political and economic actor in its own right, with a clearly defined role as custodian of the broad 'public interest' that is 'more than a mere aggregation of private interests and compromises among them' (Keating, 1998, p. 166). There are also differences in government structure. In the United States, the various state governments have a high degree of political and functional independence from the federal government and in turn local governments have a high degree of autonomy within the individual states. By contrast, in Europe government is much more centralized, and the same is true of the public service and administrative units. European countries have large, professionalized and rather unitary bureaucracies at both a central and a local level, with strong linkages between the levels, whereas the United States has a fragmented bureaucracy. American state and local government administrations are thus less dependent on senior governments, but by the same token they are more dependent on private capital – hence the need for them to mobil-ize PPPs.[4]

Some, like Keating, would argue that these very different starting points and traditions ought to lead European states to be very wary of PPPs, the rush to which is dismissed as 'a naïve adulation of American privatism' (ibid., p. 168), and 'often no more than a very expensive way for government to borrow money' (p. 170). Thus Keating concludes:

> It may be that, where local government has a weak resource base and a problematic bond rating, and faces mobile capital, it will have no choice but to go aggressively into public–private partnership. This is the case of many American jurisdictions. The European state, however, is more autonomous of private capital and potentially better able to define investment priorities. It has less need to rush into American-style partnerships and, where it does enter into partnership, should be more able to define its terms. (ibid., p. 170)

Yet the reality would seem to be different. Consider, for example, the Netherlands. Despite the fact that a PPP is not a recognized concept in Dutch law, the Netherlands has put in place a framework for PPPs including a dedicated PPP unit, the 'Kenniscentrum' or Knowledge Centre which was set up in 1999 within the Ministry of Finance (Linklaters and Alliance, 2001). Three major PPP projects have reached the procurement stage: HSL (the high speed train line between Amsterdam and the Belgian border), the A59 (between Oss and Den Bosch) and Delfland (new Hamaschpolder waste water purification installed by DBFO). Partnerships also lie at the heart of current EU economic development and competitiveness initiatives because they are seen to facilitate innovation, bring diverse interests together and enable public authorities to cohere around common objectives (Jacobs, 1997), and the development of trans-European transportation, telecommunications and energy infrastructures is recommended for major partnership programmes (European Commission, 1995). Since the late 1980s, the European Investment Bank (EIB) has approved more than 100 projects in EU countries which can be considered to be PPPs in a broad sense, and as of October 2003 another 50 projects are in the pipeline (European Investment Bank, 2004).

In the United Kingdom there is no strong tradition of organizing public–private relations through joint participation in institutions, and PPPs are often dismissed as a byproduct of a particular brand of ideological Conservative thought (despite the fact that the PPP programme has expanded under the Blair Labour government). Nonetheless, the 'nationalize/denationalize' cycle and the 'privatize or not' argument that lasted for much of the post-war period would appear to have given way to a more considered debate about how best to ensure that certain organizations, irrespective of whether they are in public or private ownership, can be made to work in the public interest (Harding, 1998). This has led to a great number of experiments with different forms of PPP, covering virtually the whole gamut of government activities. The description PPP has now come to be used as an umbrella term for arrangements involving the private and public sectors, with PFI projects and DBFO contracts one sub-set of such arrangements.[5]

Nevertheless, Keating's misgivings about PPPs are shared by many in academic circles and in addition the general public remains deeply sceptical about, and even hostile to, PPPs. As the Commission on Public Private Partnerships (2001, p. 23) notes, the 'public good, private bad' position when it comes to public services provision commands a great deal of emotional support. Such attitudes prompt a series of questions. What is wrong with traditional public procurement methods? Can PPPs be structured to achieve value for money, and how is this to be done? How are risks in PPPs best to be allocated?

Another set of questions relate to the governance of PPPs. The fact that one of the participants in a PPP is a public body creates a need for the inclusion of mechanisms of accountability quite different from those that would exist if all the participants were private. Yet, one reason for a partnership agenda is to break away from the political and bureaucratic processes that might exist if the activities were purely public. How are these potentially conflicting demands to be balanced? Can governments transform themselves from purchasers of infrastructure assets to managers of long-term contractual relationships? What are the administrative requirements needed for them to do so?

In this volume we address many of these questions and more, not only to try to set the record straight on some issues, but also to provide a comprehensive overview of PPPs, what they are and how they work. A feature of the book is that it seeks to combine an academic perspective on these issues with practitioner-based experience of organizing PPPs and advising government bodies. This experience is reflected directly in some of the examples given, and while the whole volume draws on this practical knowledge of the PPP market, there are also seven specific case studies. Two examine road projects (Chapter 2), one relates to prisons and custodial services (Chapter 5), two consider hospital projects (Chapters 5 and 6), and the other two case studies look at water projects (Chapters 7 and 9). Reflecting the diversity of models that make up the partnership approach to infrastructure services delivery, the case studies cover a variety of PPP approaches in some different countries.

NOTES

1. Office of Government Commerce (2002b, p. 11).
2. We follow the UK tradition of using the abbreviation PPP. Many US authors use P-P partnership, perhaps to avoid confusion with Purchasing Power Parity, also invariably abbreviated to PPP.
3. According to the Correctional Facility Census (Thomas, 2003), in September 2001 there were 151 private prisons in the US, 14 in Australia, ten in England and Wales, two in South Africa, and one each in Canada, the Netherlands Antilles, New Zealand and Scotland, accommodating 142,521 detainees. Experience with private prisons in the United States is examined by McDonald (1990), Gallagher and Edwards (1997) and Schneider (2000). Dissatisfaction with the operation of some private prisons in Victoria, Australia led to an independent review (Kirby, 2000). It was concerned about the fragmentation of the correctional system into public and private prisons, and recommended the development of uniform operational standards across all operators. Since then, two new prisons in Victoria have been commissioned under the Partnerships Victoria programme, but under a different approach, the 'serviced infrastructure' model. See Chapter 5.
4. US commentators have attributed the emergence of public private partnerships to the greater burdens placed on local government, especially in terms of urban governance (Beauregard, 1998). This is consistent with the development of PPPs in Australia, where the initiatives have all been at the state rather than the federal level (Grimsey and Lewis, 2002b). However, in contrast, the PPP programmes in the UK and the Netherlands began at the national level, and in the case of the UK were subsequently taken up at the local authority level.
5. It may be useful to distinguish PFI and PPP in the UK context. The Private Finance Initiative (PFI) was announced by the then Chancellor, Norman Lamont, in the 1992 Autumn Statement with the aim of increasing the involvement of the private sector in the provision of public services. In 2000, the Labour government published 'Public Private Partnerships – the Government's Approach' which defined public private partnerships (PPPs) into three categories:

   - the introduction of private sector ownership into state-owned businesses, using the full range of possible structures (whether by flotation or the introduction of a strategic partner), with sales of either a majority or a minority stake;
   - PFI and other arrangements where the public sector contracts to purchase quality services on a long-term basis so as to take advantage of private sector management skills incentivized by having private finance at risk. This includes concessions and franchises, where a private sector partner takes on the responsibility for providing a public service, including maintaining, enhancing or constructing the necessary infrastructure; and
   - selling government services into wider markets and other partnership arrangements where private sector expertise and finance are used to exploit the commercial potential of government assets (HM Treasury, 2003b, p. 3).

2. The revolution in infrastructure

THE NATURE OF INFRASTRUCTURE

For most of the post-war period, government has been the principal provider of infrastructure (at least outside the United States). Over the last decade, that position has begun to change. Faced with budgetary stringencies and, at the same time, pressure to expand and improve public facilities and services, governments have turned to the private sector, in order to harness private finance and achieve better value for money. Private sector entities have entered into long-term contractual agreements to construct or manage public sector infrastructure facilities, or to provide services to the community (using the infrastructure facilities). The techniques have been developed at national level, used to promote investment in local government services and in infrastructure projects more generally elsewhere, and have been extended to joint ventures and infrastructure projects for regional regeneration.

When considering infrastructure projects, 'infrastructure financing' and 'infrastructure investment' need to be distinguished. The former can arise from the privatization of existing facilities, whereas infrastructure investment involves development, operation and ownership either by the private sector alone or in a joint venture between government and the private sector entity. The distinction is analogous to buying an existing office block, already fully let, as opposed to developing a new site – the financing requirements and risks are obviously quite different in the two cases. Our interest is with infrastructure investment, and in the case of a PPP contract it incorporates:

- the construction of a new infrastructure asset (or the refurbishment of an existing one) to be designed, built and financed by the private sector to the procuring agency's services specification, within a particular deadline and to a fixed price;
- long-term (25- to 35-year) contracts for the provision of infrastructure services associated with the asset; and
- collection of revenues by the operator or the payment by the public sector body to the private body of a fee or unitary charge, allowing the contractor to make a return on investment commensurate with the levels of risk assumed.

But what is infrastructure? Obviously, we do not have PPPs for the production of coal or steel or motor vehicles. But why not? What is distinctive about infrastructure? Investment in infrastructure on some definitions is said is to provide 'basic services to industry and households',[1] 'key inputs into the economy',[2] and 'a crucial input to economic activity and growth'.[3] However, what is 'basic', 'key' and 'crucial' varies from country to country and from one time to another. For example, steel production was once regarded as essential infrastructure in many countries. In early post-war Britain, coal, iron and steel were regarded as constituting parts of the 'commanding heights of the economy', but few would describe them in these terms today.

Public ownership is another suggested characteristic. For example, Gramlich (1994) in his survey article on infrastructure investment focuses on ownership and defines 'infrastructure capital' as 'the tangible capital stock owned by the public sector' (p. 1177). Highways, ports, bridges and other transport facilities, power generation and distribution, water and sewerage treatment, and telecommunications systems would be regarded by most commentators as part of a country's infrastructure. Yet, in England today, only roads and motorways among these items remain publicly owned, and even then some motorways and bridges are privately operated, including in December 2003 the new 42 km M6 toll road, Britain's first tolled motorway. As we shall see in the next chapter, the private sector has a long history of being involved in providing such infrastructure facilities and services to the public (including toll roads). With the current shift toward a return to more involvement by the private sector in infrastructure services, ownership cannot in itself be a defining characteristic as to what should be seen as public infrastructure. In any case, the public ownership definition is not especially helpful unless we can bring into the picture those factors that have led certain assets to be brought at some time within the ambit of government and thus become, by definition, infrastructure.

While there would be a general consensus that tangible capital assets such as bridges, roads, streets and tunnels are infrastructure, others would cast the net much wider. A distinction is often made between 'economic' and 'social' infrastructure and within each of these between 'hard' (physical) and 'soft' infrastructure (Argy *et al.*, 1999). On this basis, there are four categories:

1. hard economic infrastructure
2. soft economic infrastructure
3. hard social infrastructure
4. soft social infrastructure.

These classifications are set out in Table 2.1.

Table 2.1   Classification of infrastructure by type

	Hard	Soft
Economic	roads motorways bridges ports railways airports telecommunications power	vocational training financial institutions R & D facilitation technology transfer export assistance
Social	hospitals schools water supply housing sewerage child care prisons aged care homes	social security community services environmental agencies (EPAs)

Economic infrastructure is considered to provide key intermediate services to business and industry and its principal function is to enhance productivity and innovation initiatives. 'Hard economic' facilities include roads, highways, bridges, ports, railways, airports, public transport, telecommunications, electricity and gas generation, transmission and distribution. 'Soft economic' infrastructure encompasses vocational training, financial facilities for business (payments, credit, equity, derivatives, venture capital, etc.), the facilitation of R & D and technology transfer, and organizations encouraging export orientation and productive cooperation among individuals and entities. Notably, many of these are privately owned and operated, some provided by individual institutions (e.g. credit rating organizations) and others by groupings of private entities forming cooperative networks (e.g. payments systems).

Social infrastructure is seen as providing basic services to households. Its main role is to improve the quality of life and welfare in the community, especially among those of limited means. 'Hard social' facilities embrace hospitals, education and training buildings, water storage and treatment facilities, housing, sewerage and drainage pipes, child care and aged care institutions and prisons. Again, some of these are provided by private sector bodies (e.g. private hospitals and private schools). 'Soft social' infrastructure takes the form of the social security system, a range of community services, and environmental protection agencies. Many of these services are viewed by the community as 'essential' and tend to have, in the description of Musgrave (1959), the characteristics of 'merit goods' in that they are regarded as socially desirable.

As to the importance of these categories, the OECD (1993) describes 'hard economic' structures such as road and rail networks, waterways and ports, airports, energy and water utilities, and telecommunications as 'core' physical infrastructure, as compared with 'other' infrastructure such as education and health, or intangible investments. In Australia, the services from economic infrastructure are estimated to account for more than 10 per cent of GDP (Productivity Commission, 2001). Also, economic infrastructure represents around 70 per cent of the stock of infrastructure in Australia by value. However, to some degree this comparison may be misleading, since economic infrastructure contains items that are more easily priced and appreciated in narrow economic or financial terms, whereas social infrastructure contains many investments where the gains are less tangible or less easy to price or value in economic or financial terms (Allen Consulting Group, 2003).

While the distinction between 'economic' (hard or soft) and 'social' (hard or soft) may be a useful one for organizing thinking about infrastructure policy, the categories do overlap. Some forms of social infrastructure such as those that enhance the skills, health, productivity and morale of the work force and the quality of life may have as much bearing on the productivity of industry as economic structures. Economic infrastructure such as roads and transport networks can impact on the quality of life, even if this is not the intent. Moreover, both types of infrastructure incur relatively high initial capital costs, have relatively long lives, and need to be managed and paid for on a long-term basis.

Others would cast the infrastructure net wider still. One such definition is 'those physical and social structures that support the life and interactions of a society'.[4] Along these lines Jochimsen (1966), cited in von Hirshhausen (2002), defined infrastructure as 'the sum of material, institutional and personal capacities available to economic agents' (p. 100), identifying three categories:

1. *Material infrastructure* is that part of the physical capital stock of an economy used as a fundamental input into other directly productive activities. This type of infrastructure corresponds to what has been called *social overhead capital* in development economics (Hirschman, 1958). Examples are equipment and structures in telecommunication, transport, energy, water and sewerage.
2. *Personal infrastructure* comprises the entrepreneurial, mental and other skills of the people that contribute to economic production. Commercial skills can include accounting, banking and finance, procurement, management and marketing.

3. *Institutional infrastructure* corresponds to what new institutional economics[5] calls the 'institutional environment'. It includes internal and external norms (or formal and informal institutions) that shape economic behaviour and decision-making processes. These norms are governed by what Buchanan and Tullock (1962) would call the constitutional framework (choice of rules governing economic and social interactions), as well as unstated conventions and various forms of implicit behaviour, the 'choice within rules'. Examples are the legal system, the economic constitution, banking and finance regulation, the bureaucracy, along with informal institutions such as trust, culture, business networks, and acceptance of social norms.

Jochimsen's definition of infrastructure and his emphasis on institutional aspects recognize that the key foundations of a market economy are the markets themselves, institutions and policies that support and enhance markets and market-based behaviour, skills and enterprise, not just physical structures. An infrastructure project can create a new market or alter the structure of a market, expand competition in other markets, widen market-oriented conduct and innovation and contribute to the reform of policies and government institutions and practices that alter the investment climate in the country (Stern and Lankes, 1998). While in principle such impacts could be incorporated into cost–benefit analysis,[6] in practice cost–benefit analysis seems unlikely to capture all of the effects of institutional change resulting from infrastructure investment.

THE EFFECTS OF INFRASTRUCTURE

Despite these likely difficulties in measuring the full impact of infrastructure projects, some writers have discerned differences between infrastructure investment (defined as public capital formation) and private investment (Aschauer, 1989; Munnell, 1992). Aschauer found evidence that infrastructure was distinguished by being roughly twice as productive as private capital, due to the nature of the relationship between the two. The impact of public capital accumulation on private investment can be regarded as falling into two broad categories, depending on whether the public investment 'crowds out' or 'crowds in' private investment.

The 'monetarist' view is that public capital expenditure simply 'crowds out' private expenditure by a number of direct and indirect mechanisms, including higher inflation.[7] To the extent that publicly provided capital is a substitute for private capital in private production technologies (public health facilities leaving less room for private initiatives), firms require less private capital to produce the same level of output. In addition, higher public sector demand in the capital goods-producing sector raises the price of capital goods, thereby lowering the quantity of these goods demanded by the private sector. Finally, the increased government demand in the economy creates a general scarcity of current resources, inflationary pressures, a rise in nominal and real interest rates, and a further contraction of capital spending.

But the crowding out argument is based on the assumption of an unchanged rate of return to private capital in the face of higher public capital accumulation. If public capital devoted to infrastructure purposes is in fact complementary rather than competitive to private capital in the production of goods and services, then a rise in the public capital stock makes private capital more productive. New motorways and trunk routes allow faster transportation of goods from factory to markets. Power stations lower the cost of running machinery. As a result, higher levels of public investment might filter into higher profit rates for the private businesses, more than offsetting the adverse consequences. Aschauer found that while an increase in public investment initially crowded out private investment, in the medium term it improved productivity levels in the private sector (both labour and multi-factor productivity) to such an extent that it had a net positive effect on private investment.

Aschauer's findings stimulated a bevy of research and discussion on the topic in the early 1990s that, to a large degree, was responsible for the 'rediscovery' of infrastructure as a major public policy issue (Hieronymi, 1993, p. 76). Some studies supported Aschauer's findings and estimated supranormal returns for public infrastructure. In particular, the World Bank in 1994 found evidence which overall confirmed that the role of infrastructure in growth is substantial, and frequently greater than that of investment in other forms of capital. Their summary and assessment of 14 studies on this question covering within-country and cross-country data suggested significant likely benefits from investment in public infrastructure.

Others, however, were less sure and argued that the statistical basis for these estimates is weak. A number of papers published by the European Investment Bank found that there was sufficient contrary evidence to counsel against simply attributing large indirect benefits to public investment. It was argued that the empirical results are not robust to changes in model specification, and that there is actually some evidence to suggest that excessive public investment can hinder growth – presumably because of the distortions due to higher taxes, or the crowding out of private investment (Gruber, 1994; Girard *et al.*, 1994; Hurst, 1994).

Aschauer has revisited the topic on several occasions (Aschauer, 1995, 2001) and defends his original estimates. In 2001, he pointed to empirical support, for a range of countries, that investment in public infrastructure has positive spillover effects on an economy's productivity and thus on economic growth. For example:

the results of the empirical analysis: substantiate the notion that the relationship between public capital and economic growth is nonlinear; provide reasonable estimates of a positive impact of public capital on economic growth; uncover positive growth effects from both core (highways, water and sewers) and other (primarily schools and hospitals) public capital, with particularly high impacts of urban infrastructure such as water and sewer capital. (Aschauer, 2001)

His early work indicated that cross-country differences in productivity growth can be explained in part by differences in levels of infrastructure spending (Aschauer, 1989). More recent studies confirm a statistically significant positive relationship between productivity and infrastructure and suggest that infrastructure may be a key determinant of comparative advantage between countries (Yeaple and Golub, 2002). Also, Milbourne *et al.* (2001) found a positive effect on economic growth from public investment, with particular evidence of gains from investment in transportation, communication and education.

A further feature of the recent evidence is the finding that it is not only economic infrastructure investment that is valuable. Again it is Aschauer (2001) who provides most support for this view.

Previous studies of the relationship between public capital and the economy have tended to find support for the notion that 'core' public capital – typically comprised of highways, water and sewer systems – is more important than 'other' public capital.

When he estimated output and employment growth where allowance is made for the separate impacts of core and other public capital, the results indicated that the output and employment growth effects were positive for both core and other public capital, as was evident from the earlier quotation.

These studies are predominantly at a national or multi-country level. When the effects of infrastructure investment are considered at a less aggregated level, it may be more difficult to establish that rates of return on infrastructure are appreciably larger than those on other investments. That, at least, is the conclusion of Flyvbjerg *et al.* (2003) who warn of 'overselling' projects in terms of regional and economic growth effects (pp. 65–72).

Consider, for example, transport. Transport infrastructure is used by both businesses and private individuals, and it can be seen as an input into the production of a transport service, which in turn is used as an input into a final product or service demanded by consumers, such as a visit to a friend or the availability of a certain commodity in the local shops. Investment in transport facilities should produce a reduction in the cost of the input, either through decreased outlays for undertaking a trip or decreased time spent on a trip, which may also translate into reduced outlays, or both. In effect, the investment reduces the 'price' and this lowering of the price of infrastructure services will have two consequences in the short term. First, it will increase the demand for that service by both private individuals and businesses, and second, it will add to the level of profits made by businesses generally, as a result of cheaper transport costs reducing overall production costs for firms in the area. For this impact to be significant, transport costs need to be an important element in total production costs, and the change in transport costs as a result of the road has to be large (Parkinson, 1981).

In the longer run, transport investment can generate a relocation of industry and economic activity. This occurs when a firm decides to relocate because of a change in accessibility brought about by road investment. As in the short run, the change in transport costs has to be significant to matter. However, the evidence would indicate that transport costs are a relatively small component of the final cost of goods and services. Parkinson (1981) found transport costs to be typically only 5–10 per cent of total production costs, although they do vary from one industry to another and from firm to firm.[8] The upshot is that even large-scale investments, that give rise to large savings in expenditure, time and inconvenience, may have a small impact on company profitability (Flyvbjerg *et al.*, 2003).

That is not to say that investment in public infrastructure is unproductive – no one would advocate a country without roads, for example. Part of the difficulty is that investment in infrastructure is not a continuous process but tends to be 'lumpy' and discontinuous. Once an economy reaches a certain stage of development it needs a good road system. Major investment may then take place in building motorways and trunk routes. Until the system is nearly completed its full benefits are not available to the economy or society. However, once completed, the capacity may be adequate for many years to come. The result is that at certain stages in economic development infrastructure may be a constraint on growth, but once the constraint is dealt with, further investment does little to expand productive capacity. Measuring the overall economic effects of infrastructure investment may be a very difficult task (FitzGerald, 2003).

It may also be the case that high returns apply to some forms of infrastructure but they do not carry across the board to all types of infrastructure. Aschauer in his early studies identified streets, highways, airports, mass transit systems, water and sewerage, as well as power and electricity, all of which can be viewed as inputs into production with the capacity to reduce exchange and transactions costs. Later, he found evidence of high returns from social infrastructure, but these effects may be more difficult to identify at a local or regional level when there is significant mobility of the work force. At a regional level, the impacts on development may be greater the more the investment is geographically concentrated, creating a cluster of firms in related industries all drawing on similar regional infrastructure and resources. Nevertheless, economic impacts are not the only consideration, for infrastructure has significant socioeconomic and organizational characteristics. Some infrastructure services are considered to be a citizen's right, and government is expected to ensure a minimum availability to everybody (for example, health care) to some degree, irrespective of their capacity to pay. This leads us to the public characteristics of infrastructure.

PUBLIC CHARACTER OF INFRASTRUCTURE

There remains broad agreement among economists that infrastructure is an area in which government economic policy is required. In the past, that consensus meant that infrastructure had to be provided by government-owned enterprises (the predominant approach in Europe) or by privately owned utilities subject to rate of return regulation (the approach in much of the United States). This conviction derived from a number of inherent features of infrastructure.

First, there is the presence of network services, providing activities that bind economic activity together. The notion of a network providing integrative threads is often identified with the 'hard economic' facilities of communication, energy supply, water supply, sewerage treatment and transport. Often these services constitute a small, but indispensable, part of the total cost of the wide range of products in which they are used, yet the losses that result from service failure can be very large relative to the basic cost of service provision, for example a restaurant losing its power while meals are being served. Serious disruptions such as those that took place in the summer of 2003, blacking out much of north-east Northern America and the whole of Italy, make the point more strongly. In these cases, due to the integrated grids and transnational interconnectors, failure of a number of local power lines created power losses over much larger areas that lasted almost a day in each case. In this respect, these infrastructure services can be described as being of 'strategic importance' (Kay, 1993, p. 55).

Second, infrastructure frequently provides public goods. This means the benefits are shared across the community in such a way that those who do not wish to buy the service cannot be excluded from the benefits created by those who do. Generally, competitive markets will tend to underproduce these services. A prison is a good example of this, and so is a lighthouse or an aircraft beacon; once built, it is very difficult (and perhaps not desirable) to limit the protection afforded by these devices to those who paid for its construction or who pay a price for its service (the non-excludability principle). Other types of activity, for example, technological or information infrastructure, may have many of the characteristics of a public good. First, technology is a *non-rival* good. When one entity uses technology to produce a good or a service, this action does not preclude others from doing so, even simultaneously. This feature distinguishes technology from, say, a piece of capital equipment, which can only be used in one place at a time. Second, technology in many cases is a partially *non-excludable* good. That is, the creators or owners of technical information can experience difficulty in preventing others from making unauthorized use of it, at least in some applications. Again, this attribute of technology distinguishes it from capital equipment, which is readily excludable. Such non-excludability of knowledge suggests that industrial research and development (R & D) may generate 'technological spillovers'. By technological spillovers one understands that firms can obtain information created by others without paying for that information in a market transaction and also that the creators (or current owners) of the information have little effective recourse, under prevailing laws, if other firms use it.

Third, there may be network externalities, whereby benefits and costs are conferred on those not a party to the transaction (e.g. spillovers, such as those discussed above). In general, competitive markets are likely to overproduce goods imposing negative externalities and underproduce those with positive externalities. Many goods may have both positive and negative spillovers. A road, for instance, confers positive externalities to those firms whose distribution system has been improved, even though they have not paid for the road. Contrariwise, the road may generate a negative externality, for example on residents around a new road who have their views spoiled, or peace disturbed, and have not been recompensed for the cost they are bearing. The difficulty with externalities is that they arise to a greater or lesser degree in virtually all economic activities, and if every service that produced external benefits or costs had to be supplied by government, it would produce virtually everything. Nevertheless, the network characteristic of infrastructure, which links it to many parts of the economy, means that the spillovers arising from an infrastructure project are of a much larger order of magnitude than for many other activities. Indeed, they almost define the nature of infrastructure (Threadgold, 1996).

Fourth, infrastructure gives rise to natural monopolies, when scale economies make it practicable to have only one provider (for example, of an electricity grid to a particular area). It is more cost effective to have one provider of an electricity grid, rather than multiple small providers who individually cannot realize the economies of scale involved. Because of the high fixed capital costs involved, the competitive provision of the infrastructure itself is costly, often prohibitively so. Related to this characteristic, the development and delivery of many infrastructure services require the acquisition of land for transport routes or rights above or below ground to install conduits, pipes and cables. Often only government has the capacity to cede these negotiation rights. Nevertheless, the natural monopoly characteristic need not exclude competition in the use of infrastructure, and public control over property rights does not necessarily require government to own or operate the infrastructure services.

Fifth, infrastructure usually involves very large investments. Capital costs of infrastructure are generally large relative to the running costs, and the sunk costs of establishing an infrastructure asset are substantial. This means that a high proportion of the total cost of a service has already been irrevocably committed before the service is made available.

Many of the items widely recognized as infrastructure – such as the distribution networks of public utilities and the development of road and rail systems – generally meet all five of these conditions. Other activities, still widely regarded as infrastructure, such as postal services and financial payment systems, have several features in common with utility distribution facilities: they involve networks, have significant sunk costs and are widely used, are indispensable, and have a relatively low user cost.

Together, these five characteristics traditionally have been seen as casting doubt on the viability of private-sector, competitive market provision, despite the fact that some infrastructure is privately owned and operated. Two of the characteristics, natural monopoly and the predominance of sunk costs, simply suggest that competitive supply is unlikely to emerge. The network feature of infrastructure raises the possibility that efficient provision will not be achieved unless mechanisms of central coordination are put in place. Finally, the strategic importance of the service to the economy means that governments traditionally have been unwilling to rely on supply by the competitive private sector. In the presence of externalities and public good features, the benefits of an increased supply of the good in question may be greater than what can reasonably be charged to users. Toll roads and inland waterways are the classic illustration. In theory, these could be, and in the past have been, built by private entrepreneurs charging tolls. But the charges might have to exceed the cost of the existing modes of transportation, so the profitability of the venture would be threatened by the unwillingness of users to switch to a higher cost mode of transport. Nevertheless, the greater efficiency of the new transportation facility would provide considerable benefits to many non-users across the whole geographical area.

Public finance and public provision have thus been seen as necessary to ensure that these efficiency gains will be realized, and in most countries the outcome was that a large number of infrastructure activities were owned, managed and financed by the public sector. However, this government monopoly of infrastructure activities has come under increasing scrutiny and mounting pressure for change, resulting in the growing commercialism of infrastructure.

THE COMMERCIALISM OF INFRASTRUCTURE

The trend away from public to private provision of infrastructure has been underpinned by a marked change in thinking and practice, reinforced by technological changes and institutional innovations. Over the past two decades, a worldwide movement has taken place towards privatization and deregulation, signifying an intellectual revival of faith in free markets. There has been growing dissatisfaction, particularly in Anglo-Saxon countries and developing countries, with the performance of state-owned enterprises, and in some cases a recognition that state-led development programmes simply have not worked. Government budgets have come under pressure, and with that development have come two responses. One has been a desire to reduce the impact of infrastructure spending on government budgets, both as a means of minimizing government borrowing and as a way of protecting economically necessary but politically dispensable infrastructure expenditure from general budgetary pressures. The other response has seen governments turn to private capital markets for infrastructure funding.

Infrastructure itself is becoming more commercially oriented. There has been the perception, for example, that a move from 'taxpayer pays' to 'user pays' (i.e. from ability-to-pay to the benefit principle)[9] in the provision of infrastructure services (water, power) is likely to be associated with a better economic use of the services. Many industries considered to be natural monopolies, such as electricity generation and telecommunications, have been broken up geographically into different regional firms or, with deregulation, separated into competitive (or potentially competitive) sectors *vis-à-vis* those sectors that remain natural monopolies (the distinction between power supply and high-voltage transmission). As a consequence, competition among power generators to supply transmission grids is becoming increasingly common. In telecommunications, microwave links have made it economic to provide long-distance connections at relatively low volumes, and so have eroded the natural monopoly previously enjoyed by the public telecommunications companies.

In fact, it has become apparent that most of the industries commonly regarded as natural monopolies bundle together activities in which competition is inherently imperfect with activities in which competition is possible. Efficiency in these industries can be enhanced by promoting competition in those components of the 'bundle' that are susceptible to the benefits of market-based activity. Examples come from the deregulation of supply inputs in the energy sector, the splitting of local networks and long-distance operations in telecommunications, the division of coaching and coach terminals, the separation of air transport and computer reservation systems, and of train services and track infrastructure. Even in those activities that retain natural monopoly characteristics, substitution of price-cap regulations for rate-of-return regulation (i.e. fixing of maximum prices rather than the mark-up over costs) has created strong incentives to reduce costs, while third party access to certain facilities that are not economic to duplicate has widened competition in the upstream and downstream markets served by the facilities.

At the same time, technological changes have been challenging traditional methods of operating infrastructure and allowing a wider application of economically more appropriate pricing mechanisms. Like any market, that for infrastructure services (in transport, energy, water, etc.) will not work efficiently unless all the costs and benefits are fully represented and made apparent to users and operators. The clearest way to achieve this is through the price mechanism. However, efficient pricing of infrastructure provision is still incomplete and there is a wide range of infrastructure for which prices bear no relation whatsoever to consumption by end users. Roads are the most striking examples. Their construction and maintenance are financed almost entirely from general and dedicated taxes and vehicle licence fees. With the exception of some motorways, bridges and tunnels, and even fewer cases of urban roads, pricing of road use is largely undeveloped. Yet its potential for relieving congestion, for identifying where the provision of additional infrastructure would be beneficial, and for raising the financial resources for maintenance and new investment is considerable.

With new technology, there is the ability to impose toll financing and pricing on many bridges, motorways, and even streets, and vary the toll according to traffic conditions. Electronic toll collection systems are now operating or being experimented with in many locations around the world, including the City Link project in Melbourne with which both authors are familiar.[10] Electronic toll collection is a set of technologies that automates the manual, in-lane, toll collection process so that drivers do not have to stop and pay cash at a toll booth, thereby reducing the cost to the user. Three major technologies are employed: automatic vehicle identification, automatic vehicle classification, and video enforcement. Electronic transactions take place between nodes – transponders[11] and collection points – both tied back to the rest of the financial network. Use of electronic toll collection increases toll lane or motorway capacity, thereby reducing toll processing time and queue lengths at toll booths. Opening pre-payment accounts eliminates the need for patrons to be concerned with having cash ready for each toll booth. Having dedicated electronic collection lanes or whole roads operating on this basis means that transponder-equipped vehicles have no need to slow down or stop when paying tolls, which can reduce noise pollution, air pollution and fuel consumption.

Another example is the use of electronic devices to control entry to city centres. In February 2003, a £5 a day congestion charge was introduced in London for those driving into an eight-square-mile segment of central London bounded by Park Lane, Euston Road, Commercial Street and Vauxhall between 7 am and 6.30 pm on weekdays. The scheme relies on 700 video cameras installed on every road into the city centre scanning the licence plates of all motorists entering the area. This information is then matched each night against a data base of those who have paid the charge either by phone, internet or at shops and garages, and those who fail to pay by midnight are fined £80. Rome has also introduced an electronic tagging system to ensure that entry to its centre is restricted to residents and essential services.[12]

From an economic viewpoint, there are obvious merits in these developments. Charging for the use of roads ties the revenue stream directly to road use (or need) and should result in more effective and less political road financing decisions. Since electronic tolling collects revenue from users of a specific facility, it can also be used to provide incentives to reduce the inefficiencies associated with excess use. For example, wear and tear on roads increases directly in proportion to the cubic power of vehicle axle weight (Small *et al.*, 1989). Tolls could be based on the likely damage to roads by levying a higher charge on heavy trucks. Large, heavy four-wheel drive vehicles pose greater risks in accidents to pedestrians and drivers and passengers in smaller cars, and could be tolled more heavily in urban environments. To reduce congestion, tolls could be adjusted according to the time of day or week.

For the future, video cameras could be replaced with technology utilizing global positioning satellites.[13] Motor cars fitted with satellite receivers could be charged for road use via digital on-board maps according to type of vehicle, time of day, location and the distance travelled, allowing flexible pricing across a whole city or urban conurbation. This would be more efficient than 'one size fits all' pricing regimes (Levinson, 2002, p. 203). Two examples of privately operated toll roads using new tolling technology are outlined in the final section of this chapter.

PRIVATE INVOLVEMENT IN INFRASTRUCTURE

Associated with the commercialism of infrastructure, there has been the recognition of the value of introducing the discipline of the private capital markets to improve efficiency in construction and operations, particularly in order to ensure that projects are completed at the best value without unnecessary delays. Along with this acceptance, it has also been acknowledged that there is not an either–or, public or private, choice to be made. Many of the benefits of the market can be obtained by combining public and private resources in infrastructure projects.

If the private sector is to take a greater role in the provision of infrastructure services, it can provide capital, management, or both. If it provides either capital or management, then the existing structure of public sector management and control will have to be changed to a more explicit system of regulation and monitoring of private sector bodies by public agencies. If neither is provided, then private sector ideas and thinking may need to be borrowed instead.

In broad terms there are three ways by which infrastructure can become commercially oriented (Stern and Lankes, 1998). First, at the most basic level, the public sector can be operated in a manner that resembles more closely the ways the private sector works. This means paying close attention to revenues, costs and market demands. It also involves creating a management structure that provides clear goals, makes managers responsible for performance and allows them independence to carry out their tasks. Introduction of these changes may require bringing in a private sector consultant on an advisory basis, and overcoming the peculiar difficulties that governments face in providing incentive schemes for managers of government enterprises. Second, governments can seek the limited entry of new private providers through various forms of PPP. This approach implies a more active private sector participation, usually as a provider of services, as well as a constructor and designer of facilities. The basis for this involvement is usually some type of concession. Finally, the third alternative is for governments to opt for full privatization of some public services.

Obviously, our interest lies in the partnership route. One of its attractions to many people is that it is not privatization. It thus fits in with the strong political preference in some quarters that a nation's fundamental assets should not be permanently alienated from public ownership. However, it is often overlooked that the partnership route signals a marked change in infrastructure policy. It also brings with it new responsibilities for government agencies.

Infrastructure policy can be thought of as covering three levels:

- *network planning* (this means long-term planning of infrastructure at central and regional levels);
- *financing*; and
- *operation* (construction, operations, maintenance, and so on).

In the past, these three aspects were all governmental activities. Adoption of a partnership agenda is tantamount to admitting that in the areas of financing and operation, there are no persuasive market-failure arguments against a competition-oriented supply of infrastructure (von Hirschhausen, 2002). High sunk costs make direct competition less likely, but do not prevent it completely, so long as the economic policy framework remains competition-oriented and includes competition, if not in the market, then at least for the market (Demsetz, 1968).

In fact, this last point should be couched in more positive terms. Market competition is a form of coordination with intrinsic advantages over bureaucratic organizational forms, and the discipline and incentives embodied in market contracting arrangements are valuable for injecting greater efficiency into infrastructure delivery, in the following ways:

- Agency problems, which arise due to the divergence between ownership and control of assets, are easier to deal with in the private sector through managerial incentives and market disciplines.
- The transfer of risk to the private sector provides an incentive for private entities to maximize efficiency.
- Resources are more efficiently allocated in cases where clear markets for property rights can be established.

The latter two are especially important in a partnership arrangement. An effective transfer of risk from the public sector to the private sector is needed, since it is the acceptance of risk that gives the private entity the incentive to price and produce efficiently. But for this transfer to happen, a clear property right needs to be created. The conventional analysis of property rights suggests that the creation of a market for ownership rights results in an allocation of assets to owners who maximize efficiency in their use (Alchian, 1965). Within the ambit of a PPP, this suggests an allocation of responsibilities that might have the government retaining those areas where it is difficult to establish a clear contractual specification, leaving the private sector to undertake those activities for which a clear and unambiguous contract or property right can be formed.

Government, as partner in the PPP, must manage these contractual relationships and also provide the network planning function. Externalities of various sorts (e.g. environmental side-effects) may require some sort of public coordination and corridor planning, but participation of the state in network planning does not rule out the private supply of the infrastructure assets and associated services.

Finance is another attraction of the partnership option. Governments have looked to forge partnerships to provide an increasing array of infrastructure, social services and regional development programmes that neither they nor the private sector are likely to have the resources to offer by themselves. The PPPs with which we are primarily concerned utilize project financing techniques in order to deliver the required private finance in a form that meets the risk–reward requirements of private financiers and suppliers of risk capital, drawing on the experience of using DBFO/BOT techniques for highways and other transport schemes. These structures achieve two purposes. First, they are devised to spread risks across a number of participants (sponsor, constructor, suppliers, financiers) including the government, which typically provides the site, reduces legal uncertainties and purchases the output. Second, they are mechanisms for monitoring risk, and the explicit incorporation of a risk premium by private investors aids this process by making project risks more apparent.

A further attraction of partnerships is their versatility. Earlier we noted that infrastructure is often classified into 'economic' or 'social' and within these into 'hard' or 'soft' (see Table 2.1). PPPs in the UK were originally used for 'hard' economic infrastructure projects such as roads, bridges, ports, and so on. They then spread to social infrastructure such as schools, hospitals, prison and detention centres, sewerage and so on. Now the 'hard hats' have become providers of 'soft services' (D & P, 2001). Instead of being interested only in the construction contract and the first two years of a project, the facilitators are now servicing the asset throughout its life. Major UK construction companies, for example, have become more like facilities management companies, re-inventing themselves as project operators and service providers. They have effectively started to be infrastructure services companies, a development which helps to insulate their bottom line from cyclical construction markets. Much the same trend is occurring across Europe and in other locations where the UK-type model has been adopted. This is an indication of the flexibility of the PPP arrangement, and its ability to engage the private sector in a number of different ways.

TWO PRIVATE TOLL ROADS

This section gives some details of two privately operated toll roads employing the new automated tolling technology outlined earlier in this chapter. The two roads are Express Lane SR 91 in California, USA and City Link in Melbourne, Australia.

Express Lane SR 91

The 22.4 km long Dulles Greenway in Virginia that opened in late 1995 was the first major privately funded toll road in the United States for more than 50 years. However, the 16 km long SR 91 in the Orange County area of southern California that opened soon afterwards was the first fully automated toll facil-ity to be provided in North America. SR 91 was fully operational with the automatic vehicle identification (AVI) based electronic system (ETTM) and began revenue service in early 1996.

Under the project, a four-lane tolled section was built within an existing, congested freeway right-of-way near Los Angeles. This $125 million project moved relatively quickly, largely owing to the fact that no environmental impact statement was needed as new lanes were simply being added to the median of an existing and operating eight-lane freeway (Lockwood *et al.*, 2002). A private investor is in charge of financing and operating the new lanes, which are priced and tolled, whereas the rest of the highway can be used free of charge. In line with congestion pricing rules, the toll for the express lanes is increased in peak periods. The operators' concession is to run for 35 years and, beyond a certain threshold, profits are shared between the state and the concession company. According to the operator, a major factor of success is the high demand on this particular route at peak hours, along with public acceptance of the idea of congestion pricing and other charging incentives to users. For example, the 91 Express Lanes offer discounted tolls to 3+ car-poolers, motorcycles, zero-emission vehicles, and vehicles with disabled persons licence plates.

Toll charges are levied using the FasTrak system, which is the electronic toll collection system that enables a customer to drive on the 91 Express Lanes without having to stop at toll booths. The FasTrak system comprises three elements: an electronic transponder that is mounted on the inside of a vehicle's windscreen; toll recording equipment located on the road; and an enforcement system. When passing through the toll zone, the transponder is read by an overhead antenna, and the posted toll amount is automatically deducted from the customer's account. Since there are no toll collection booths on the express lanes, California state law requires that all vehicles be equipped with a prop-erly mounted FasTrak transponder allowing tolls to be collected electronically. Travelling on the 91 Express Lanes without a transponder properly mounted on the vehicle could result in toll-evasion fees of $100 for the first violation, $250 for the second violation, to $500 for each additional violation within one year. As part of the California State Highway system, the 91 Express Lanes are subject to the same laws that apply to other California State Highways, and are enforced by the California Highway Patrol.

Express Lanes account holders are responsible for maintaining a minimum value in their account as described in the application and agreement to become an account-holder. The prepaid toll account is automatically replenished by the amount of $30 to a holder's credit card, or the average of the monthly toll usage, whichever is greater, each time the account falls below the minimum balance. The minimum balance is equal to the average toll usage for a ten-day period as calculated by the 91 Express Lanes, or $10, whichever is greater.

Neither trucks nor cars with trailers can use the toll lanes. The only over-sized vehicles that are allowed on the 91 Express Lanes are motorhomes and buses. Large trucks are prohibited for several reasons:

- Caltrans has approved a maximum vehicle weight of 10,000 pounds for the 91 Express Lanes.

- Under Californian law, a variety of vehicles, including vehicles towing a trailer, and trucks with more than two axles, may only use the right two lanes of a four lane limited-access highway such as the 91 freeway. Therefore, these vehicles may not used the 91 Express Lanes.
- Most larger trucks using the 91 freeway must stop at one of the weigh stations which are not accessible from the 91 Express Lanes.

Melbourne City Link

By contrast, although at 22 km in length it is not much longer than SR 91, Melbourne City Link is a much larger and more ambitious project, being a totally new development, which was financed, designed and built by the private sector, and uses much more advanced tolling technology. In fact, the Aus$1.8 billion/US$1.2 billion venture was, at the time, Australia's largest ever privately financed public infrastructure project (since surpassed in size by the Western Sydney Orbital at Aus$2.2 billion). The City Link project sponsor is Transurban, a single project company listed on the Australian stock exchange in 1996. Transurban has a 34-year concession with the government of the State of Victoria, to design, build, own and operate the toll road. At the end of this time, the project is to be transferred back to public control at no cost to the State.

In the words of Arndt (1998), the concession agreement was hard fought, detailed and expensive to negotiate, forcing the creation of novel risk-sharing mechanisms. By the time of financial closure, the successful tenderer had committed Aus$24 million, including design costs. Presumably, the losing bidder (the 'reserve' tenderer) had committed nearly as much. Obviously, those tendering for projects on this scale cannot bear these high bidding costs indefinitely, and must seek to recoup costs accrued on unsuccessful bids when they win projects by factoring them into the required rates of return (a fact often overlooked by critics who focus on the apparently high 'gross' returns).[14] In this particular instance, the other tenderer, CHART Roads, which was kept on 'active reserve' status until financial closure was reached, was paid $3 million by the state government, partly compensating it for extra costs incurred due to the protracted bidding process.[15]

Sponsors of the private company Transurban include Transfield Infrastructure Investments Pty Ltd, Hastings Fund Management Pty Ltd and Obayashi Corporation of Japan. Financial closure was achieved in March 1996, and the project marks significant innovation in the issue of infrastructure equity placements, infrastructure revenue bonds and significant non-recourse financing on the basis of the toll revenue. The Victorian government saw this agreement as a basis for future ventures, including projects in industries other than roads, and the Victorian auditor-general has generally been in favour of the agreement (Report of the Auditor General, 1997). Despite a later change of government, the project in reality did serve as a precursor for other large projects undertaken as public private partnerships.

Overall, the project entails a 5 km long tunnel and six toll zones, using automated electronic toll collection. It involved significant construction, including the widening of existing, formerly public freeways,[16] new elevated sections, and major new bridges and tunnels under densely populated areas and the Yarra River. Essentially, City Link connects existing publicly funded freeways and allows traffic to bypass the Central Business District (CBD). Previously, traffic approaching the CBD from the north (Tullamarine Freeway), the east (Eastern Freeway), the south-east (South Eastern Arterial), and the west (West Gate Freeway) had to pass through already congested city streets. City Link widens and upgrades the Tullamarine Freeway (which serves Melbourne airport) and the South Eastern Arterial, and connects both of these formerly public roads with the West Gate Freeway. In all, about 22 kilometres of road were built or upgraded.

City Link is one of the first urban toll roads to be developed as a BOOT (build-own-operate-transfer) project. Urban toll roads are generally more constrained on right-of-way availability than interurban or country roads. This may sometimes preclude toll plazas altogether, as it did with this project. A fully automated tolling system therefore was required, but such a system had never been used on a real project at the time when the City Link negotiations began, and thus an entirely new system had to be developed.

In some automated tolling systems, the cars need to pass through toll plazas, slowing down to 50 kph as they pass through the gates. This was impracticable in the City Link application. Tolling technology is also relatively easy in SR 91 because the vehicles are travelling in a dedicated lane and cannot switch to and from the untolled lanes in the freeway. In the City Link case, cars could move between lanes on the freeway system. The problem was thus one of devising a system to 'capture' for tolling purposes cars that are travelling at 110 kph (or more) and switching from one lane to another and from one route to another at high speeds.

In the event, a system that would do the job, Transroute, was designed by French engineers. The result is a tolling system for the project that is completely automated, so there is no need for motorists to slow down approaching tolling plazas or to stay in one lane. A transponder in the car registers even high speed lane changes at tolling points and payment is transferred from the road user's account by direct debit, according to 'user pays' principles.

The City Link project embodies many significant innovations in terms of project financing arrangements and risk management, and the interested reader is referred to the article by Arndt (1998) which is reprinted, along with many other of the articles to which reference is made in this volume, in

Grimsey and Lewis (2004). However, in view of the discussion that takes place in the next chapter, two aspects of the risk allocation are noteworthy. This history of private sector involvement in transport infrastructure investment suggests that private initiatives are particularly vulnerable to two things: (1) technological and economic developments that lead to demand risk, and (2) changes in government regulations. Both risk factors are explicitly addressed in this case.

Traffic demand is probably the largest single risk for an urban toll road. In situations where there are many alternate routes available for toll-averse drivers, there is ample opportunity for those drivers to avoid tolls. This is particularly true for the City Link facilities, since there are many alternative routes in and around the CBD. One preliminary study estimated a 40 per cent diversion rate if manual tolling was introduced, which was an additional spur for the contractors to ensure that the (untried) automated tolling system was easy to use and worked effectively. Often, in such circumstances, demand risk guarantees are sought from public sector bodies. Significantly, Transurban explicitly accepted the risk of traffic demand, which it considered to be the most critical risk to the project's viability once construction was completed. There are no state-provided minimum usage or revenue guarantees.

The government stuck to the policy of accepting only those risks that it is best placed to control and manage, while adhering to the concept of risk–reward, in which the party assuming a risk should have access to associated rewards. Conversely, it is argued that the party to whom the rewards flow should accept the risk. Consistent with this position, the government took on the risk of changes in the state-controlled road network that connects to City Link, adversely affecting City Link patronage. It is also important that this risk allocation be symmetrical. That is, if one party accepts the consequences of a downside risk, it should also gain the benefits of an upside risk. Thus the government agreed fully to compensate Transurban under the Material Adverse Effect regime for any detriment to the project resulting from publicly sponsored changes in the transport network. However, if any modifications result in increased traffic volumes and profits for Transurban, only 50 per cent of these are passed back to the State.

NOTES

1. Martini and Lee (1996).
2. Threadgold (1996).
3. East Asia Analytical Unit (1998).
4. The Allen Consulting Group (2003, p. 4).
5. The leading luminary is Douglass North (1990). For later contributions see Deepak Lal (1999) and Rodrik (2003).
6. Cost–benefit analysis is the appraisal of an investment project that includes all social and

financial costs and benefits accruing to the project over its expected life, to determine whether the discounted value of the benefits exceeds the costs. For a classic analysis of the issues involved, see Mishan (1971).

7. For an overview of monetarist views, see Lewis and Mizen (2000, chapter 7).
8. For example, a US study found that transport costs as a percentage of product prices ranged widely, from 3 to 27 per cent. The actual proportion of industry that falls into the transport cost sensitivity range may be relatively small (Hurdle, 1992).
9. The ability-to-pay principle is that taxes or charges for public services should be levied according to the user's capacity to pay, whereas the benefit principle holds that individuals should pay taxes or charges in line with the benefits each would receive from the services, akin to transactions in the marketplace (see Musgrave, 1959).
10. The City Link (linked motorways and tunnel) project is analysed in Arndt (1998).
11. A transponder is a small battery-powered radio device which is mounted inside the vehicle on the windscreen and identifies the customer's prepaid toll account. When travelling through the toll zone, the transponder is read by an overhead antenna, and the posted toll amount is automatically deducted from the customer's account. The transponder can be easily moved from one vehicle to another. In addition, it is possible to add other vehicles to the account even if not equipped with transponders, so long as the licence number is advised to the relevant operator.
12. See *The Economist*, 15 February 2003, pp. 51–3.
13. A system currently using global positioning system (GPS) technology in a limited way is the 'distance-based heavy vehicles fee' (LSVA), which was introduced in Switzerland in 2001. Trucks travelling through Switzerland are charged per kilometre travelled. GPS is used as an auditing tool to check the distances recorded on the truck's on-board unit, which is activated and deactivated as the truck enters and leaves the country. A more developed GPS-based truck tolling system is being developed in Germany for possible implementation in 2005. See *The Economist*, Technology Quarterly, 12 June 2004, pp. 22–4.
14. This is, in fact, an issue for government because tenderers must recoup costs on other works, either other government projects or private projects. In the former case, the government pays directly in the longer run. In the latter case, it is an additional burden on the economy which raises the costs of doing business.
15. A recent review of PPPs in Victoria recommended that the government should give consideration to creating a fund to compensate bidders where a particular design innovation becomes the property of the state or where additional costs are imposed on participants due to 'process changes' by the state (Fitzgerald Report, 2004).
16. This particular aspect drew criticism from those who objected to paying tolls on stretches of road which were previously free. The critics overlooked that public roads are heavily subsidized in many different ways. Not surprisingly, some of the strongest criticism came from the road haulage contractors who ignored the fact that trucks do more than ten times the damage to roads than motor cars, yet do not pay commensurate taxes for road use.

3. The origins of partnerships

INTRODUCTION

This chapter mainly is concerned with the increased involvement in recent years of the private sector in the provision of infrastructure-related services. Our particular focus is on the variety of forces that lie behind and have come together to underpin and to inform this trend. Here we refer to the 'new public management' agenda, dissatisfaction with traditional procurement methods and the development of the private financing model, and the conceptualization of 'partnering' as a management process. But we begin with history, for there is a rich tradition of private sector investment in infrastructure. It is important to understand this history, and why so many of the projects come to grief, in order to appreciate the special risks that infrastructure investment poses to private entities.

Many people would think of the 'railway mania' of the mid-nineteenth century as the grand era of private sector involvement in infrastructure investment, and with good reason because the railway construction boom 'overshadowed all other economic developments of the period' (Briggs, 1959, p. 296). Some idea of the extent of private activity in this infrastructure sector can be discerned by the calculation of Thomas Tooke, the Victorian economist, that at the height of the railway construction boom in Britain in the late 1840s, as many people were employed in railway construction activities as the total population engaged in factories in the whole of the United Kingdom at that time (Court, 1962). In addition, railway construction in Britain was soon followed by the construction, using British finance and equipment and often British management and labour, of railways abroad, especially in the Americas.

Yet, roads and water projects provide some of the earliest examples of private activity in infrastructure, and it is on these that we focus in the first part of this chapter by examining the turnpike system of toll roads in Britain and the United States, and the concession approach to infrastructure in France, first used for water distribution. In terms of railways, we look briefly at the early history of the London underground, which is arguably from today's perspective a more interesting example than the 'age of steam' in view of the UK government's recent decision to use public private partnerships to rebuild and refurbish the London underground 100 years after much of it was originally constructed. In fact, the PFI contracts with the Tubelines and Metronet consortia to modernize London Underground, signed in 2002 and 2003, represent the largest PFI contracts by capital value (HM Treasury, 2003b, p. 19). It is this recent resurgence of private sector involvement in infrastructure that is the subject of the rest of this chapter.

HISTORY

Early Roads

Tolled roads are no new thing. The Greek historian and philosopher Strabo (63 BC–AD 21), writing in *Geographia* at the time of Caesar Augustus records there being tolls on the Little Saint Bernard's Pass. The Salassi tribe was given a toll concession by the Roman Empire, in return for maintaining the pass and providing guidance and porterage across the mountain range. In the Middle Ages, tolls were used to support the cost of bridge construction, and as early as 1286 London Bridge had tolls. Tolls were less common on roads, although in 1364, Edward III of England legislated tolling rights on the Great Northern Road from London to Philippe Litchfield in return for his work on improving the roadway (Levinson, 2002).

However, for the most part, roads in the Middle Ages – at least in Britain – were very different from today. The principal 'highway' was the sea in combination with rivers. Many major cities (e.g. London, Paris) are located on the first practicable river crossing in from the sea (Kindleberger, 1974). Large numbers of small craft plied the waters around Britain carrying coal, stone, slate, grain, wood and even groceries. Such was the state of the roads that some of them were described by a pamphleteer as being 'what God left them after the Flood' (Ashton, 1955, p. 78). In general, roads were more of a right of passage on another's land to avoid damage to crops than a constructed surface, and the tracks were kept clear mainly by continual usage much like footpaths, bridleways and other public rights of way are today except that then traffic came from farmworkers and pilgrims rather than ramblers and ponytrekkers (Mountfield, 1976).

It was not until 1555 that legislation was passed in Britain to ensure that roadways would be maintained, but the administrative body responsible was unfitted to the task. The duty of caring for the highways was put on the local parish. Each parish appointed surveyors – unpaid and unskilled – to supervise the labour of the parishioners who were called on to contribute services to the repair of the roads in their own area. Those with property were obliged to send horses, carts and ploughs to help maintain the roads, while others had to work on the roads for six consecutive days each year under the surveyor's authority. This system of compulsory labour was not finally abolished until 1835. A similar requirement operated in the United States where the laws requiring highway labour lasted into the twentieth century in some rural areas (Goddard, 1994). In both countries the system proved to be inefficient because the local community had neither the resources nor the motivation to carry out road maintenance effectively. People were put to work, but few of them had any special qualifications, and in parishes where through traffic was growing the condition of the highways probably deteriorated. The demand for better quality roads led to the next development – the turnpikes.

British Turnpikes

Turnpikes have been described by Adrian Smith as 'the precursors of the modern build, operate and transfer systems' (Smith, 1999, p. 11). A turnpike is a road partly or wholly paid for by fees collected from travellers at tollgates. It derives its name from the hinged barrier (spiked spear or English 'pike') that was stretched across the road and prevented passage until swung open for toll-payers. Turnpikes comprised both new and reconstructed roads.

Although, as we have noted, tollgates in England were first authorized by law in 1364, the first turnpike was established in 1663. The justices of Hertfordshire, Huntingdon and Cambridge petitioned Parliament for the passing of an Act enabling them to raise funds for the repair and improvement of a section of the Great Northern Road running through the three counties. The Act gave the justices the right to place three tollgates to collect tolls at a specified rate on vehicles and livestock passing on the particular section of road over a period of 21 years, within which time it was expected that the debt would be cleared and the road would revert to being free of charge (Cossons, 1934). It was not until early in the eighteenth century, however, that the customary formula vesting the administration of roads in *ad hoc* local bodies, and of transferring the cost of maintenance from the public to the users, was firmly established.

One of the first so-called 'turnpike trusts' was formed in 1706–7 to improve the section of the London–Holyhead highway between Fornhill and Stony Stratford. Its success led to the passing of hundreds of Acts extending the system to almost all parts of England. By the 1840s there were nearly 1000 Turnpike Acts in force, promoted by town councils, merchants, manufacturers, farmers and landowners, including those responsible for maintaining at least a part of the road in question.

Trustees of the turnpike trusts were given powers to raise capital, usually at 4 or 5 per cent, and to apply this to making a new road (or, more often, to improving an old one) in a particular locality. Actual maintenance and construction were left to the management of an appointed surveyor, who was usually involved in supervising the operations of a number of turnpikes. Collection of the tolls was franchised to toll 'farmers' who paid a fixed sum to the trust in return for the right to collect tolls on particular gates on the turnpike (an early example of outsourcing or subcontracting). After 1773, toll farming leases were auctioned, initially to local businessmen and eventually to larger groups which might buy leases to a number of turnpikes.[1]

Construction techniques were left to the discretion of the local engineer. One famous road constructor, John Metcalf, the blind engineer of Knaresborough, engineered about 180 miles of turnpike road in the north of England. His method was to dig out the soil, lay bunches of heather on the bed of soft earth, cover these with stone, and dress with a layer of gravel to form a convex rather than a flat surface, so that the rain water ran off to the ditches made at each side. But there were many others, each adapting to variations of sub-soil and local needs (Ashton, 1955, p. 81).

While the turnpike trusts were relatively small undertakings, each concerned with ten or twenty miles of road, it was expedient to attract not only local, but also through traffic, and hence the trustees of each turnpike sought to link up their road with others. For example, by 1765 there was a line of turnpikes from London to Berwick-on-Tweed, with only a short break in the neighbourhood of Doncaster (Cossons, 1934, p. 12). But since tolls had to be paid every seven or ten miles, long-distance traffic consisted largely of passengers and of goods of small bulk and high value.

Under the General Turnpike Act of 1773 an elaborate system of differential tolls was established. Vehicles were classified according to the breadth of their wheels. Rates fell as the breadth rose, and wagons with 'rollers' of between 13 and 16 inches in width were exempted from tolls for a year and given preferential treatment thereafter in part because they created fewer ruts in the surface (Cossons, 1934, pp. 20–2). Moreover, not every traveller was subject to tolls. The mails and the clergy were exempt, as were the construction workers for turnpike maintenance and improvement. The government paid an annual fee in lieu of tolls, as did the residents in the locality of the road. Revenues obtained were used to pay off mortgages incurred by the trusts for extending, resurfacing, straightening and widening the roads.

Despite the general improvements to the highway infrastructure, opposition to the turnpikes was strong. As is the case with tolled motorways today, the turnpikes were seen as a transfer from the poor, who had been able to travel free with their carts and horses before the turnpiking of the road, to the rich, who had the most to gain because they travelled over longer distances and their carriages could now pass more easily on the better roads. Several turnpike riots took place.

US Turnpikes

It was not until after the War of Revolution that turnpikes were introduced in the United States. The first turnpike road was actually a state enterprise, authorized by a Virginia act of 1785. The first to be constructed and operated by a private corporation was the Philadelphia–Lancaster Turnpike, chartered in Pennsylvania in 1792 and completed two years later. Thereafter the movement gathered pace, and by the 1840s a total of nearly 1600 turnpike companies had been chartered. There were also private toll bridges. The early roads were rough and ready by present-day standards, but served the purpose. Construction would usually begin with felling trees and removing stumps, while swampland was crossed by logs laid side by side ('corduroy'). The surface of the turnpike was sometimes of earth, but often of broken stone or planks. Estache *et al.* (2000) claim that 'in the first half of the nineteenth century, private toll roads outnumbered public roads' (p. 10).

As in Britain, not everyone paid the tolls. Massachusetts legislation exempted people going to church, those on military duty, and those doing business within the tollgated town. In New York, toll booths were placed at ten-mile intervals, allowing many locals with short journeys to be free-riders. Also, 'shunpikes', illegal tollgate bypasses, arose which allowed people to avoid the section of the road with the toll booth. Tolls were an annoyance to those travelling and many supported the idea that roads were public utilities and should be free to all.

Free-riders and shunpikes contributed to the low returns on turnpike investments. Dividends and capital returns on turnpike stocks were at best 8 per cent annually, with 3 per cent per annum returns being more common (Levinson, 2002). It has been argued that turnpike 'subscribers were usually more interested in the possible benefits the new lines of communication would bring them than in the profitability of the investment' (Durrenberger, 1931, p. 100 cited in Levinson, 2002, p. 25), because the towns and their leading citizens were looking to economic spillovers to their locality from the improved transport and communication. Certainly, the economic prosperity of the towns waxed and waned with the success of the turnpikes, which went into sharp decline with the advent, first, of canals, and then the railroads. As the turnpikes declined, the fortunes of the towns on the turnpikes declined, while those on the canals rose. Later, competitive pressures on the turnpikes came from the improved free public parallel roads. By the late nineteenth and early twentieth century, public operation and financing of roads had again become dominant.

When the turnpikes in the United States were chartered it was envisaged that ownership would revert to the states, typically at the end of a 99-year lease. In fact, few lived out their charters, and most were abandoned or decommissioned by sale with a fair and just price paid to the turnpikes' owners. In the early 1900s, the remaining toll roads were acquired by state and local governments as the states established state highway systems. Much the same scenario occurred in the UK. None of the turnpike trusts in the UK succeeded in paying off all their debt within the initial 21-year term, and the trusts were more or less automatically extended (rather like in the Chilean least-present-value-of-revenue tender system for BOT franchises today[2]). With the arrival of the railways from the late 1820s, the share of intercity transport moving by road declined sharply, and the case for acceding to public demands for the removal of tollroads became more compelling. Toll revenue was replaced by local taxes in Ireland in 1858, tolls were abolished in Scotland from 1865, and turnpike trusts in England were dissolved at a rapid rate. By the late 1880s, most of the British road system had been taken back into public ownership. The last turnpike toll was collected on 1 November 1895 on the Shrewsbury to Holyhead road.

The London Underground

A similar pattern of enthusiastic growth followed by competitive pressures is evident in the history of the London Underground. Each of the companies engaged in the building of the seven 'electric tube' underground lines[3] between 1894 and 1907 first had to be chartered by means of a Private Act of Parliament. For this to take place, representation had to be made to a Joint Select Committee of the House of Parliament and the Lords involving expert witnesses (engineers, statisticians, financiers, etc.) set up to adjudicate between the various proposed Bills. Once the Act was passed, capital had to be raised, rights of way negotiated,[4] and the construction undertaken (normally over four years). Some of the companies had great difficulties in raising the capital,[5] and a number of rationalizations eventually saw ownership of the lines concentrated in two hands. The financial difficulties of the companies stemmed from two sources, one technological, the other regulatory. These two factors – technological improvements and regulatory changes – pose threats to any transport infrastructure investment.

When the companies obtained their charters and began construction, petrol-driven buses broke down frequently and could not withstand the rigours of everyday use and constant stopping and starting in heavy traffic. They appeared to pose little potential threat to underground trains. By the time the underground system finally had been put in place in 1907, buses were more reliable. The X-type and improved B-type motor buses introduced in 1909 and 1910 respectively could average 12 mph and, with the advantage of running on public roads, operated at considerable profits while the underground lines were struggling to pay.

Trams provided the other source of competition. While overhead trains were excluded from the grid formed by the Metropolitan and District lines, a change to the regulatory environment allowed electric trams, some private, others municipal (e.g. London County Council), to operate within the 'inner circuit' or 'circle'. London County Council electric cars were allowed to cross Westminster Bridge and run along the Victoria Embankment for the first time on 15 December 1906.

On both scores, the underground railway lines by the time they were built faced competition from two sources, neither of which had been anticipated in their business forecasts.[6] While some of the companies provided steady returns, most of the investors in the public share issues probably breathed a sigh of relief when the underground rail companies were effectively nationalized with compensation when the London Passenger Transport Board, a public corporation, took over operations in July 1933.

From this brief account it would seem that private supply of infrastructure, or at least of transport facilities, has had a chequered history. The ventures made significant contributions to the improvement of transport infrastructure, but the companies themselves (or more correctly, the shareholders) faced serious risks. Their financial viability was vulnerable to competition from new technological advances, and to changes in the rules of the regulatory game. Thereafter, public provision and financing was dominant for most of the twentieth century, but in the last two decades, private financing has returned to the top of the agenda. France is a country that evidences this cycle most clearly.

FRENCH CONCESSION APPROACH[7]

Unlike some other European countries (e.g. the UK, the Netherlands), France does not have a PPP policy today. This is due to the fact that PPPs are considered an 'old concept'. The French PPP model goes back more than a hundred years in the form of *Societes d'Economie Mixtes* and *Concessions*, and the concession system remains one of the most popular modes of constructing and managing 'commercial' public services and public infrastructure in France. In fact, in 1995, 75 per cent of the population was provided with water under PPP contracts. Two PPP operators, Lyonnaise des Eaux and Vivendi (now Veolia Environment) controlled 62 per cent of water distribution, 36 per cent of sewerage disposal, 75 per cent of urban central heating, 60 per cent of refuse treatment, 55 per cent of cable operation, and 36 per cent of refuse collection, all under PPPs. In most countries, these figures would be remarkable. They are not in France because PPPs have been around for a long time – dating back to the seventeenth century. Most of the railway network, water provision facilities and street lighting were developed under PPPs (Ribault, 2001).

The first concession contracts were awarded for the construction and financing of the Mediterranean–Atlantic Channel (*Canal du Midi* launched in 1666) and *Canal de Briare* (1638), but also for much other public infrastructure such as bridges and tunnels. Under a concession contract, entrepreneurs were effectively given a franchise to provide public services for a specified period of time. France's long involvement with water concessions can be dated back to 1782 when the Perrier brothers were granted the first water supply concession to provide a water distribution system to parts of Paris (although it was subsequently revoked following the Revolution). Another famous example of private sector involvement in infrastructure utilizing the concession system was the 160 km long Suez Canal (Smith, 1999). The concession was granted by the Turkish Viceroy of Egypt in 1854 and the canal was completed in 1869 with a 99-year concession period, which began when the canal was opened (but was terminated when the Suez Canal Company was nationalized in 1956 by the Egyptian government).

In the second half of the nineteenth century, France employed concession schemes extensively to finance its infrastructure networks. Railways, water, electricity and tramway networks were designed, financed and operated by private operators and banks. Most of these projects were realized in the form of long-term concession contracts, under which the property of the infrastructure was to return to the public entities at the end of the contract. Later, the system was generalized to numerous activities considered in France as 'commercial public services', such as water supply and sanitation, waste management or urban transportation. This model has influenced many civil law-based systems, in particular in continental southern Europe and the francophone African countries.

Infrastructure concessions in France experienced a period of relative decline as a consequence of the 1929 crisis and World War II when public services and public infrastructure sectors returned to the state. Numerous concessionaires were nationalized, in particular those operating on a nationwide basis, such as the railways and the energy sector. This period saw the creation of state-owned monopolies such as EDF, SNCF, ADP or RATP, which remained closely linked to central and/or local government by concession contracts. Major infrastructure projects were launched on an exclusive public funding basis, usually in the form of public works contracts.

As a result of this heritage, public services and infrastructure in France came to be divided between two opposite systems: the PPP-based private concession system known in France as *delegation de service public* and the dirigiste system of *gestion directe*, where the infrastructure or service is built and/or operated directly by a public or state-owned body (Lignieres, 2002). A large amount of infrastructure has been managed and developed under the form of a concession contract granted to a public concessionaire, whereby a special purpose public corporation is created to construct and operate the infrastructure. An example is the concession holding companies formed to develop the French motorway network during the 1950s, with equity provided by local authorities and a public credit institution, a device that enabled central government to circumvent its own budget restrictions. However, the tolls charged were regulated and rose at a rate lower than inflation, damaging the companies' revenue and balance sheets, and most were taken over by the government when they got into financial difficulties (Smith, 1999; Levinson, 2002).

Purely private concessions, however, never completely disappeared, and survived under various contractual forms, especially in the municipal services sector. Water supply, sanitation, urban heating, waste management, urban transportation and contracted food services have generally been operated in France under PPP schemes. Since the end of the 1990s, the use of PPP schemes to finance and design infrastructure projects has made a strong comeback and French utilities such as Vivendi (Veolia), Suez Lyonnaise, Bouygues, Vinci, SAUR, Sodexho and Connex have taken advantage of this new climate. The French government has opened to private concessionaires projects such as the Millau Viaduct, the High Speed link between Perpignan and Figueras, as well as several highways sections (A19, A86, A28). At the local level, almost all public services are open to concession arrangements. Sewage disposal, refuse collection and management, cable, urban transport, sporting facilities, school canteens, funeral services, and water provision can be organized under *delegation de gestion* contracts (Ribault, 2001).

This changing tapestry has left France with a legislative structure for PPPs very different from that in the Anglo-Saxon countries. There is no legislation as such, but there is a long-standing tradition of concessions in France, and the administrative courts have drawn the lines of a coherent legal framework, in particular concerning the division of responsibilities between the operator and the public bodies (Lignieres, 2002). This framework, elaborated by the Council of State (*Conseil d'Etat*) is based on the following principles:

- the contract remains subject to the principles governing public services activities, i.e. the supremacy of the general interest over private interests;
- the public entities are therefore placed in a position of superiority towards the private partner;
- infrastructure and buildings necessary for the provision of the public service, even if financed, designed and operated by the private sector, are placed under the regime of public properties which means that they are the property of the public entity *ab initio* and are to be returned (*biens de retour*) to them at the end of the contract;
- as a counterpart to these powers given to the public entity, French courts

have awarded the private partner rights to be indemnified when its situation is affected by unilateral decisions founded on the general interest and the right to be indemnified when unforeseeable circumstances (*imprevision*) affect the financial balance prevailing at the date of the signature of the contract;[8]

- contracts have to be submitted to the general principles of French public law and to the jurisdiction of the administrative courts.

The effect of the last principle is that as soon as a PPP contract involves the general interest or the management of an activity considered as a public service, it is generally subject to French public law. French public law has strict rules concerning the use of public funds and public properties, which have a strong impact on the nature of the legal and financial schemes available to design a PPP project. In particular, rules pertaining to public properties (*domaine public*) render difficult, if not impossible, the implementation in France of long-term leases and BOOT contracts, in which the property of the infrastructure is to be private, at least during the contract.

In general, however, the flexibility of case-law and the realism of the Council of State and the administrative courts, make possible the adoption of the new structure of PPP projects allowing a precise and adequate breakdown of risks, funds and responsibilities between the project's main parties. For instance, most of the Anglo-Saxon rules concerning project finance schemes can be implemented under French law. Nevertheless, French administrative courts sometimes seem reluctant to admit innovative forms of PPP schemes outside the traditional concession contract. The Council of State has adopted a strict position concerning the possibility to admit private financing schemes for railways in order to protect the public properties.

RECENT DEVELOPMENTS

Our principal focus in this volume is with the model of PPPs that has evolved in the UK, Australia, Canada and South Africa, and that applies to many project-level partnerships in the United States (e.g. BTO/BOT roads). However, this is not the only approach to the private financing of infrastructure. In Europe, Ireland has followed the UK lead. By contrast, countries like France, Spain, the Netherlands and Belgium use concessions, and this approach has been adopted elsewhere. A case study of a water concession project in Bulgaria is given in Chapter 9. While the French and the Dutch experiences, in particular, constitute significant examples of alternative PPP approaches based around design, construction, finance and operation of facilities, there are considerable differences in the contractual arrangements in the two countries. Also, at an operational level, the Netherlands uses a PPP Knowledge Centre as a point of contact and adviser for government agencies interested in PPPs, whereas France does not. Nevertheless, while it is not possible to identify a common European PPP model and the details differ, there is a family resemblance between the various public/private arrangements. Moreover, it is apparent that the role of partnerships seems to be expanding in most European countries.

What is behind this growth (and in many cases, revival) of PPPs? At a general level, PPPs have a basic appeal simply because they combine private sector and public sector approaches to infrastructure development. The private financing of infrastructure drew many visionary entrepreneurs into the construction and operation of the facilities, and saw many diverse groups join forces at the local level. But the ventures often had difficulty raising enough capital to get off the ground, they were vulnerable to changes in technology and regulation, and risked haphazard development of the transport networks (e.g. duplication of routes, railway 'gauge wars', and different canal widths, etc.).

Purely public approaches to infrastructure, however, brought their own problems – projects bogged down by bureaucracy, political meddling and interference, new investment starved of funds, and often poor management and maintenance of facilities. Berg *et al.* (2002, p. 2) make the point well. They argue that a fundamental lesson of economics is Milton Friedman's dictum that there is no such thing as a free lunch. To this they add that a fundamental lesson from political science is that the next election becomes an important time-horizon for public policy. Taken together, these dictums suggest that policymakers may promote programmes that benefit today's constituencies at the expense of future groups. The costs show up in a number of ways. In the case of infrastructure sectors such as telecommunications, energy and water, the sunk costs associated with investments mean that opportunistic behaviour by government and private parties can result in sub-optimal levels of investment and poor management of programmes. Infrastructure performance can suffer because of the time it takes to get new programmes off the ground. Historically, it is also the case that state, local and national governments have often become involved with the financing, pricing and provision of network infrastructure in ways that can run counter to economic efficiency and even to widely accepted views of fairness.

Against this backdrop, a PPP seeks to get the best of both approaches to infrastructure, employing private sector innovation and business acumen where appropriate, while allowing overall planning, coordination and regulatory control of the infrastructure networks to reside in public hands. Of course, the same short-term political pressures can surface in public private partnerships and, in the case of Japan actually did.[9] But a well-constructed PPP policy in an open, pluralistic society can do much to open up these pressures to public scrutiny.

In this endeavour to use private sector resources in tandem with government, the evolution of the PPP concept has been aided by developments in a number of fields that have coalesced to inform the arrangement. Here we trace the intellectual origins of PPPs to three influences which we first outline and then discuss in more detail in the remainder of this chapter

- *The changing market for public services.* The first influence is changing attitudes to the ways in which public services are produced and delivered to the public. A PPP is simply a method of procurement (although of infrastructure services rather than the infrastructure itself) and as such its application is seen as an extension of a liberalization agenda that has become known as the 'new public management' or 'marketization' of the public sector (Broadbent and Laughlin, 2003). These terms embrace the corporatization, privatization, commercialism, managerialism, outsourcing and downsizing of public sector activities. PPPs are one exemplification of these trends, and of changing markets for public services, in that they allow for public services to be provided by public and private sector bodies working in partnership.
- *The private financing model.* In addition, in our view, two other factors have been instrumental in the growth of PPPs over the last decade. One is the refinement of the private financing model and the development of project finance techniques to 'engineer' the finance to suit PPP structures.
- *The concept of partnering.* The third influence we identify is little known to most economic commentators. PPPs have been shaped by concepts of 'partnering' developed in the engineering construction industry that lie on the border between engineering and management. Our contention is that the partnering concept has provided an intellectual backdrop and support to the organization of PPPs.

CHANGING MARKET FOR PUBLIC SERVICES

PPPs can be seen as one component of a rearrangement of the public sector with a management culture that focuses on the centrality of the citizen or customer, accountability for results, investigation of a wide variety of alternative service delivery mechanisms, and competition between public and private bodies for contracts to deliver services, consistent with cost recovery and achievement of value for money (Manning, 2002). Partnerships are part of a broad shift in the workings of government and the search for new forms of governance. In this reorientation, the image of government as the direct provider of services is transformed to one in which government is the enabler, coordinating provision and actions by and through others. The emphasis is on 'the task rather than the actor', 'outcomes rather than inputs'. Government becomes 'more about steering and less about rowing' (Stoker, 1998, p. 34).

In order to understand the distinctive contribution of PPPs, we need to consider a broader range of government business models in the context of the commercialism or marketization of the public sector. Hood (1995) outlines the various dimensions of what has become known as the 'new public management', under seven headings:

1. A shift towards greater disaggregation of public organizations into separately managed 'corporatized' units for each public sector 'product' (each identified as a separate cost centre, with its own organizational identity).
2. A trend towards greater competition both between public sector organizations and between public sector organizations and the private sector.
3. Greater use within the public sector of management practices drawn from the private corporate sector, rather than public-sector-specific methods of doing business.
4. An increased emphasis on parsimony in resource use and on the active search for finding alternative, less costly ways to deliver public services, instead of laying the stress on institutional continuity.
5. More 'hands-on' control by visible top managers wielding discretionary power, as against the traditional 'hands-off' style of relatively anonymous bureaucrats at the top of public sector organizations.
6. A move towards more explicit and measurable (or at least verifiable) standards of performance for public sector organizations, in terms of the range, level and content of services to be provided, as against trust in professional standards and expertise across the public sector.
7. Attempts to control public organizations in a more 'homeostatic' style according to preset output measures (particularly in pay based on job performance instead of on rank or educational attainment), rather than by the traditional style of 'orders of the day' coming on an *ad hoc* basis from the top.

Implementation of this agenda has spawned a number of different public sector business models, and widened the interface between public and private agencies. Table 3.1 sets out a list of public/private business models, starting from complete public provision ('collectivization') at one end of the scale, through service provision contracts and outsourcing to, at the other end, outright privatization where the ownership of the asset is transferred fully to the private sector entity. Traditional public procurement is covered by design

Table 3.1   Range of public/private business models

- Public provision of collective goods
- Service provision contracts
- Outsourcing/contracting
- Design and construct (D & C)
- Sale and leaseback
- Operate and maintain (O & M)
- Operate maintain and manage (OM & M)
- Build transfer operate (BTO)
- Build operate transfer (BOT)
- Build lease transfer (BLT)
- Build lease transfer maintain (BLTM)
- Build own operate remove (BOOR)
- Build own operate transfer (BOOT)
- Lease renovate operate transfer (LROT)
- Design build finance operate (DBFO)
- Design construct manage finance (DCMF)
- Design build finance operate manage (DBFOM)
- Build own operate (BOO)
- Franchise
- Concession
- Joint venture (JV)
- Regeneration partnership
- Outright privatization

and construct contracts, while sale and leaseback arrangements are often driven by taxation advantages, rather than any partnership motives (Grimsey and Lewis, 2002b). Most of the other models encompass some form of PPP arrangement, with wide variety being based on some form of lease, franchise or fixed-term concession, using different combinations of private sector resources to design, renovate, construct, finance, operate, manage and maintain facilities. Except in the case of a BOO when ownership remains with the private sector virtually for ever, at the end of a concession the public body usually takes over (or resumes) responsibility for the ownership, operation and management of the asset. Nevertheless, the public entity may then effectively extend the concession by means of an O & M, OM & M, or LROT (lease-renovate-operate-transfer) contract.

On this basis, relationships between the government and the market can be viewed as a continuum. Traditional public funding and provision of services constitute one pole, and purely private activity the other. Partnerships cover most of the points between the two, with each position representing a slightly different mix between the public and private sectors. For example, contracting could constitute a 'partnership' depending on the precise nature of the responsibilities assigned to the private and public entities under the terms of the contract.

This leads us to three questions. First, how do PPPs differ from privatization? Second, in what ways do PPPs differ from contracting out? Third, what do partnerships contribute to public sector management?

PPPs and Privatization

Consider, first, the question of whether, and how, PPPs differ from privatization. One reason is that within a PPP the public sector acquires and pays for services from the private sector on behalf of the community and retains ultimate responsibility for the delivery of the services, albeit that they are being provided by the private sector over an extended period of time (i.e. 25 years or longer). By contrast, when a government entity is privatized the private firm that takes over the business also assumes the responsibility for service delivery. In this case, it would be wrong to say that the government is indifferent as to the quality of services provided by the newly privatized entity. Rather, two other mechanisms come into play, since the private firm is subject to disciplines from both product and capital markets in the form of competition from other firms and competition when raising finance. Moreover, if these market constraints do not exist effectively, perhaps because the privatized firm has some form of natural monopoly, then the government will usually impose some type of regulatory regime, typically over price or rate of return.

In this latter case, however, the regulation imposed on the privatized firm is quite different from that under a PPP, and this difference is another reason why PPPs are not privatization. A PPP is a formal business arrangement between the public and private sectors. The nature of this business activity, the outcomes required, the prices paid for the services (and thus the scope for profits) along with the general rights and obligations of the various parties are specified in considerable detail in the contract or concession agreement. Consequently, regulation does not come from some statutory regulatory agency or from unseen market forces, but is a direct result of an explicit contract subject to performance indicators and quality standards, with abatement attached to any failure to maintain service standards on a continuing basis.

These two differences – regulation through contract and the lack of government disengagement – define much that is distinctive about a PPP. Nevertheless, PPPs might still be seen as privatization in all but name, as they are by many public sector unions. At issue is how privatization is defined.

Starr (1988) notes that privatization has generally come to mean two things: (1) any shift of activities or functions from the state to the private sector; and, more specifically, (2) any shift of the production of goods and services from public to private. The first, broader, definition includes all reductions in the regulatory and spending activity of the state. The second, more specific, definition excludes deregulation and spending cuts except when they result in a shift from public to private in the production of goods and services. This second definition is the one preferred by Starr.

Starr goes on to argue that four types of government activities can bring about a shift in production from the public to the private sector. First, the cessation of public programmes and withdrawal of government from specific responsibilities can represent implicit privatization. At another level, the restriction of publicly produced services in volume, availability, or quality may lead consumers to shift to privately produced substitutes (called 'privatization by attrition' when a government lets public services run down). Second, privatization may take the explicit form of transfers of public assets to private ownership, through sale or lease of public land, infrastructure and enterprises. Third, instead of directly producing some service, the government may finance private services, for example, through contracting out or vouchers. Fourth, privatization may result from the deregulation of entry into activities previously treated as public monopolies.

None of these four policies in itself directly covers the example of PPPs. Some transfer of assets, especially by way of leasehold, forms a component of most PPPs, but it is not a defining characteristic. There is procurement, certainly, but normally under a PPP this covers much more than an operations and maintenance (O & M) contract. Deregulation of entry is important for many PPPs, for example when a private toll operator is allowed to levy tolls, and to utilize public law enforcement officers to enforce payment and impose fines. Yet a PPP allows for a contractual relationship between the public entity and private provider that far exceeds deregulation alone.

PPPs and Contracting Out

In considering the second question of how PPPs differ from contracting out, we note that privatization and contracting out are often used synonymously, particularly in the USA, as we saw with Starr's definition. Elsewhere, and especially in the UK and Australia, privatization refers to the transfer of ownership of physical assets from public to private hands (that is, 'explicit' privatization in Starr's terminology). The sale of a public utility via a share float constitutes straightforward privatization in these terms. However, the privatized organizations may or may not operate in a competitive environment. In this respect, privatization can be essentially independent of the promotion of competition. How much competition there is post-privatization will depend largely on the structure of the industry and on government regulatory policy.

By contrast, contracting out involves opening up to competition a set of economic activities that were previously excluded from it. Organizations are invited to submit bids for contracts to provide particular services to the client. The distinctive feature of contracting out is the element of *ex ante* competition – competition for the market as opposed to competition in it. The market in this case is defined by the contract specification, and the bidding process resembles an auction (Domberger and Rimmer, 1994, Domberger and Jensen, 1997). A formal contract binds the parties to an exchange of services of a predetermined quality and quantity for agreed financial payments. The contract itself becomes the instrument through which relations between the parties are managed and regulated.

Domberger *et al.* survey the type of activities outsourced, encompassing 'brush and flush' cleaning services and refuse collection predominantly but also air traffic control, buses and business services. Lengthening the term of the contract and widening its scope to incorporate operations, maintenance and management (OM & M) of the public facility over an extended period, say five years, would see some similarities emerge between contracting out and a PPP. Such an OM & M contract operates for the Haldimand–Norfolk, Ontario, Canada wastewater treatment facility whereby the operator is responsible for all aspects of operating, maintaining and managing an existing facility, including decisions about personnel, energy use, chemicals and sludge disposal. Yet there remains some gap between this OM & M contract and that of another water treatment project in Moncton, New Brunswick, Canada. This PPP incorporates two contracts, one for the design, building and finance of a new water treatment plant, the other a 20-year operations and maintenance contract for the facility which, when combined, make it effectively a design-build-finance-operate (DBFO) project. Quite clearly, PPPs like these involve some elements similar to those involved in contracting out, but at the same time are much more complex in that intricate financing and organizational/contractual issues are intertwined.[10]

Contracting out is normally associated with saving money. Substantial evidence has emerged since the mid-1980s, and is surveyed by Domberger *et al.*, that suggests that governments can save in the order of 20 per cent of expenditures on services by putting them through a competitive tendering process. The benefits are therefore substantial, and have been sustained by the growth of specialist private sector firms providing a wide range of business and managerial services. Not surprisingly, the policy has gained currency as an instrument of public sector reform – achieving better value for taxpayers' money. Nevertheless, because of their wider scope and sophistication, PPPs introduce many more elements into the equation. Achieving value for money is obviously an important issue, but it is not the overriding consideration. A PPP is not just about producing an asset or a service. Rather it is about attempting to achieve a social outcome that may not be obtained by government or private sector forces acting separately. This brings us to our third question.

PPPs and Public Sector Management

The third question concerns the impact of a PPP agenda on public sector management. In a way, the whole of this volume addresses this issue and it would be premature to try to answer it now. Nevertheless, it may be valuable at this early juncture to outline what PPPs are meant to do.

In broad terms, a PPP is a method of producing and delivering public services that brings together the public and private sectors in a long-term contractual relationship in which each retains its own identity and set of responsibilities. Public and private sector resources are combined on the basis of a clearly defined division of tasks and risks. The purpose of this collaboration is to bring added value to infrastructure through innovation, enabling the government to deliver either a qualitatively better end product for the same outlay or the same quality at a cost saving. PPPs are predicted on the assumption that there exist in the private sector certain core competencies that can be drawn into infrastructure projects and that incentives can be written into the contractual arrangements to encourage the participants to find other parties who can bring extra value by way of complementary skills and synergies. To this end, PPPs are designed to maximize the use of private sector skills where these are needed to supplement the existing skills of the public sector, while ensuring clear accountability and risk transfer for both project delivery and operation (American Chamber of Commerce, 2002). In the words of Linder and Rosenau (2000),

> They [PPPs] are a means to finance and deliver publicly demanded services, qualitatively different from private and public, and superior to either one alone. For example, they may be structured to get around the deficiencies of extreme privatization that include important conflicts of interest. They may be structured to overcome, as well, public sector difficulties with lackadaisical performance and inefficiency due to monopoly status. (p. 9)

Drawing on the US experience of partnerships, Linder (2000) goes on to suggest six ways in which PPPs can introduce change into the public sector. First, PPPs are a tool for management reform. As such a device, they can alter the way government operates by introducing market disciplines into public services. Second, PPPs encourage what is termed 'problem conversion', so that the task for public sector managers becomes one of reframing the constraints they face so as to facilitate the entry of private sector operators and their commitment of funds. The focus becomes one of the outcomes to be achieved, rather than the processes by which things are done. Third, once this is done, PPPs can produce a 'moral regeneration' by widening the number of participants in the outcomes and building market experience for public service managers. Fourth, PPPs allow for financial risks to be shifted from public to private investors. Fifth, partnerships can be a vehicle for restructuring public services, streamlining administrative procedures and substituting a private workplace for public servants. Sixth, as power sharing arrangements, PPPs can alter business–government relations in fundamental ways. One is that an ethos of cooperation and trust can replace the adversarial relations endemic in command-and-control regulation. Also, any relationship between partners will involve some mutually beneficial sharing of responsibility, knowledge or risk. In most instances, each party brings something of value to the others to be invested or exchanged. Finally, there is an expectation of give-and-take between the partners, negotiating differences that were otherwise litigated. This is the essence of partnering considered later in this chapter.

THE PRIVATE FINANCING MODEL

A feature of many PPPs is the commitment of private sector finance to the construction or renovation of the facilities. Underpinning the development of the PPP concept has been an appropriate model for channelling the supply of private finance for infrastructure projects – a need highlighted by the difficulties often experienced by those seeking to raise capital for private infrastructure in earlier times. The methods developed for 'design and build' road contracts pioneered techniques now used for a range of PPP projects.

Traditional public sector procurement methods have generally resulted in the award of design and/or construct contracts. However, as Hodgson (1995) concludes on the basis of the UK experience with such contracts,

> the public sector's record in the design and construction of capital schemes is poor. Time and cost overruns are common. Part of the reason lies in the attitudes and culture of the public sector. In the construction sector this often results in conservative or over-engineered designs. (p. 68)

Traditional methods also leave the government with a number of risks including that of asset ownership. This is the risk that the asset will be inadequately designed, maintained and refurbished so that its effective life will prove shorter than anticipated, and its economic value will vary from that on which the financial structure of the project is based.

These findings are not confined to the UK. In a survey of major infrastructure projects in a large number of countries, the majority of which were
undertaken under the 'conventional approach' with the use of public money,
Bruzelius *et al.* (1998) discovered that cost overruns of 50–100 per cent in
fixed prices are common for major infrastructure projects, and that traffic
forecasts that are out by 20–70 per cent compared with actual developments
are not unusual. Forecasts of the viability of the projects are also overoptimistic. They attribute much of this to weaknesses in the conventional public
approach to infrastructure projects, coming from an overcommitment of
political prestige to projects, costly changes to project specifications at a late
stage in the project cycle, the 'capture' of the project by special interest
groups, and a failure to articulate policy objectives and carry out risk analysis. These points are analysed in more detail in the next chapter.

The DBFO Model

The critical innovation of a contract such as a DBFO (Design, Build, Finance,
Operate) road comes from it not being a conventional capital asset procurement but a service procurement policy where the service outcomes and
performance standards are clearly specified. DBFO is a term coined by the
UK Highways Agency to describe their concession-based road schemes let
under the Private Finance Initiative and a DBFO contract has the following
features:

- it is long term, with a contract term of 25 or 30 years being common;
- it has detailed provisions on payment, service standards and performance measurement, providing an objective means to vary payment
  depending on performance;
- there will usually be one public sector and one private sector party to
  the contract. While there may be other private sector entities involved,
  executive responsibilities will generally be delivered through subcontracts to the principal private sector party to the DBFO contract.

The DBFO concessionaire has to assume substantial risk, the intention being
that the government body will be buying a road service and not just a new
road. Concessionaires have to be capable of long-term commitment and, as a
result, need to be both robust and committed to quality of performance in this
market. To encourage this high quality of service, the payment system
includes both incentives for good performance and abatements for bad
performance.

In the UK and some other parts of Europe (Finland, Portugal and Spain)
the main form of payment mechanism has revolved around shadow tolls.

Shadow tolls involve payment per vehicle using a kilometre of the project road, in accordance with a pricing structure. They are shadow, as opposed to real, tolls because the payment for usage is made by the government rather than the road user. Typically, different payments are due for traffic with different traffic bands and are dependent on the length of the vehicle. Under the UK model, bidders would be asked to bid the parameters of traffic levels for a maximum of four, and a minimum of two, bands, with the proviso that the top band – anything exceeding X vehicle kilometres per annum – must have toll levels set at zero to ensure that the maximum liability to the state under the DBFO contract is effectively capped. Bidders set the bands and tolls from their own assessment of traffic levels. Most have opted for four bands with the lowest band representing a cautious view of traffic and tolls within that band set at a level that would cover debt service requirements (but would not provide a return on equity). Shadow tolls are therefore essentially volume-based payments by the government that in theory allow the public sector to transfer usage risk to the private operator without introducing direct user charges and the associated traffic diversion effects.

The UK's National Audit Office (NAO) has been critical of shadow tolls in its review of the DBFO roads programme. Its criticism is largely directed at the appropriateness of transferring volume risk to a private operator when the operator is unable to influence demand for the road through direct pricing measures as would be the case with explicit user charges. In effect, there is little that a private operator of a road can do to increase traffic usage under the shadow toll mechanism. In addition, the way the bidders have structured their pricing levels results in a reduced payment per vehicle in the higher traffic range. Ultimately, because of the zero cap in the top payment band, additional traffic flows do not receive a toll payment despite them resulting in extra maintenance costs to the private sector (National Audit Office, 1998). The NAO goes on to conclude that it is likely that the premium paid for transferring volume risk via a shadow toll mechanism outweighs the benefit. The issue of whether shadow tolls provide the most appropriate basis for payment is further highlighted where traffic is consistently heavy and there is consequently little traffic risk, as is likely in an urban situation.

It is important to appreciate that shadow tolls were originally conceived in the UK as a transitory mechanism for moving to a system of real tolls at some time in the future. They were invented at a time when the future of road user charges was uncertain, and were seen as an interim measure that would make it easier to vary the contract to user tolls at a later stage. However, the move to real tolls has not come about largely because there is no recent history of toll roads in the UK and therefore such a move is highly sensitive. Also, it is only relatively recently that the technology has advanced to a state that makes possible electronic tolling like that discussed in the previous chapter.

Most recent DBFO road projects have focused more on availability payments and performance payments. Implementation of the availability mechanism requires determining when a section of road is deemed unavailable, and the level of deduction for the deemed unavailability. Unavailability includes a section of road being closed for maintenance by the road operator or a third party, and blockages due to it not being operated to a specified standard because of the provision of signing, lighting, communications equipment, crash barriers, and so on. The basic idea is to encourage the operator to respond quickly and efficiently to incidences of non-availability.

Performance payments can cover a number of aspects, such as relating payment to the operator's successful performance of individual tasks (e.g. surface conditions, maintenance, and aspects such as drainage, lighting, verge conditions); and to the operator achieving key overall objectives (e.g. fewer accidents). Usually, objectives would be set as pre-determined outputs measured against pre-specified key performance indicators (KPIs). The payment stream by these means is performance based and will vary depending on whether, and to what extent, each of the KPIs is met. A bonus or abatement regime would be developed in line with this concept. In setting KPIs reference would be made to the criteria associated with:

- lack of congestion (average travel times),
- road accidents (number of traffic incidents),
- ride quality (pavement surface condition),
- environmental impacts (number of incidents of breach in noise/air quality requirements),
- provision of traveller information (accuracy and frequency), and
- vehicle breakdown services (availability and response time).

The goal is to encourage the operator to design for safety and to pursue safety through additional works and changes to the road over time.

These types of approach are generally in accordance with the principle of transferring road operating risk to the private sector. Obtaining an appropriate transfer of risk is a primary objective of DBFO models, and includes all or some of these factors: design risk, construction risk, opening date risk, traffic risk, legislative and *force majeure* risk, and operational risk. These features, pioneered in the case of road schemes, have now become standard. Examples of the design and build approach for roads come from the Dartford River Crossing, the second Severn River Crossing, the M8 St James Interchange, Glasgow and the Birmingham Northern Relief Road. As we shall see in some of the case studies examined later, the DBFO-type payment mechanism based on some combination of shadow tolls, availability measures and performance indicators features in most PPP arrangements.

Project Finance

Another characteristic of DBFO-type projects is the participation of private risk capital, with the expectation that those with money at risk will require there to be a harder-nosed approach to project evaluation, risk management and project implementation. Project-financing techniques are employed and a mixture of instruments and methods is available, including asset-based financing, leasing, hire purchase, and the use of special-purpose non-recourse financing vehicles. The underlying premise is that projects are income-producing and borrowings can be serviced from these proceeds. Future income from the investment is earmarked for the service of the borrowings, providing security to the financiers by decoupling the servicing of the loans from the financial fortunes of the owners or sponsors of the investment. A fairly standard approach is for the sponsors of a project to establish a special purpose vehicle company (SPV) in which they are principal shareholders. Each sponsor holds a sufficiently small share of the equity in the joint venture so that for legal and accounting purposes the SPV cannot be construed as a subsidiary. Funding of the project is then routed through the SPV.

Due to the low capitalization of the SPV, there is consequently a reliance on direct revenues to pay for operating costs and cover financing while giving the desired return on risk capital. The senior financier of private finance looks to, and evaluates the adequacy of, the cashflow and earnings of the project as the source of funds for repayments. Funding security against the project company is not sought because the company usually has minimal non-project specific assets and because the financing is without call on the sponsor companies behind the project company. The aim is to achieve a financial structure with minimum recourse to the sponsors, while at the same time providing sufficient support so that the financiers are satisfied with the risks.

In this respect, the financing of a PPP project must be 'engineered' to take account of the risks involved, sources of finance, accounting and tax regulations, and so on. Project design requires expert analysis of all of the attendant risks and then a structuring of the contractual arrangements prior to competitive tendering that allocates risk burdens appropriately (a task usually assigned to a financial adviser or investment bank). Project implementation then requires expert management of all of the components parts of the delivery of the services, such as construction, commissioning, operation and maintenance. From a senior financier's point of view, this stage is essential to the successful treatment of all the attendant risks and thereby realizing control of the sole source of security against the cashflows.

In our view, this combination of upfront engineering and downstream management of project execution plays a defining role in bringing about the outcomes required. These outcomes are projects that give value for money, that are delivered on time and to budget, and that provide services to the required standards. Without the market disciplines brought to bear on projects, and the benefits that flow from them, highly geared project finance might simply be dismissed as another form of finance, more expensive than state debt. To do so would be to ignore that the whole basis of the PPP process is about assessing the risks and putting in place appropriate evaluation procedures and management methods to deal with them. In effect, having the privately provided finance at risk acts as a catalyst to inject risk management techniques into the project in a way that is not possible under government financing.

As we have already seen, using the future revenues of an investment to secure financing for it is a very old idea, dating back to tolls for bridges and the turnpikes discussed earlier. Its heyday was undoubtedly during the boom of railroad construction financing in the nineteenth century, when bondholders in general had no security other than the railway itself and its revenues. What differs now is the range of financial instruments employed in financial engineering and the computer programs used to forecast cashflow projections and stress test the likely outcomes.

Revenue Streams

When private financiers commit funds under PPPs for infrastructure, they need to be convinced that a viable revenue stream can be tapped. In a public–private arrangement, revenues to the private firm can come from two sources, namely consumer payments, or public entity payments (or from some combination of both). The source is important because it determines (1) the incentives of a private firm to adjust the cost and quality to consumers' willingness to pay for them, (2) the amount and timing of public expenditures, and (3) the nature of the risks to which revenues are exposed.

PPP projects for roads provide illustrations of both, and indicate the diversity that exists within what might otherwise seem to be similar partnership modes. In the United States, three basic types of PPP have been used for roads (Lockwood, 1995). Under a BOO scheme, a private consortium agrees to finance, build, own, operate and collect toll revenues for access to the facility for a limited period of time. The Dulles–Leesburg Toll Road Extension (the Dulles Greenway) in Virginia is an example of such a facility. Privately owned and operated, all pre-construction development costs have been at the expense of the owner. The road is being financed by toll-backed debt, private equity and some state sub-debt support. All the right-of-way has been either provided under grant or purchased by the project sponsor.

The other PPP arrangements for US roads are BOT or BTO schemes, differing only in the timing of the government's financial responsibility. Under

BTO, the private consortium leases the constructed facility from the government, operates it, collects toll revenues sufficient to retire the project debt and earns a reasonable return on investment, after which all rights are passed back to the government. Although the government formally owns the facility from the first day of operation, full financial responsibility remains with the private consortium. The BTO system may be preferred to the alternative BOT model when some form of government ownership of the facility is advantageous, since in the US a government-owned project is covered under sovereign immunity laws for tort, and this will avoid exposing the private consortium to uninsurable risk during operations.

Under both types of arrangement, a private consortium approved by the government agency submits a competitive proposal and, if chosen, the consortium is allowed to proceed with negotiations that lead to the signing of a concession or franchise agreement. In the concession agreement the private consortium is authorized to plan, design, finance, build and operate a toll road for a limited time period (usually 20 to 40 years). After this period, ownership of the facility is transferred to the sponsoring government free of charge (under the BOT scenario), or the transfer can occur straight after the completion of construction (under the BTO scenario).

Many recently constructed UK roads are built under DBFO contracts. As we have seen, the concessionaire is responsible for design, construction, maintenance, and operation, and it has to finance the project. But no rights of ownership are conferred on the developer, neither does the developer at any point acquire any interest in the land – the Secretary of State remains the highway authority throughout the contract period. Instead, the DBFO contractor is merely given a right of access to the road, and effectively a 'licence' to operate it, normally for a period of 30 years. Unlike in French-style concessions, this right does not include the collection of user charges. Payment is made on some combination of 'shadow tolls', availability measures and performance indicators.

Clearly, there are differences between the arrangements in terms of the nature of the revenue stream and the attendant risks. When private entity revenues consist of prices or user fees (user charges, tolls, electricity prices), project revenues are governed by commercial risks, as in any market context, although the firm may be subject to regulatory risk if fees or rates of return are regulated. There are also collection costs and externalities to be taken into account, although the use of electronic tolling systems has altered the cost–benefit calculus of the former.

On the other hand, if the public sector entity is the source of the revenues, there may be little or no commercial risk, but there may be contractual disputes, which result in a failure to pay. Daniels and Trebilcock (1996) argue that government bodies can pose contractual difficulties for two reasons. First, governments can expressly abrogate contractual commitments and nullify contracts by passing legislation. Second, a whole range of government changes, such as environmental policy, health and safety provisions, transport, regional development, can alter the franchise value of a concession to the private investor. Add to this the difficulty of imposing financial conditions on the public body, and either seizing the assets or suing the public agency involved, and there may be some reluctance on the part of the private firm – or its backers and investors – to bear public payment risk. In these circumstances, careful design of the contract is needed. Some of the conciliation and risk mitigation elements are considered in later chapters.

In the meantime, we may note that although DBFO/BOT arrangements were refined in transport projects, the techniques carry over and form the basis of PPPs in other infrastructure applications. As Adrian Smith (1999) observes: 'The operation of a toll road is not conceptually very different from operating a railway, a hospital or a prison, in that all must provide specified services to a guaranteed and measurable standard within a predetermined budget' (p. 138).

PARTNERING

So far we have examined the origins of the PPP concept in terms of the commercialism of the public sector under the heading of the 'new public management' and the fashioning of 'build and design' (or, more correctly, DBFO) arrangements, with the associated need to refine financing techniques. Now we examine what we regard to be a third influence – the concept of 'partnering' itself.

In the middle of the 1990s, a number of studies appeared in the engineering management literature, reviewing and assessing the conceptual basis of a recent development in the construction industry – that of partnering (Crowley and Karim, 1995; Hellard, 1995; Wilson *et al.*, 1995). It has long been recognized in the project management literature (e.g. Kerzner, 1989) that time spent early in the process of building an integrated project team is likely to lead to more successful outcomes in terms of project procurement, construction planning and construction processes. The aim of team building is to develop a project-based culture and ethos that is carried down through all levels of the organization. Partnering seeks to extend this idea across organizations, breaking down organizational barriers by developing a structured management approach to facilitate team working across contractual boundaries. Its fundamental components are formalized mutual objectives, agreed problem resolution methods, and an active search for continuous measurable improvements.

Advocates of partnering have as their starting point that the construction industry is marred by adversarial relationships. Earlier contracting methods and project management practices, whether involving private or public sector projects, have had the effect of putting the participating parties – owner, designer and contractor – into adversarial situations in which common project objectives get lost. This failure of communication and cooperation leads to disruptive conflicts, the results of which are cost and schedule overruns, lost time, wasted money, poor quality, low morale and ultimately litigation. Partnering, by contrast, centres around conflict management, team building, trust, commitment and mutual goals. The studies on partnering suggest ways of bringing about these results.

Crowley and Karim (1995) define partnering as a means of resolving inter-organizational conflict, with two or more organizations maximizing resource effectiveness in achieving common project objectives. The key elements introduced into the relationship are trust, commitment and a shared vision. Trust is important for confidence and encouraging a communication of ideas. Commitment allows for mutual improvements in technology and methods. Achievement of a shared vision comes from consensus in realizing objectives in common. A successful partnership is marked by openness, innovation, equity, shared risk and conflict resolution through problem solving. While partnering can apply to both public and private sector entities, the authors note that public sector agencies may have difficulties in overcoming traditional bureaucratic structures if they are to partner successfully.

In the other major article on the topic, Wilson *et al.* (1995) argue that partnering represents a significant cultural change for most organizations. A major hurdle is that project partnerships are single events and do not in themselves generate the cultural change mechanisms required for the partnering process. The authors seek to move partnering beyond a single-event project arrangement, and investigate partnering from the strategic aspect of a partnering process embedded in an organizational change model in which strategic change is driven by a transformation leadership team. Such a team is responsible for defining the goals to be achieved from partnering, managing the partnering process and undertaking continual diagnosis, coordination and problem resolution. The aim is to institutionalize change by placing common goals, trust and teamwork at the heart of all contractual agreements for construction. But for this to happen an appropriate framework is needed to initiate and implement change within the organizational structure of the partnership.

This framework is not simply the result of appointing people to work together in coordinating a project. The idea is to wrap the major participants into an alliance that centres attention on the project, and not on the individual parties involved, in such a way that the resulting culture necessitates that these organizational barriers must be modified. Partnering of this form is especially important in a PPP because flexibility and permeability tend to be greater in private sector organizations, whereas in public sector bodies the boundaries tend to be more rigid, and overcoming them can be difficult. Also, those on the lower rungs of the public sector ladder may not share the enthusiasm for 'privatism' of ministers and senior officials.

Partnering is not a contract as such; nevertheless a partnering approach is usually supported by a written partnering agreement, a non-contractual agreement, signed not by the organizations but by the actual people who will be directly involved, which sets out the essence of the parties' mutually agreed obligations. Smith (1999) gives an example of what a partnering agreement might look like for a BOT tolled road concession (see Table 3.2). It would be normal for the parties to employ an outside facilitator to aid the process and help formulate the agreement. The role of the facilitator is to help the parties to develop the required 'team ethos' to articulate and fashion the partnering agreement, and to help the parties to stick to the bargain they have made by recognizing that every contract incorporates an implied covenant of good faith

Table 3.2   An illustrative project partnering agreement

Partnering agreement

We, the partners of the Blanktown Bypass toll road concession, agree to work together for the whole period of the concession in such a way as to ensure the design, construction and operation of a high quality project. We hereby affirm that we are one team, and that we are jointly committed to achieving the following objectives:

- Design, construct and operate a high quality scheme to the continuing satisfaction of all concerned.
- Achieve or better all programme targets.
- Maintain an effective team relationship.
- Operate effective communications systems.
- Resolve any contentious issues at the lowest possible level in a timely and progressive way.
- Achieve or better all environmental objectives.

We also jointly agree to use our best endeavours to develop specific action plans to improve problem resolution procedures and to ensure successful completion of the project.

Signed:

Source: Smith (1999, p. 137).

(Hellard, 1995). Partnering agreements are part of the alliance approach that partnering represents – they are not needed in PPPs where the partnership arrangement itself serves this purpose, and cements in place the same shared goals.

Perhaps the best way to think of the transition from partnering to PPPs is to adopt Peters' conception of partnerships as 'institutions' (Peters, 1998). Rather than relying on the bargaining of individuals in a series of negotiations to generate collective action, the entities involved instead choose to create an organization (or an 'institution') for the purpose of the partnership. Instead of there being transient relationships among governments and private sector actors,

> these partnerships can be conceptualized as stable institutional structures that are governed by shared understandings of priorities and values, as well as by sets of rules that have been mutually agreed upon by the two (or more) actors. This stability and institutionalization can be seen as a mechanism for reducing transaction costs and for facilitating decisions through creating common perspectives on policy. (p. 19)

CONCLUDING REMARKS

PPPs draw on this heritage of 'partnering' and 'design and build', but add additional layers of complexity. These come from, first, the fact that many PPPs are of the DBFOM (design, build, finance, operate, manage) character, combining (limited) ownership with operation and management, and also design and construction. Second, PPPs cover many areas of infrastructure services (e.g. prisons, hospitals, courts) where tolls, user fees, and so on cannot be levied in the form of consumer payments. Third, in some PPPs, such as those for regeneration and regional development, non-government organizations (NGOs) participate along with public and other private sector bodies, while for many projects the sponsoring parties are obliged to consult widely with community groups and other interested parties. For all these reasons, the organization of PPPs becomes a central issue, and later chapters focus on this aspect.

NOTES

1. In 1825, one partnership was collecting three-quarters of the tolls in London (Levinson, 2002).
2. Usually with an auction for a concession the length of the franchise (e.g. 30 years) is fixed in advance of the tender. The fixed-term concession can lead to demand risk for the franchise-holder; it is possible for the franchise to lose money even when the road is profitable

in the long run simply because the term of the franchise may be too short given the state of demand. An alternative mechanism advocated by Engel *et al.* (2001) is a least-present-value-of-revenue (LPVR) auction. With such a system, the winner is chosen on the least present value to toll revenue required over the project lifetime. But the time span of the concession is not fixed in advance and can vary in response to economic conditions, ending when the present value of toll revenue is equal to the franchise-holder's bid. An LPVR auction takes advantage of the fact that roads may eventually pay for themselves even when traffic turns out to be less than expected by the device of allowing the franchise term to lengthen. The LPVG auction technique has been instituted for highways franchises in Chile (Engel *et al.*, 1999).

3.   These were Waterloo and City, Central London Railway, Great Northern and City, City and South London, Baker Street and Waterloo, Charing Cross, Euston and Hampstead, and Brompton and Piccadilly Circus Railway. We are indebted to Owen Covick of Flinders University of South Australia for supplying us with information about the London Underground. Additional details came from studies of London transport by Barker (1990) and Taylor (2001).

4.   The railway companies found it easier to negotiate rights of way with one or two authorities than with each of the many individual property owners above the line. Thus the lines were built to follow below ground the course of the streets and roads above.

5.   Four of the seven companies failed to raise capital on the first attempt and were either taken over by other interests or needed financial support from others.

6.   Interestingly, similar problems plagued the Sheffield Supertram project in the 1990s. Its passenger demand was forecast to be 22 million per year, whereas the initial out-turn was only 8 million passengers per annum. By the time the system opened a housing scheme it was designed to serve had been demolished. However, one of the features of the Sheffield Supertram has been the vigorous competition from the rival bus companies which was not envisaged at the planning stage. The Supertram was forecast to have a speed advantage over rival bus services. However, due to junction delays and route variations, these speed advantages have not materialized (Mackie and Preston, 1998).

7.   The authors are indebted to Paul Lignieres, Directeur du Departement Partenariats Publics/Prives/Droit Public Economique, Landwell & Associes, Paris for his assistance in preparing this section.

8.   These provisions are not dissimilar to the Material Adverse Effects clauses that have been used in some PPP contracts in Australia.

9.   Kagami (2002) examined the political and economic problems that plagued the so-called 'third sector' projects in Japan. These were joint ventures between private and public sector bodies whereby, in the words of the author, 'parks and resort areas spouted like mushrooms throughout Japan' under tax incentives and political pressures from local government authorities, only to crash when the bubble economy burst (p. 37).

10. In this case, the private partner (US Filter Operating Services and the Hardman Group) took on the risk of design, construction, operations and maintenance. Uninterrupted service was guaranteed as was water quality meeting or exceeding Canadian drinking water guidelines. The water fee charged to the municipality was fixed for term of the contract. The savings over the 20-year term of the project were estimated to be in excess of $12 million compared with the City's own estimate of what it would cost to undertake the project itself.

4. Partnerships and conventional procurement of infrastructure

INTRODUCTION

In this chapter, procurement by means of a PPP is compared with that by conventional means in terms of the steps involved, procedures followed, and overall procurement performance. Before doing so, it is perhaps worthwhile restating and reiterating some of the factors that have led to PPPs being employed for infrastructure projects. The previous chapter traced the changing involvement of the private sector in infrastructure investment in Britain, the United States and France. In all three countries, and in others as well, the dominant public sector role in producing, delivering and financing infrastructure services, which held sway for most of the twentieth century, has given way in recent years to experimentation with a variety of means of engaging private sector resources for infrastructure. Part of this regeneration of interest in private sector participation must be seen as a continuation and extension of public sector reforms, which have seen the commercialism of many activities previously regarded as state monopolies. But this is not the only factor.

Much of the revival can be attributed to dissatisfaction with traditional methods of public procurement of infrastructure. Infrastructure policies after World War II had been driven by a faith that governments could succeed where markets appeared to fail, in the words of the World Bank, but the reality proved to be different. Public sector infrastructure projects in many parts of the world were marked by inefficiency, unreliability and poor fiscal control (World Bank, 1994). This performance, indifferent at best, led to the growth of BOT/DBFO-type arrangements in road construction and to the search for more cooperative 'partnering' approaches in construction projects. Both are seen by us as forerunners of the PPP concept.

WHAT'S WRONG WITH CONVENTIONAL PROCUREMENT?

Hodgson (1995), as we saw, put a lot of the blame for the poor record in the design and construction of capital works on the attitudes and culture of the public sector, which result in time delays and costs overruns being common-place. Since then, more complete – and damning – evidence has come to hand on the extent of cost overruns and revenue shortfalls on infrastructure invest-ments – phenomena that have come to be known under the heading 'appraisal optimism'.

Appraisal Optimism

In particular, two recent studies (Flyvbjerg *et al.*, 2002; Mott MacDonald, 2002) confirm the results of earlier research (Pickrell, 1990; Fouracre *et al.*, 1990). Attention has already been drawn to the Danish study by Flyvbjerg *et al.* which examines 258 large transport infrastructure projects covering 20 countries, the overwhelming majority of which were developed using conven-tional approaches to public procurement.[1] Costs were found to be underesti-mated in 90 per cent of the cases. For rail projects, actual costs were on average 45 per cent higher than estimated, for tunnels and bridges they were on average 34 per cent higher, while for road projects, actual costs averaged 20 per cent higher than estimated. They also found no evidence that this posi-tion has changed over the past 70 years. Table 4.1 summarizes the overall results from their study.

In the other major study conducted in 2002, the UK Treasury commis-sioned Mott MacDonald to review the outcome of 50 large public procurement projects in the UK over the last 20 years. A wide range of infrastructure projects was covered, including offices, hospitals, prisons, airport terminals, major refurbishments, roads, rail, IT facilities and tunnels. Table 4.2 summar-izes the results for projects procured by conventional (i.e. traditional) methods. There is substantial evidence of what the UK *Green Book* (2003 edition) calls 'optimism bias' – the estimated difference between the business case and the final outcome for each category of project (HM Treasury, 2003a). For all projects, time overruns exceeded the estimated duration by 17 per cent. In the case of capital expenditure, actual costs exceeded those estimated by 47 per cent on average, and for operating expenditure, they exceeded estimated costs by an average of 41 per cent (although the sample was much smaller than that for capital expenditure).

Considering the different project types, it might be expected that standard projects would have smaller optimism bias levels when compared to non-stan-dard projects, and this is so for buildings. However, for civil engineering projects, the study shows a higher works duration optimism bias for standard as opposed to non-standard projects. Standard civil engineering projects comprise mainly road projects, which may be susceptible to unexpected envir-onmental impacts, giving rise to the relatively high works duration optimism bias discovered.

Table 4.1   Differences between actual and estimated costs in large public works transport projects

Project type	All regions		Europe		North America	
	Number of projects	Average cost escalation (%)[a]	Number of projects	Average cost escalation (%)[a]	Number of projects	Average cost escalation (%)[a]
Rail	58	44.7 (38.4)	23	34.2 (25.1)	19	40.8 (36.8)
Fixed-link[b]	33	33.8 (62.4)	15	43.4 (52.0)	18	25.7 (70.5)
Road	167	20.4 (29.9)	143	22.4 (24.9)	24	8.4 (49.4)
All projects	258	27.6 (38.7)	181	25.7 (28.7)	61	23.6 (54.2)

Notes:
[a] Figures in brackets are the standard deviation of the cost inaccuracies.
[b] Fixed-link projects consist of tunnels and bridges.

Source: Based on data in Flyvbjerg *et al.* (2002).

Table 4.2 Estimates of average 'optimism bias' for conventional public procurement in the UK, by type of projects

Project type	Works duration[a]	CAPEX[b]	OPEX[c]	Benefits shortfall[d]
Standard civil engineering	34	44	No info	No info
Non-standard civil engineering	15	66	No info	5
Standard buildings	4	24	No info	No info
Non-standard buildings	39	51	No info	1
Equipment development	54	214	No info	No info
Outsourcing	N/A	N/A	41	No info
All projects	17	47	41	2

Notes:
[a]The percentage by which the time taken for the actual works programme exceeds the estimate for time allowed in the business case.
[b]The percentage by which the actual capital expenditure exceeds the expenditure expected in the business case.
[c]The percentage by which the actual operating expenditure exceeds the expenditure anticipated in the business case.
[d]The percentage by which the delivered benefits fall short of the benefits expected in the business case.

Source: Data from Mott MacDonald (2002).

Optimism Bias in Transport Projects

A variety of reasons can be put forward to account for such results. In fact, an earlier study by Mackie and Preston (1998) of the transport sector identified no less than 21 sources of error and bias in transport projects. These are:

1. Failure from the outset to clarify project objectives and, when there are conflicts between stated and actual objectives, to order the aims in terms of priority.
2. Political commitment to a project at too early a stage, particularly before there can be an appraisal at sufficient depth to allow a graceful exit to be made by politicians and their backers.
3. An inability (or unwillingness) to obtain good data on factors like actual (and likely) traffic routes used, bus and rail usage, and sources of low transport demand that are up-to-date and 'typical'.
4. Difficulties in defining the catchment areas affected by new motorways (e.g. the M25), new bypasses, additional train stations, park and ride systems etc.
5. Omitting a full appraisal of the 'do minimum' or 'do something else' options. Is a new bypass really needed, or will junction improvements suffice? Alternatively, if current maintenance levels are sustained, will train services suffer from reduced speeds, late running, deteriorating ride quality, and still lower passenger demands?
6. Over-engineering or 'gold-plating' of the 'do something' option of new infrastructure facilities. How much excess capacity needs to be built in to airports (HongKong, Kuala Lumpur) or bridges (Humber Bridge)? How long does a building need to last?
7. False planning assumptions based on complementary investments such as occurs when traffic forecasts are based on new towns that fail to eventuate (M65) or housing schemes that are demolished (Sheffield Supertram), or access to air rights over land that is not granted (Concord).
8. Overestimating external factors, such as population growth, income, economic activity and car ownership, impinging on demand usage (e.g. Tyne and Wear Metro, M1 Motorway in Hungary).
9. Forecasting errors resulting from specification errors in models (e.g. incorrect assumptions about the price elasticity of traffic to toll charges, failure to consider substitute services).
10. Optimistic forecasts of the performance of new transport facilities in terms of travel speeds, service frequencies, service quality and fare structures which do not eventuate (e.g. Sheffield Supertram on all accounts).
11. Underestimating the consequences of intensified competition from rival

transport operators (e.g. buses versus light rapid transit systems, ferry companies and cheap air services versus Euro-tunnel).[2]

12. Forgetting that teething problems, temporary disruptions and other events can do long-term damage to traffic flows (e.g. the consequences for Eurostar of the tunnel fire, asylum seekers, and the delayed high speed link).

13. Overestimating asset lives when technological advances and rising maintenance costs significantly lessen the economic or market life of an asset relative to its technical life (e.g. Victoria line, Bradford Interchange, rail modernization in the 1950s).

14. Ignoring in cost–benefit calculations the disruption effects on traders and the loss of goodwill of the construction phase (e.g. in urban transit systems) and the increased walking times (e.g. due to interchange locations).

15. Difficulties of evaluating environment impacts, such as valuing antiquities and historical monuments, in cost–benefit analysis.

16. Problems of weighting the economic, non-economic and political consequences of projects (the third London Airport inquiry, the choice of location of the high speed rail link to the Channel Tunnel in terms of north or east London routes).

17. Benefits counted twice or even three times in different parts of the appraisal when the secondary and tertiary impacts are really ramifications of the primary impact (e.g. reduced travel times).

18. Ignoring the hidden costs of inducements such as tax breaks, grants, subsidies, and reduced rentals on a project's viability, along with factors such as the redistribution of wealth from changing property values and the transfer of employment from one area to another.

19. Excessive focus on the appraisal of individual projects in isolation, while overlooking the consequences for the network as a whole (e.g. bypasses, upgrades of trunk routes, individual airports).

20. Downplaying the risk that because of the long gestation period for projects (10 years or more in some cases such as the Manchester Metrolink), they are vulnerable to changing political, financial and economic circumstances.

21. Systematic appraisal optimism, resulting in benefits being overestimated and costs underestimated.

Although 'appraisal optimism' is listed as a factor in its own right, at least 12 of the other 20 factors interact to contribute to it. For this reason, the authors single out appraisal optimism as being the greatest danger in transport investment analysis. They argue that it happens because the information contained in the appraisal tends to be generated or commissioned by scheme promoters who have obvious incentives to bias the results – knowingly or unconsciously – in one or more ways that inflate benefits or understate costs. This is seen to be a particularly acute problem if the scheme is in the public domain rather than the private sector, since the normal commercial checks and balances on excessive optimism do not apply.

Three antidotes are suggested by Mackie and Preston. The first is to have within organizations, groups whose function it is to 'own' the appraisal regime rather than the projects, and to ensure that the appraisal has integrity (much like risk management in a bank has to be kept separate from the trading floor). The second is to expose projects to open scrutiny at public inquiries, with adequate resources available to cross-examine the scheme promoters. The third is to spend a lot more time on after-the-event evaluation than is currently done. Systematic comparisons of what actually happened relative to forecast would be an important discipline on future decision-making and strengthen the hand of the sceptics.

Problems and Solutions

Returning now to the more recent studies, many of the same factors recur. In the Mott MacDonald report, by far the most significant factor identified was the inadequacy of the business case. The various project risk areas contributing to optimism bias in recorded capital expenditures are listed below, ranked according to the maximum average percentage contribution. They are:

- inadequacy of the business case (58%)
- environmental impact (19%)
- disputes and claims incurred (16%)
- economic influences (13%)
- late contractor involvement in design (12%)
- complexity of contract structure (11%)
- legislative and regulatory changes (7%)
- degree of innovation (7%)
- poor contractor capabilities (6%)
- project management team (4%)
- poor project intelligence (4%).

The next most important contributors are environmental impacts; disputes; economic conditions; and a failure to involve contractors in design. Recommended solutions to the problems are better risk management and greater diligence at the project definition stage, with the aim of reviewing the project objectives, scope, specifications and definitions detailed in the business case to ensure they are fully comprehensive and address all the project requirements in the short, medium and long term. Since the third most significant project risk area, disputes and claims, can also be seen a result of inadequate specification giving rise to variations and consequently claims, there is clearly a need to put considerable effort into ensuring that the business case represents the interests of all project constituents, in terms of the scope of the project and its objectives.

Many factors that feature in the Flyvbjerg *et al.* (2002) analysis are the same as in the Mott MacDonald report, and the study by Mackie and Preston. In particular, the authors identify the overcommitment of political prestige at an early stage, late changes to project design, failure to engage interest groups and consider external effects, lack of attention to regulatory impacts, and an overemphasis on technical aspects. However, they explicitly reject the idea that the differences between forecast and actual costs and revenues can be attributed to the innate difficulty of predicting the future. Rather, they look to three contributors.

1. *Short political tenure.* Because of the time frame of major project development, politicians involved in advocating projects on the basis of overoptimistic forecasts are often not in office when actual viability can be checked.
2. *Rent-seeking behaviour.* Special interest groups can promote projects at no cost or risk to themselves as others will be financing the projects, and often taxpayers' money is behind that in the form of government guarantees.
3. *'Putting on a good spin'.* Contractors are keen to have their proposals accepted during tendering, and the penalties for producing over-optimistic tenders are often low compared to the potential profits involved. Costs and risks are often underestimated in tenders only to surface once construction is underway.

In short, project promoters appear to think that a degree of deception and delusion is necessary to get projects started, and they are aided by engineers with a 'monument complex' and by 'empire-building politicians' with access to public funds (Flyvbjerg *et al.*, 2003, pp. 45–8).

Flyvbjerg *et al.* look to four basic remedies. The first is increased transparency and public involvement. A second is the use of performance specifications, substituting a goal-driven approach based on outputs in place of the conventional technical-driven procedures that focus on means rather than ends. Third, there is the need to formulate a clear set of rules governing the project development, construction and operation. The fourth is the inclusion of private risk capital in public infrastructure, so that projects are subject to the market test.

ARE PPPS THE ANSWER?

All these suggested ways of improving public procurement are core elements of a well-structured PPP programme. The PPP agenda focuses on clearly defining outputs, revolves around a detailed business case and project development phase, puts in place project and contract management plans, and involves market testing at a number of levels. A PPP structure also militates against 'ownership' of the appraisal system by one group and should provide for public scrutiny at a number of points. PPPs actually add a fifth element to the four remedies suggested by Flyvbjerg *et al.* – which is a rigorous and robust competitive tendering process.

Flyvbjerg *et al.* (2003) themselves propose two organizational mechanisms for bringing about their four suggested remedies, especially their aim of drawing private sector capital and risk assessment disciplines into infrastructure investment. One proposal is the formation for each project of a state-owned enterprise established under the Companies Act, with the ability (and expectation) to mobilize private capital participation in the capital market without guarantees, or to enlist private equity capital as a minority stake. While this device seems to be the authors' preferred option, it must be noted that the experience of this approach in France and Spain in the 1960s was not a happy one (Smith, 1999). Such mixed models can lead to difficulties in determining the 'rules of the game'. What is the government's role as major shareholder? Should it adopt a 'hands-off' or 'hands-on' role? What does it do if the enterprise gets into financial difficulties, and people are clamouring for something to be done? What are the expectations of the private parties on this score? Are private financiers relying on an implicit government guarantee, and anticipating that ultimately its funds are not really at risk? If this is the case, then the disciplines of the market are blunted.

The other organizational model examined by Flyvbjerg *et al.* (2003) is the concession approach whereby a consortium of private companies would be required to bid for a concession to design, build, finance and operate (DBFO) a particular infrastructure facility for a specified period of time. The authors are less keen on this approach, and their misgivings about this route are on three accounts. First, there is the question of whether the operating company will face sufficient competition from other alternatives. This concern boils down to one of whether competition for the market is an effective substitute for competition within the market. Second, they worry about whether the government has the capacity to think through all of the issues related to a project and build in stratagems to deal with them. Third, and related to the second, the authors question whether the private interests are fully committed, over the long term, to carrying through their obligations once the construction phase is completed. Here we would note that a partnership approach, as opposed to a DBFO concession, is explicitly designed to provide a cooperative framework to deal with and negotiate contract variations, while ensuring that the participating private parties remain committed to the project objectives over the contract period. A PPP also normally (although it is not true of all) ensures that the various subcontractors involved in the later stages are entrenched in the ownership and management structure of the project company from the very beginning.

In the companion Danish study, Flyvbjerg *et al.* (2002) consider that there are as yet insufficient data to decide whether private projects perform better or worse than public ones, although the concession method based on DBFO contracting (design-build-finance-operate) is one approach that they see as at least worthy of investigation. By contrast, 11 of the 50 projects examined by Mott MacDonald were undertaken under the UK PPP/PFI models. The results are striking. On average, the PPP/PFI projects came in under time (compared to 17 per cent over time for those under conventional methods), and capital expenditure resulted in a 1 per cent cost overrun on average for PPP/PFI projects (relative to an average of 47 per cent for traditional procurement projects). These results are attributed in the report to the better risk allocation in PPP/PFI projects, and the high level of diligence demanded to establish the business case.

Following those studies, further evidence has been published on the performance of PPPs. In its July 2003 review of PFIs, HM Treasury (2003b) presented the results of its research into 61 PFI projects covering a wide range of service areas (prisons, police stations, roads, bridges, trains, hospitals, schools, defence accommodation and defence equipment). The key findings were as follows:

- Overall 89 per cent of projects were delivered on time or early.
- All PFI projects in the HM Treasury sample were delivered within public sector budgets. No PFI project was found where the unitary charge had changed following contract signature – other than where user requirements changed.
- Three-quarters of public sector managers stated that their project was meeting their initial expectations.
- While there is scope to reduce procurement times, there is evidence that new initiatives to tackle this problem are having an impact.

The UK's National Audit Office (NAO) undertakes a rolling review of all government procurement, including PFI procurement, and in February 2003 it examined PFI construction performance. An earlier NAO study in 1999 had found that only 30 per cent of non-PFI major construction projects were delivered on time and that only 27 per cent were within budget. By comparison, its investigation into PFI construction outcomes showed that in contrast to traditionally procured projects, the PFI projects were largely being delivered on time or early (76 per cent versus 30 per cent) and on budget (78 per cent versus 27 per cent). The results are shown in Table 4.3. Moreover, in no case did the public sector bear the cost of construction overruns, a significant improvement on previous non-PFI experience where the financial costs of projects that ran into difficulties were borne by taxpayers.[3]

While the preliminary evidence does seem to indicate strongly that PPPs offer one solution to the public procurement problem, there is an important sense in which Flyvbjerg *et al.* are right in having some misgivings at this stage about concession-based approaches (they do not canvass partnership arrangements as such). Construction of the asset is only one part of a public–private infrastructure arrangement, and the obligations of the sponsors do not stop at the completion of the facility. The authors are also correct to highlight that public–private sector contractual agreements place very different, and more testing, demands on the public sector bodies involved. This can be appreciated by considering the procedural steps involved in public procurement and PPPs.

Table 4.3   Construction performance of PFI and conventional projects

Projects	PFI projects 2002 NAO census	Government procurement 1999 survey
Percent		
on time	76	30
on budget	78	27

Source: National Audit Office (2003).

THE CHANGED ROLE OF GOVERNMENT UNDER PPPS

A switch from traditional public procurement methods to infrastructure provided under a PPP signals a changed role for the public sector. This section examines the different role for government occasioned by the PPP procurement process relative to the conventional procurement method. The following section then outlines the features of PPPs that can help to bring about the better outcomes indicated in the previous section.

Public procurement involves the following procedures.[4]

1. establish alternatives
2. appraise options
3. draft terms of reference; recruit consultants for feasibility study
4. carry out feasibility study (involves consultants)

    • preliminary design and cost estimates
    • market analysis
    • economic analysis
    • financial analysis

5. undertake safety study (consultant)
6. arrange environmental impact study (consultant)
7. project recommendation (consultant)
8. parliamentary decision
9. create project team to implement project
10. apply for required permits
11. raise the finance
12. preparation of detailed design (consultants)
13. appoint contractors
14. supervise construction (consultants)
15. commission works
16. begin operations.

With a PPP, however, there are a number of different steps involved in getting the project to market and initiating construction and the operational phase:

1. undertake policy study
2. appraise options
3. publish policy document
4. prepare terms of reference
5. draft performance specifications (consultant)
6. commission consultants to undertake feasibility study
7. direct consultants to prepare plan for public involvement (public hearings, stakeholder group involvement, peer review, etc.)
8. evaluate feasibility study
9. Consultation Document issued for wide consultations with public and stakeholders
10. consultation with public, stakeholders and regulatory bodies
11. involve consultants in proposed regulatory regime; further analysis of associated costs; risk management plan

12. second Consultation Document for consultation with public and stake-holders
13. Decision Document to identify

    - performance specifications
    - financing conditions for operation
    - risk management
    - mode of operation
    - tender procedures
    - regulatory regime
    - cost estimates and financing conditions for associated costs

14. legislation to go to Parliament
15. undertake pre-qualification of bidders
16. prepare shortlist and ask for bids (consultant involved)
17. evaluate bids
18. select concession holder, negotiate and sign preliminary agreement (consultant involved)
19. circulate Information Document subject to review by Auditor-General.
20. selected private party to initiate final designs to obtain

    - final permits from regulatory authorities
    - bids from contractors

21. negotiated agreement to be approved by relevant authorities and concession holder
22. detailed design
23. final clearance from environmental and safety authorities
24. implement agreement
25. audit and manage contract.

These steps will normally be divided into a number of distinct phases, and in each of them the government will assume different roles and thus wear a number of different 'hats'. As managers of contractual relationships, public bodies authorize contracts (government as concession grantor), evaluate infrastructure needs (government as network planner), provide supporting facilities (e.g. land) and pay for services (government funding), define performance outcomes and standards (government as customer), undertake detailed procurement planning (government as project manager), ensure facilities are constructed, used and maintained satisfactorily (government as inspector), require compliance with standards and specifications (government as overseer), monitor business and financial viability (government as contract manager), assess environmental impacts (government as protector of the environment), and guarantee community access and achieve social policy objectives (government as representative of the public interest).

Table 4.4 sets out the major stages involved in developing a typical PPP project and indicates the different perspectives that the government must apply in each stage. At the same time, very different obligations are placed on the private sector entity because the government is not acquiring and taking immediate ownership of infrastructure assets but, rather, is contracting to buy infrastructure and related ancillary services from the private sector over time. Among the key ingredients of such an arrangement are:

- a focus on services, with the emphasis on the delivery of infrastructure services using new or refurbished public infrastructure assets;
- planning and specification, so that government's desired outcomes and output specifications are clear to the market;
- creating a viable business case for the private party;
- certainty of process, ensuring that any conditions to be fulfilled are clearly understood before the project proceeds;
- project resourcing to enable government to advance the project and address issues in line with published timeframes;
- clear contractual requirements, centred on key performance specifications, to create incentives that promote performance and minimize disputes;
- formation of a partnership to encourage good faith and goodwill between government and the private party in all project dealings; and
- contract management to monitor and implement the contract.

These features give emphasis to the risk management and the output-based project definition cycle advocated by the Mott MacDonald (2002) report. They also embody the checks and balances and incentives (public perusal, performance specifications, clarity of rules and the involvement of risk capital) recommended by Flyvbjerg *et al.* (2003) as a solution to the problems of conventional procurement. In particular, there is the opportunity for complete integration – under one party – of upfront design and construction costs with ongoing service delivery, operational, maintenance and refurbishment costs. Moreover, the approach focuses on output specifications, providing enhanced potential and incentives for bidders to fashion innovative solutions in meeting these requirements. With traditional procurement of infrastructure the detailed design work is normally completed in advance of calling for tenders, so removing scope for innovative new technologies or cost-saving devices. A PPP is in this respect an incentive-oriented, performance-based arrangement in which contractors are given responsibility for design as well as construction,

Table 4.4   Major stages in a PPP contract

Stage	Main tasks	Government role
Define service need	• identify service needs • determine outputs • consider network effects, corridor planning • allow scope for innovation	customer, network planner
Appraisal	• examine various alternatives (refurbishment, reconfiguration, new assets) • evaluate financial consequences, risks and other impacts	network planner, protector of environment, representative of public interest
Business case	• quantify risks and costs, establish net benefit • cost–benefit analysis, PSC • obtain funding and project approval	network planner, funding
Project development	• assemble project resources (steering committee, project director, probity auditor, procurement team) • create a project plan	project manager
Bidding process	• develop and issue expression of interest invitation • evaluate responses and prepare a shortlist • issue Project Brief • evaluate bids	concession grantor
Project finalization review	• confirm value for money and achievement of policy intent	network planner, representative of public interest
Final negotiation	• establish negotiation framework and team • probity review • execute contract • financial close	concession grantor, funding
Contract management	• handover to contract management team • formalize management responsibilities • finalize project delivery • handle variations to contract • monitor the service outputs • maintain the integrity of the contract	inspector, overseer, contract manager

along with operations and maintenance over extended periods of time (sometimes 25–30 years). By specifying in detail the service outcomes required, the government body signals that it will no longer be responsible for cost and time overruns or systems that are inefficient or fail to work (Smith, 1999).

ADVANTAGES OF PPPS

However, a partnership arrangement aims to be much more than an outcome-driven contracting system, and Lockwood *et al.* (2000) argue that PPPs have clear advantages over DBFO/BOT-type arrangements as well as conventional procurement. These authors' focus is on road transport infrastructure development, and they begin by noting that governments have two basic choices when it comes to financing investment in road expansion: using general funds on a pay-as-you-go basis or using toll roads (by which they mean mainly explicit tolls rather than the shadow toll system that has been used in the UK). Financing roads out of the general budget means that the demand on funds for the road allocation fluctuates greatly from one year to the next, creating difficulty in equitable and efficient allocation of financial resources among other sectors. It can also have the effect of keeping the risks from view and from being acknowledged. There are also the problems already discussed, such as determining the economically appropriate scale of facilities and instituting the incentives to control costs.

Under a BOT concession, the government grants to a private company (normally a consortium) the rights to finance, develop and operate a revenue-producing toll road for a defined time period after which the facility is transferred back to the public sector. This works well under the EGAP principle, that is, when 'Everything Goes According to Plan' (Flyvbjerg *et al.*, 2003, p. 80), and costs can be controlled, road users can afford toll rates that will pay for the road, and the commercial and economic contexts are relatively neutral. But the reality is that many things can go wrong, and often do, with difficulties in securing right of way, delays in meeting environmental impact process requirements, inadequate design, planning changes, slowness in securing permits, underestimation of project construction and operations costs, over-estimation of traffic-based revenues, 'teething' problems, and a slow build-up of patronage. These problems are compounded by a failure of the contracting parties to adopt a realistic and cooperative approach to the assessment, mitigation and sharing of risks (Lockwood *et al.*, 2000, p. 80).

PPPs are seen by Lockwood *et al.* as an evolving approach to government–private sector business relationships for road development that has certain advantages over the conventional BOT concession method. Partnerships are not seen by the authors as constituting an entirely new 'model', but rather as a variant of earlier models of private sector involvement in infrastructure incorporating a higher level of cooperative cost and risk sharing. One of the major differences is that the public sector plays a significantly increased role in providing resources, in effect becoming an actual development 'partner' rather than a 'client' (p. 77).

The PPP works as follows. The parties commit themselves at the outset to a more cooperative relationship, with the expectation that they will each contribute something of value to the project. The public sector has command over assets such as land, property and the negotiated right-of-way and brings to the development process the authority to implement the infrastructure acquisition within a planning process. The private sector brings access to outside capital, technical expertise and an incentive structure to develop projects in the most effective manner. As a consequence of the 'discipline' of the private capital markets, there is pressure to improve efficiency in construction and operations, and complete projects at the lowest cost and in the shortest time period. There must then be close control of the operational phase of the facility to ensure security of the cash flows that are needed to repay the project finance. As we said in the previous chapter, a PPP is all about putting in place appropriate strategies for appraising and managing the risks. Having equity capital and borrowings at risk introduces into the calculation an element of realism that it is not possible to obtain when the project is being publicly funded.

Rather than there being a 'model' of a partnership, PPPs should be thought of as a process, designed to ensure that all the risks are valued and taken into account in a meaningful way. Because both parties have committed resources and prestige to the success of the project, the partnership relies on a detailed step-by-step analysis of cost-sharing arrangements, risk mitigation and risk allocation. Abdel-Aziz and Russell (2001) propose a framework for this process revolving around rights, obligations and liabilities. This threefold classification encompasses key features of any PPP project. Under the agreement, various rights are ceded to the private entity in return for it taking on and committing to a specified set of obligations. Consider first the rights. One set of rights ceded relate to possession, when the public sector transfers ownership of land and property in its possession to the private sector. The other right refers to revenues, when the government entity gives the private sector body access to revenues during the operational stage of the contract. In return, the private firm is obliged to undertake certain functions. These obligations relate to planning, design, construction, improvement, operation, maintenance, financing, environmental aspects (biophysical), labour issues and regional and other business impacts. Finally, the liabilities dimension refers to the actual and potential liabilities and risks shared or assumed by parties under the agreement. Included under this heading are general liability (tort, third party and facility damage), liability for taxation, and risk liabilities. The latter arise from the risk allocation process. The various factors are listed in Table 4.5.

Table 4.5 A framework for assessing public private partnerships

Definition	Dimensions	Characteristics
Rights: the various rights given by government to a private entity in return for carrying out a specified set of obligations	Possession	Real assets Intellectual assets Equity Ownership Whole or part allocation of rights
	Revenues	Basis for generation Allocation to parties
Obligations: the promises that the private entity and the government agree to be bound to under the agreement	Development	Planning Design Construction Improvements
	Operating	Operation Maintenance
	Environment	Biophysical (air, marine, terrestrial) Social (labour issues, regional benefits, business impacts)
	Financing	Extent of financing Source of security Government guarantee
Liabilities: the real and potential liabilities and risks assumed by either party under the agreement	Legal liability	Tort liability Business interruption Physical loss
	Risk	Construction Business Financial *Force majeure*
	Taxes	Exemptions Liability assumption

Source: Based on Abdel-Aziz and Russell (2001).

Using this framework, Abdel-Aziz and Russell examine a number of projects in the UK, Canada and United States. From this investigation, they provide a checklist of recommendations as to attributes of the three dimensions that need to be specified in documentation for PPPs. In particular, the authors stress the need for clear articulation of government requirements in such documents and PPP agreements in order to reduce the amount of supplementary materials issued to request proposals, help consortia respond with proposals that can fit the requirements, and reduce the amount of time spent in negotiations and perhaps the need for contract amendments to reflect marketplace realities not considered at earlier stages. But, unlike in the traditional procurement process, in which all requirements are vested in government, under a PPP they are temporarily or permanently assigned to another entity.

These potential advantages of PPPs over traditional procurement come at a cost, one tangible element being the contracting costs. These contractual issues are not absent from traditional procurement but the agreements are less complex to draw up and are certainly less onerous to implement and monitor. Nevertheless, this apparently lower cost of traditional procurement methods may be deceptive because the risk analysis may be less thorough – hence the cost overruns and project delays. In this respect, it can be argued that PPPs are formalizing the sort of independent evaluation and scrutiny that ought to have been applied to procurement policies.

There is a real sense in which the application of a partnership agenda can inform other procurement methods, as well as learn from them. It has been argued, for example, by the UK Treasury Committee (1996) that 'There is no *a priori* reason why public procurement should not run to time and cost. Indeed many of the assumed benefits of PFI would appear to be available to better-managed and controlled conventional procurement' (para 33). As a statement of principle, this may be so. But it ignores the essential ingredient added by a PPP, which is to build in the incentives to avoid delays and cost overruns.

THE SCOPE OF PPPS

There is no single 'recipe' for all potential projects, and the range of applications in a variety of contexts testifies to the versatility of the concept. Nevertheless, PPPs are not for all. The corollary of the greater complexity of PPP contracts is to put a floor on the range of practicable projects. In the UK, the Treasury Review of July 2003 rules out PFI for small projects costing less than £20 million on the grounds that the bidding costs and contractual costs are too high to make the projects worthwhile. And, again considering the case of the UK, it is also worth noting that, despite all the controversy that surrounds the PPP/PFI programme and the stringent opposition from public sector unions and their supporters, the vast amount of investment in public infrastructure in the UK – over 85 per cent – still takes place by means of conventional procurement, with PFI accounting for around 10 to 14 per cent of the total investment.

The Treasury's view is that PFI is valuable, but only in certain applications. These are when there are major and complex capital projects with significant ongoing maintenance requirements. Also, PPPs are considered appropriate where private sector project management skills, more innovative design and risk management expertise can be brought in to give substantial benefits. In their opinion, however, PFI is unlikely to deliver value for money in other areas, for example where the transaction costs of pursuing PFI are disproportionate compared to the value of the project or where fast paced technological change makes it difficult to specify contractual requirements over the long term (HM Treasury, 2003b, p. 2).

An earlier report by the (self-appointed) Commission on Public Private Partnerships (2001) reaches similar conclusions. It recognizes that the PFI/DBFO route involving an SPV may be the most appropriate one for very complex projects, involving significant risks in the design and construction phase that carry over into the operational phase. Here project management disciplines and having some or all of the partners putting their equity at risk are relevant conditions, and there is a strong case for the integration of the contractors and subcontractors. The PPP model is also regarded as suitable for projects where there is considerable scope for innovation in design and also in operation. But the corollary may be that more routine projects, where the emphasis is on the delivery of an asset with routine maintenance and only a modest operational element, may best be dealt with using a Design Build Operate (DBO) model with the finance coming from the public sector (and the Commission particularly cites hospital projects in this respect). Also, the Commission suggests that routine refurbishment and maintenance – for example of schools – that do not involve significant risk and that do not require long contractual arrangements could be left to more conventional forms of contracting (pp. 100–1).

We would dispute these judgements in two ways. First, in terms of the ability of PPP/PFI to respond to changing circumstances, we note that in some PFI deals the extent of partnerships involved is not extensive in the sense that the public procurer is often cast in the role of 'client' rather than 'partner', and the private sector contractors deliver proposals that match, rather than seek to change, the requirements set out in the outline business case (Audit Commission, 2001). A more cooperative framework can provide an environment which makes it easier for both parties to negotiate contract variations in the face of changing business needs. One case study that we consider later is of a PFI hospital in West Middlesex where some flexibility was built into the contract to take account of changing health care needs, notably in a project area in which technological change is rapid. Second, we would question whether PPP contracts need be confined to complex projects. Another case study considered later is of a PPP hospital accommodation services project in Australia which is described as a 'plain vanilla' one, yet it promises to deliver good value for money. One reason for this result would seem to be that the consortium is integrated under the direction of a single entity, in this case a bank. This 'financier-led' approach to PPPs has been pioneered in Australia, and may offer the potential to lower bidding costs for relatively straight-forward PPP projects, while still delivering value for money, fast procurement times and projects delivered to budget.

However, we have jumped well ahead of ourselves, for a large number of considerations are involved in ascertaining whether a project can benefit from a partnership approach and deliver value for money. These issues are considered in the next chapter where we examine both the 'traditional' approach to structuring PPPs and the newer 'financier-led' model.

NOTES

1. The major and notable exception is the Channel Tunnel.
2. In July 2003, passenger numbers using Eurostar were half the original predictions, and freight figures were a quarter of those forecast. Competition from ferries proved to be stronger than anticipated, while Ryanair and Easyjet have emerged unexpectedly as strong competitors for passenger services (*Daily Telegraph*, 31 July 2003, p. 22).
3. Leading examples are the Guy's and St Thomas' Hospital project, the Trident submarine berth, the Jubilee Line extension, and the 25 largest equipment projects in the Ministry of Defence (see HM Treasury, 2003b, p. 31).
4. These points and those following build on and modify listings in Flyvbjerg *et al.* (2003).

5. The structure of partnership agreements

WHEN SHOULD PPPS BE USED?

Under traditional methods for procuring infrastructure, the public sector has obtained new assets – for example, roads, bridges, schools, hospitals, buildings, etc. – separately from services. The associated services have then been delivered by the public sector organizations either by using their own work force or by outsourcing or contracting out, fully or in part, the service provision to other specialist operators. External contracting out and outsourcing have grown over the last two decades as public (and private) sector organizations have searched for ways to enhance efficiency and make better use of resources. A partnership agenda takes this further and offers a different approach to traditional procurement because the acquisition of infrastructure assets and associated services is accomplished with one long-term contract, under which the initial capital outlay is financed by the private sector.

One of the major objectives of the PPP is to harness private sector management expertise, and the market disciplines associated with private ownership and finance, for the provision of public services. Of course, private sector skills are also employed under traditional procurement when the public sector engages design skills and private constructors, what the PPP adds is a different type of inducement for those involved. The private sector entity is encouraged to plan beyond the bounds of the construction phase and incorporate features that will facilitate operations and maintenance within a cooperative framework. This is one respect in which a PPP is designed to act as an incentive contract.

PPP Applications

Based on existing experience, the types of projects that could be suitable for partnerships include:

- transport (road, rail, ports, airports)
- fixed links (bridges, tunnels)

- water resources (filtration plants, irrigation, sewage treatment, pipelines)
- tourism (facility development)
- health (hospitals and specialized health services)
- specialized accommodation facilities (courts, police stations)
- educational facilities (schools, museums, libraries)
- correctional services (prisons, remand and detention centres)
- arts, sport and recreational facilities
- convention centres
- government office accommodation
- social housing.

In its latest review in July 2003, the UK Treasury argued that PFI/PPP has worked well for projects that have long-term planning horizons, require effective management of construction and delivery risks, and are sufficiently capital intensive to cover the procurement costs. On the other hand, PFI/PPP seemed less amenable to information technology applications because of the complexity of the business processes involved, the fast pace of technological change, and the often low level of operational content. Some IT projects may be suitable for PPP delivery, but these are likely to be those with sophisticated technology and a large operations element, such as emergency service centres using complicated dispatch interfaces.[1] Social housing, urban regeneration, waste management and prisons were seen in the review as areas for expanded private finance initiatives (HM Treasury, 2003b).

Three Criteria

These applications are all obviously areas where partnerships can be considered. However, whether or not a service should be delivered by means of a PPP project depends on the answer to three basic questions:

1. Which (if any) part or parts of the proposed service is a service which government itself should deliver to its citizens? (the core services question);
2. For all other aspects of the service and supporting physical infrastructure, what is the project model that delivers the best value for money? (the value for money question); and
3. Do the outcomes of the value for money question satisfy the public interest criteria articulated in the policy and, if not, can the public interest be satisfied either by building safeguards into the contract or through regulatory measures? (the public interest question).

It is the combined response to these three central questions – core services, value for money and public interest – that determines the underlying model for the project.[2] Obviously if the whole service is considered to be core, there will be no scope for a PPP arrangement. Nevertheless, one merit of a partnerships agenda is to bring into focus two dimensions of the core services question. First, what is really 'core'? Second, where do 'core' services end and 'ancillary' or related services begin.

WHAT IS A CORE GOVERNMENT SERVICE?

The question of what is really a core government activity takes us back to the essence of government itself. Under the American system of government, as fashioned by James Madison, there are three basic arms, equal but separated, in a system designed to constrain the expansion of government powers. Madison's conception divided government into three different branches which would check and balance one another: a two-house legislature, an independent executive, and an independent judiciary. Each would have specific functions and would see to it that the others did not overstep their bounds (Blum *et al.*, 1963). Translated into the British Commonwealth context (and ignoring the role of the Crown), the fundamental core of government can be seen as Parliament, the administration, and the justice system.

Establishing and maintaining a system of law and order has traditionally been seen as a fundamental role of government, acting as 'protector of the realm and guardian of civil society' – in effect, 'umpire' and 'peacekeeper' (Gray, 1989). Milton Friedman in his classic statement of the 'small government' position saw the basic roles of government as: 'to provide a means whereby we can modify the rules, to mediate differences among us on the meaning of the rules, and to enforce compliance with the rules on the part of those few who would otherwise not play the game' (Friedman, 1962, p. 25). Most (including Friedman himself) would accept that in addition to these basic functions, government has a duty of care towards the poor and the disadvantaged in society. But the four main components of the modern welfare state – education, medical services, housing and pensions – have expanded well beyond duty of care obligations to those groups. As Arthur Seldon (1990) has argued, 'the larger part of the public sector is a political artefact, not an economic necessity or a public preference'. Instead, he argues that its persistence can best be explained by 'party politics' and 'rent-seeking vested interests' (p. 170).

Most people nowadays would also accept that government should provide services when it is better than the market at doing so – what Officer (2003) calls the principle of comparative advantage in service provision. On this basis, responsibilities would be allocated between the public sector and the private sector according to which sector can add the greatest value to the community. Officer goes on to note that, on a number of scores, the government would appear to have a 'comparative disadvantage' in undertaking many business activities. Principal among these is the difficulty it has in creating incentives for managers to act in commercially oriented ways. Too often the downside risks to innovative and risk-taking activities exceed the gains, and it is easier to 'keep to the rules'. Another problem is that governments are elected with a broad mandate and this does not translate into clear objectives. Public sector bodies are confronted with a large number of often conflicting goals, with little accountability for any of them, in an environment in which many special interest groups are clamouring for attention. Having many goals is often a recipe for achieving none of them. All too frequently, the first stumbling block when a PPP procurement proposal is being formulated comes when the public sector entity is asked: 'What are the objectives of the project and what performance indicators would indicate that the aims have been achieved?'

The comparative advantage rule is, in essence, the basis of the value-for-money test applied under public procurement policies where private sector provision of infrastructure services under a PPP arrangement is compared against public sector provision. While there is no simple pass or fail with this examination, there is the expectation that the private sector bid must deliver better value for money if it is to proceed. To economic liberals, this presumption is the wrong way round. They would point to the Adam Smith principle, that government should do only what cannot be done in the market. To do otherwise and go beyond this point, they argue, is ultimately corrosive to the market, and inhibiting to the development of free enterprise. In effect, in the words of Seldon (1990),

> the classical principle, reaffirmed by Keynes, is that government should act not where it is better than the market but only where there is no market. . . . Wherever it is used, government is so disappointing or worse – inefficient, unaccountable and corrupt – that it is best not to use it at all except for functions where all its faults have to be tolerated to obtain the services required. (p. 239)

From this perspective, those things that absolutely have to be done by government are few in number, and consist largely of activities that cannot be financed by charges because they are 'non-excludable' and 'non-rival' (e.g. external defence), and those where the revenue would be exceeded by the costs of collecting it (e.g. local parks and children's playgrounds). But do the parks need to be policed and maintained by government workers? Even if one accepts that government has a duty to ensure that everyone is schooled, receives health care and is protected from criminals, on what grounds can it be argued that the actual teaching, surgery or custodial services cannot be provided by the private sector?

Services that once seemed self-evidently public in nature are now routinely being carried out by private suppliers – for example, prison and custodial services, fire services, power supply, telecommunications, roads, bridges, tunnels, and so on. Security at airports and buildings is now provided by private companies (and in many countries, like Australia, there are more private 'police' than public police). Police and emergency call lines are now managed and manned by private firms. Job centres are being run by private agencies. Water supply and sewage disposal can be provided by private concessionaires. Taxes are levied by governments but could be collected by private enterprises. Many legal disputes might be handled by private arbitration. The boundaries, it would seem, are governed by political expediency and perceived limits of public acceptability rather than any requirements of economics.

As these examples make apparent, there are hardly any public services provided to the community that are 'core' in the sense that government needs to deliver these services itself. Moreover, core services are usually supplied in a context that does not preclude participation by private parties. The services performed by doctors and nurses within public hospitals, teachers within government educational facilities and judges within courts are still widely regarded as ones which it is a function of government to provide. Yet, even if the public provision principle is to remain sacrosanct in some of these particular cases, there is no reason why supporting infrastructure and ancillary services within those areas cannot be delivered by the private sector. For example, a court needs complex systems of horizontal and vertical circulation. There have to be custody centres and secure entrance and exit points for those accused and for prisoners. Acoustics must be good, yet jurors' private deliberations cannot be compromised. Sophisticated court recording and audio visual systems need to be installed and kept in good working order. There has to be good access for visitors. All these functions, including the courthouse itself, can be designed and carried out by private operators.

THE CASE OF HOSPITALS

Hospitals are one area where private participation at a number of levels can be achieved and where PPPs involving the construction and management of public hospitals can introduce innovative ways to control costs and improve services within existing health systems. Table 5.1 lists the options for private sector involvement from outsourcing arrangements at one end, to privatization by sale at the other end, with a variety of PPP approaches in between. The various

Table 5.1   Options for private participation in hospitals

Option	Private sector responsibility	Pubic sector responsibility
Outsourcing nonclinical support services	Provides nonclinical services (cleaning, catering, laundry, security, building maintenance) and employs staff for these services.	Provides all clinical services (and staff) and hospital management.
Outsourcing clinical support services	Provides clinical support services such as radiology and laboratory services.	Manages hospital and provides clinical services.
Outsourcing specialized clinical services	Provides specialized clinical services (such as lithotripsy) or routine procedures (cataract removal).	Manages hospital and provides most clinical services.
Co-location of private wing within or beside public hospital	Operates private wing (for private patients). May provide only accommodation services or clinical services as well.	Manages public hospital for public patients and contracts with private wing for sharing joint costs, staff and equipment.
Private lease and management of a public hospital	Manages public hospital under contract with government or public insurance fund and provides clinical and nonclinical services. May employ all staff. May also be responsible for new capital investment, depending on terms of contract.	Contracts with private firm for provision of public hospital services, pays private operator for services provided, and monitors and regulates services and contract compliance.
Private construction, financing and leaseback of a new public hospital	Constructs, finances and owns a new public hospital and leases it back to government.	Manages hospital and makes phased lease payments to private developer.
Private construction, financing and operation of a new public hospital	Constructs, finances and operates a new public hospital and provides nonclinical or clinical services, or both.	Reimburses operator annually for capital costs and recurrent costs for services provided.
Sale of public hospital as a going concern	Purchases facility and continues to operate it as public hospital under contract.	Pays operator for clinical services and monitors and regulates services and contract compliance.

Source: Adapted from Taylor and Blair (2002).

97

possibilities differ according to whether the private firm manages medical services, owns or leases the facility, employs the staff, and finances and manages capital investments. A government's decision on the most appropriate arrangement will depend on hospital service needs and circumstances, the government's ability to regulate and effectively control the quality of care, and the public's view on the need for reform and the role of government in health care; that is, what is a 'core' government service? An extra dimension is provided by the involvement of mainly religious-based, not-for-profit organizations, and governments have long been willing to entrust core health care services to such bodies.

Australia is one market where almost all of these models exist. Health care is provided by individual states and territories, along with the federal government, and there is now private sector involvement in over 50 public hospitals across the country, including BOO arrangements (in which a private firm builds, owns, and operates a public hospital), conversions (in which a hospital is sold to a private operator as a going concern), concessions (private management of public hospitals that the government continues to own), build-own-leasebacks (in which a private firm constructs a new public hospital, then leases it back to the government), and co-locations (in which a private wing is located within or beside a public hospital). These initiatives were stimulated by a need for new capital, a desire to transfer operational risk, and by the search for increased efficiency (Taylor and Blair, 2002). A case study is provided later in this chapter of the design, construction, finance and facilities management of a new public hospital in Victoria.

In the UK, the National Health Service is another example of different views about the 'core' versus 'ancillary' issue in the case of health care. The model that was originally developed under the Private Finance Initiative (PFI) was one in which the NHS Trusts continued to be the employer of clinical staff, with the private sector responsible for design, build, ownership, maintenance and delivery of ancillary services. A Trust would tender for a private firm to finance and construct a new hospital, maintain the facility, and provide non-clinical services such as laundry, security, parking and catering. The operator receives annual payments for 15–35 years as reimbursement for its capital costs and its recurrent costs for maintenance and services. In this way, the private parties ensure that the facilities for clinical staff are as modern, efficient and cost effective as is possible to obtain. This allows the NHS to then concentrate on the provision of health care, its primary function. However, there is still the question of who should actually deliver primary health care, and recent experiments have challenged the traditional allocation of activities within the NHS with the development of PFI 'diagnostic centres', which are full service delivery models for elective surgery.

THE CASE OF PRISONS

Prisons are another area where there has been a diversity of approaches to the issue of what is considered to be within the capacity of the private sector to provide and what is the role of the public sector. In the UK, the model is more inclusive than has been the case for UK public hospitals and is more integrated than in some other countries in that the full range of prison and correctional services is left to the private sector entity to provide, including the management of prisons and their staffing. Figure 5.1 lists the various services that come under the heading of 'prison and correctional services' and indicates the

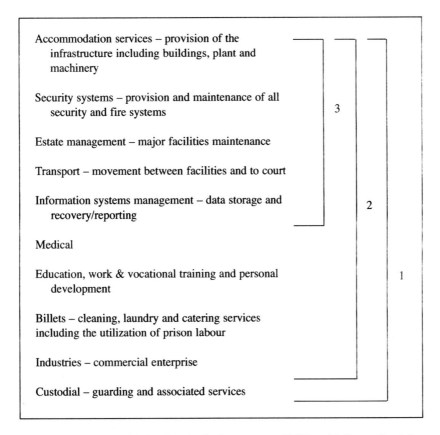

1 = UK PFI 'DCMF' model; 2 = French mixed management "DCF' model; 3 = services infrastructure model

Figure 5.1   Alternative models of private sector participation in prison services

three different models of private sector participation that have been employed. These are the UK PFI design, construct, maintain and finance (DCMF model), the French mixed management, design, construct and finance (DCF) model, and the serviced infrastructure model in the State of Victoria in Australia.

The DCMF model is the one most widely adopted in recent times for private sector involvement in prisons and has been used in the UK, the US and certain states of Australia for numerous correctional facilities. Under this model, the private sector designs, constructs, finances and manages the prison. The state may or may not own the prison site. The distinguishing feature of this approach is the transfer of all prison services to the private sector and the management of prison operations by a private firm. In the UK context, a number of features apply. Typically, there is a contract of up to 25 years between the Minister for Corrections and a shelf company established by the private sector entities as a special purpose vehicle (SPV) to deliver the project. A Crown lease for the site is usually granted for the term of the contract. The SPV enters into a turnkey fixed-price, fixed-term design and construct (D & C) contract with the construction company, and also negotiates a fixed-price, fixed-term operating contract with the prison operator. The capital costs of the construction works are raised by means of non-recourse debt on the basis of payments made by the government for prisoners handled. No payments are made until the prison is commissioned, and certain service standards must be met. If these specifications are not reached, deductions are made according to a points accrual mechanism for poor performance against key performance indicators such as temporary release, items smuggled in, prisoner self-harm in custody, and so on. Note that government duty of care responsibilities are not compromised within a private prison, for sentences of punishment of inmates are normally administered by a public servant. It is important when considering the payment regime not to mix up the duty of care itself, which is held by the state, with the financial consequences of breaches of duty of care that can be delegated and borne by the private prison operator.

The French mixed management model provides a more limited role for private sector involvement than the DCMF model. Under this model, the private sector designs, constructs and finances the prisons and manages the provision of a limited range of prison services, but excluding prison operations and custodial services. When the programme began, private sector operators were initially invited[3] to tender for the building of 25 new prisons on a design and build basis along with the operation of specific prison services over a 10-year period. The sites remained in state ownership. The specific prison services to be provided by the private sector included industries, education, catering (including staff facilities), medical, maintenance, work and vocational training, and transport. Public sector employees were to provide all custodial services, including inter-prison transfers, while the police provided prison-to-court transfer services. In relation to design of the prisons, design innovation was organized through architectural competitions, with bidders responding to standard briefs for different kinds of prisons. The state guaranteed the financing of the construction and the management and security functions. At the end of the 10-year period, the government retained the option of selecting between new private sector competition, extending the original tenders or returning to full public sector operation.

The serviced infrastructure model was developed under the Partnerships Victoria programme in 2001 when, because of dissatisfaction with the operation of private prisons under the previous government, it was decided that all new prisons in Victoria were to be managed and operated by public sector resources. Accordingly, prison services were divided into three categories:

- Core services under public sector control and excluded from the contract; that is, billets (cleaning/laundry/catering), industries, and custodial operations.
- Services provided by a private sector partner (infrastructure plus ancillary services); that is, accommodation, security systems, estate management, transport, and information systems management.
- Those services with the potential for private sector provision but excluded from the contract at the outset, namely medical, education, works and vocational training.

Under the contract term of up to 40 years, the public sector operator is responsible for specifying in output terms the custodial aspects of the design of the facilities; that is, functional content/adjacencies, but without extending this to engineering and construction responsibility for any aspect. Other than this, the SPV is responsible for all aspects of the design and construction works as a whole, including structural integrity, circulation space, foundations, air conditioning, and so on, with payments linked directly to performance and other criteria.

There are obvious differences between the models in terms of the range of services covered. Another important difference between the 'serviced infrastructure' and the 'DCMF' model relates to the encompassing framework, specifically the extent of the partnering arrangements. Under the DCMF model the contract structure has tended to be rigid and there is therefore limited flexibility for the government to vary its requirements. Under the partnership framework, the serviced infrastructure model can be structured so that flexibility is an inherent feature of the contractual arrangements. For example, contractual mechanisms could provide for upside benefit sharing where the introduction of new technology results in a reduction in cost of either core services (custodial) or those services provided under the PPP arrangements.

There could also be scope for risk-sharing in relation to prison capacity and prisoner mix within defined boundaries. The DCMF or BOOT-type approach can often be more contractual than cooperative.

PPP DELIVERY MODELS

As is apparent from these examples, in general PPPs can allow for a range of roles for the parties and in a hierarchy ranging from maximum to minimum retention of service delivery by government, the various models are broadly as follows:

- public sector delivery of services (considered to be 'core' public services) with private entities providing infrastructure-related services only (for example, a public hospital);
- public sector delivery of core services with private parties providing infrastructure-related and ancillary services (for example, a courthouse or school);
- public sector delivery of core services with private parties providing infrastructure and related ancillary services, together with some services to the community (for example, a sporting facility); and
- private sector delivery of a full range of services to the community inclusive of infrastructure (for example, some transport projects).

Table 5.2 summarizes in broad terms the range of service delivery models available. In addition, because of their flexibility, PPPs can also cover a range of commercial scenarios, varying from:

- an arrangement where demand is effectively controlled by government and the costs of service delivery are substantially or fully funded by government (for example, non-judicial court services); to
- an arrangement where government has little control over demand and shares the costs of service provision with users (for example, public transport services); to
- an arrangement where government has no control over demand, costs of service delivery are fully funded by users and government's role is limited to providing some supporting infrastructure (for example, land) or project facilitation in areas such as planning. A port project may be an example of this model.

In structuring the most appropriate approach, the focus should be on the output specifications, the public interest, the capabilities of both government and the private sector, the optimal risk allocation environment and commercial viability. The objective remains one of achieving value for money outlaid.

Table 5.2 Range of partnership models

	Role of the private sector increasing			
Private party role	Infrastructure services only	Infrastructure and ancillary services	Infrastructure and partial private-to-public service delivery	Infrastructure and service delivery to users
Government role	All public-to-public services	Delivery of core public services	Delivery of core public services	No operational role
Examples	Public buildings	Non-core hospital services, non-judicial court services	Community facilities linked to educational facilities (e.g. after-hours usage)	Rail, road, port facilities, car parks

Source: Partnerships Victoria (2001).

Related Services

'Related ancillary services' encompasses a number of operational services, including information technology services, accommodation services arising out of the infrastructure, building-related services such as maintenance and some support services. Notably, in all cases, land and property are required for the delivery of the PPP service, and often the private party can gain value from an imaginative development of the property site that is integrated with and complementary to the project. An example of this comes from the Spencer Street Station redevelopment project, designed to be fully operational for the Melbourne 2006 Commonwealth Games.

The Spencer Street Station contract provides for the Civic Nexus consortium (led by ABN-AMRO) to redevelop the station to an agreed standard and to operate it for a period of 30 years, after which ownership passes to the State government. Civic Nexus will also develop catering and retail services within the station, and it has acquired commercial development rights in neighbouring properties over which it has a 99-year lease. The project has a number of notable features including the iconic roof design. But from the outset the winning bidder did not think of the project as a station, which is what might have happened under traditional procurement. Instead, Civic Nexus saw the location as a junction point where people congregate with cash in their pockets, and it set about combining transport, retail, commercial office space, and residential inner-city accommodation in a way that will help integrate the adjoining Docklands development (which includes a major sporting facility) into the City of Melbourne and serve as a suitable structure to occupy a central position in an expanded central activities district of Melbourne. The idea is for the station to recover its historic role as the main thoroughfare to the city.

From a property point of view, it may seem that the analysis of a PPP project involves many of the same principles as a joint venture/development arrangement in an open commercial environment. Perhaps the main difference between the PPP and the various property-based public/private joint ventures that have preceded it lies in the fact that the PPP encourages participants to focus on service delivery. This contrasts with the more traditional institution-led view of regarding the assets *per se* as having intrinsic value. If the private sector can add considerable value from an integration on the property side of a project and thereby reduce the cost of service provision to the government, then it is the public that ultimately benefits. In addition, on the government side, senior management is freed from the everyday issues of infrastructure ownership and management and the delivery of related ancillary services. Management's focus on service delivery is not distracted by time and cost overruns in construction, maintenance needs, infrastructure that is not quite fit for purpose, and staff and client unrest that could be resolved by a refurbishment of facilities if only funds were available.[4] This leads into the issue of finance.

Financial Aspects

Governments frequently have been motivated to enter into PPP arrangements by the desire to reduce debt (and contain taxation), while facing pressure to improve and expand public facilities. However, the argument that PPPs are the only way of delivering the public infrastructure (and the services) that the community wants is exaggerated, for PPPs still draw on public funds when user charges do not cover the cost of services. What differs is that the public payments are made over a very different time frame. When infrastructure is provided under a PPP, the government does not own the asset but, instead, enters into a contract to purchase infrastructure and related ancillary services over time from the private sector. These operating payments must cover operating costs as well as giving the service providers a return on risk capital, therefore a project delivered under a partnerships approach will have a similar (although not identical) effect on the government's annual operating surplus to that if the asset was publicly funded.

Figure 5.2 illustrates the cashflow differences between public funding and a PPP project. From the public sector side, PPPs require little or no upfront capital expenditure but involve a larger operating expenditure over time to purchase the services. By contrast, the public asset approach requires a large

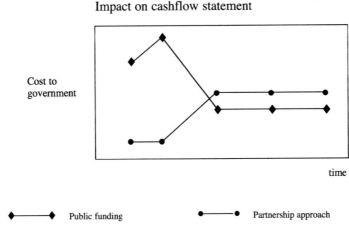

Figure 5.2   Comparison of public funding and partnerships on cashflows

upfront capital funding commitment and relatively lower operating expenditure over time. Thus the PPP route may on these grounds hold some attractions to a government with a backlog of infrastructure projects and facing an uncertain fiscal climate – a not unimportant consideration for many transition countries. But the major merit is in terms of the predictability of costs and funding. A PPP ensures that whole-of-life costing and budgeting are considered, providing infrastructure and related ancillary services to specification for a significant period, and including any growth or upgrade requirements. This provides budgetary predictability over the life of the infrastructure and reduces the risks of funds being diverted (for example, away from scheduled refurbishment) during the life of the project, impacting on residual value risk to the asset. Certainly, pricing predictability and whole-of-life costing were important considerations for the NHS Trust in the West Middlesex University Hospital redevelopment, examined as a case study in Chapter 6.

Treatment of Risk

Financing is only one element of the calculation. Infrastructure procurement has traditionally been viewed by the public sector as asset acquisition from private sector contractors, the responsibilities of which were limited to the construction of the asset, while the risks associated with the financing and operation of the facility remained with the public sector. With a PPP, the emphasis is on the purchase of infrastructure-based services, and the allocation of risks in the transaction is quite different.

In theory, the conception of risk allocation with a PPP is straightforward. The government frees itself entirely from asset-based risk (including design, construction, operation and possibly residual value risk), and becomes the purchaser of a product that is risk-free in the sense that government does not pay if the service is not delivered, or is not delivered to the specified standards. That is, the public sector purchases the long-term provision of a service of a guaranteed standard, along with the security that if the service is not provided at the right time or to a satisfactory quality then reduced payments are made or compensation is received.

That is the underlying philosophy. In practice, risk allocation in a PPP is more complex. Rather than shifting all risk to the private sector, the policy aims at allocating risk to the party that is best suited to manage it and demonstrating value for money for any expenditure by the public sector. Those in the best position to manage a particular risk should do so at the lowest price. Unloading inappropriate forms of risk onto the private entity merely adds unnecessary cost to a PPP agreement, as the private sector does not bear risk cheaply. Driven by the requirement for 'value for money', the government may agree to assume some risks for which the private party would charge too much if the risk transfer to the private party were to remain complete. Only 'efficient' levels of risk should be transferred to the private party, reducing individual risk premia and the overall cost of the project.

Thus the conceptual framework underlying PPPs is that, as service recipient paying only on satisfactory delivery, the government initially transfers all project risk to the private party. It is then a matter for government to determine, on a value-for-money basis and having regard to the cooperative framework of the partnership, what risks it should 'take back' to achieve an optimal risk position. Taking back means a deliberate decision by government to assume or share a risk that would otherwise lie at the door of the private party. The outcome of this analysis is reflected in the contract.

The upshot is that a PPP contract differs from a standard procurement contract because it is not part of a traditional product supplier/buyer relationship. Under a PPP, the parties allocate risks between them and work together in an ongoing relationship to meet project objectives. It is also more complex than a procurement agreement. For example, the contractual framework for a County Court in Victoria included a Crown lease, a court services agreement, a multi-party agreement for financiers, a commercial site and building, bond issuance contracts, and subcontracts for operation, maintenance and finance.

Whole-of-Life Cycle Contract

When considering risks and negotiating a risk allocation position, the public sector party would prefer to deal with a single entity which is fully accountable for all contracted services. From a government point of view, risk transfer is most effective if there is a 'whole-of-life cycle' contract with a single private party, to give that party the strongest possible incentive to ensure that the design and construction phase converts into a highly effective operations phase. Behind the private party, however, there may be a number of private sector interests. The distinctive feature of current PPPs is the bundling of finance, design, construction, operations, and maintenance. Because these functions are highly specialized, private sector providers tend to be consortia consisting of engineering and project management firms, construction companies, financial underwriters, and operating enterprises that come together to develop a particular facility.

Generally speaking, private entities take on risks if they can be appropriately priced, managed and mitigated, which often involves transferring the risk to a third party, by way of subcontract or insurance. Should there be a risk, say, that an innovative design for a project may not be suitable for the designated purpose, that risk may be partly mitigated by appointing an experienced (and insured) designer. The consortium then accepts the risk, provided it can earn a commensurate return.

However, if the risk is one which carries a significant probability of interrupting or diminishing the payment stream that will service the debt, a significant premium may be demanded to assume that particular risk. This in turn greatly increases the cost of financing the project. The private party's uneasiness becomes more acute when the risk is not within its control. In such cases, it may be possible to change the nature of the risk so that it can be taken on. If this cannot be done, it may well be more cost-effective for government to 'take back' the risk and reduce the costs of financing the project.

Hence one way to get value for money in a PPP is through sensible risk allocation, but it is not the only means. One of the appeals of PPPs is that they may be a vehicle through which the 'can do' mentality of the private sector is imported into public services, and the integrated PPP structure creates incentives to realize 'synergy' gains (such as fewer disputes between builder, operator and owner and a closer examination of capital/maintenance costs) that are not available if the owner is government and the other functions are simply contracted out. Effective use of public funds on a capital project can accordingly come from private sector innovation and skills in asset design, construction techniques and operational practices, as well as from shifting the responsibility for design risks, construction delays, costs overruns and finance and insurance to the private sector entities. Without the risk transfer the incentives would be blunted, and all parties need to understand the implications of the risks to be managed. The value-for-money test, considered in Chapter 6, is one way of drawing attention to the risks. So is the development of a risk matrix for the purpose of risk management and allocation, examined in Chapter 7. For the moment, we consider the parties to a PPP and their respective functions.

THE ORGANIZATION OF PPPS

A PPP is an organizational structure that brings together a number of parties for an infrastructure investment, typically in the form of a 'special purpose vehicle' (SPV) created specifically for the project. The main participants are:

- the public sector procurer (the government, local governments and agencies, state-owned entities);
- the sponsors who as equity investors normally create a special purpose vehicle (SPV or project company) through which they contract with the public procurer, and the principal subcontractors;
- financiers;
- subcontractors; and
- other involved parties such as advisers (legal, financial, technical), insurers, rating agencies, underwriters, etc.

In a project, each retains its own identity and responsibilities. They combine together in the SPV on the basis of a clearly defined division of tasks and risks.

Special purpose vehicle

An SPV is simply a separate legal entity, generally a company, established to undertake the activity defined in a contract between the SPV and its client, in this case the public procurer. Execution of the activity generally requires the involvement of a number of parties, and the SPV enters into subcontracts with a number of organizations for the execution of these activities. SPVs are used in PPPs for the following reasons:

- to allow lending to the project to be non-recourse to the sponsors by virtue of the limited liability nature of the SPV;
- to enable the assets and liabilities of the project not to appear on the sponsors' balance sheets, by virtue of no sponsor having more than 50 per cent of the shares in the SPV and the application of normal consolidation principles when preparing the group accounts; and
- for the benefit of the project lenders, to help to insulate the project from a potential bankruptcy of any of the sponsors ('bankruptcy remoteness').

Two approaches

Figure 5.3 illustrates the generic form of the consortium, which is likely to include debt financiers (often in a syndicate arranged through a bank), equity investors and sponsors (who invest in the fortunes of the project and are therefore exposed to both the 'upside' and 'downside' risks), a design and/or construction contractor and the operator. In terms of which parties take the lead in organizing the arrangement and putting together the bid, there are two alternative approaches: the traditional construction and facilities management-led approach, and the new financier-led approach.

Traditional approach

The traditional approach, commonly seen in the UK, is for the contractors and the service providers to sponsor the SPV and to take equity stakes in it as a sign of their commitment to the project and its delivery. Financiers are involved in the consortium, and they may take minority equity stakes in the SPV and, as long run investors with a strong financial interest, may assume a more prominent role in the project after the construction phase is over. Nevertheless, the initial organization and bidding process is directed by the engineering and construction companies in tandem with the facilities managers, third party equity investors and debt investors.

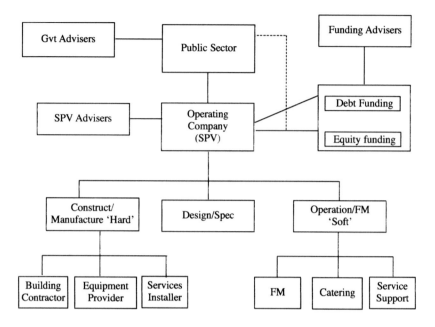

Figure 5.3   Typical private sector consortium

Financier-led approach
Under the newer financier-led approach that has developed in recent years in Australia, specialized investment banks have taken a more active role in managing the SPV from the outset. The bank invests the equity in the SPV, manages the bid, decides on the pricing, guarantees the commercial revenue from the project, underwrites the senior debt and subcontracts to the contractor and the operator under a letter of credit issued to debt-holders. Obviously, the bank cannot perform all the functions and must liaise and conclude agreements with the other parties that come together contractually to form the consortium. Nevertheless, it is the investment bank that takes 100 per cent of the equity in the SPV and underwrites capital market issues and all other elements of the contract.

Pros and cons
It is fair to say that the development of the financier-led approach has caught the PPP industry by surprise and there has been some disquiet about its novelty and lack of road-testing, although there was an earlier precedent in the international capital markets for the issue of new securities where the 'bought deal' (whereby one investment bank bids for a mandate at a fixed price and amount and places these in advance with institutional investors) superseded the old,

cumbersome and drawn-out issue procedures organized by a syndicate of participating banks (Lewis and Davis, 1987, pp. 327–8). The bought deal gave greater certainty of process, faster placement and keener pricing, and much the same reasons underpin the financier-led model.

In the case of PPPs, of course, we are dealing not with a process over a matter of weeks but with procedures governing contractual arrangements lasting 25–30 years. Concerns have been raised about the nature of the partnership created, and who bears the service performance risk, when the components are 'unbundled' by the financier into subcontracts after the bid is successful. Equity participation in the SPV is one way of aligning the interests of those involved in delivering the project with policy objectives and the long-term partnership with the government. Certainly, in the traditional approach, connectivity exists between service delivery outcomes, those providing the services (and taking the risks), and the extent and proportion of equity investment from the contractors and service providers in a way that is not so readily apparent in the financier-led model.

Against this, there are clear pricing benefits when the whole process is an integrated one under the direction of the bank, one aim of which is to reduce transactions costs and generate a competitive bid. It also enables the bank to control the various elements that underpin the financing deal. This is a reflection that financing in the PPP market is changing from traditional project finance to corporate financing methods, with the end process being the issue and underwriting of bonds that are placed directly with institutional investors. In addition, some leading banks have created special 'social infrastructure' pooled investment funds and it remains to be seen to what extent they will look to direct the cash flows from the projects to those funds, tapping a wider investment market for infrastructure financing.

These two issues are taken up later when case studies of the two alternative approaches are presented in the final section of this chapter. One case study relates to the 'traditional' PPP project approach and involves privately built and operated prisons in Bridgend, Wales and Fazerkerley, Merseyside. The other case study is of a 'financier-led' PPP for the construction of a public hospital in Berwick, Victoria. In the meantime, bearing the distinction between the two models in mind, we now outline the role of the various participants.[5]

THE ROLE OF PARTICIPANTS

Public Sector

In the previous chapter we noted that the government must wear a number of different 'hats'. In a PPP, unlike with privatization, the government retains a permanent interest in the delivery of an asset or service. It is ultimately responsible for determining the objectives, seeing that the outcomes are delivered to the required standards, and ensuring that the public interest is safeguarded. Consequently, while the execution of many elements of service delivery may transfer to the private sector, the public sector procurer remains accountable for many aspects. These include:

- defining the business and the services required, and the public sector resources available to pay for them;
- specifying the priorities, targets and outputs;
- executing a carefully planned procurement process;
- determining the performance regime by setting and monitoring safety, quality and performance standards for those services;
- governing the contract by enforcing those standards, taking action if they are not delivered;
- managing community expectations;
- providing the enabling environment; and
- reacting, in cooperation with the private sector, to changes in the project environment while remaining focused on pre-defined objectives.

Public sector regulatory bodies and other public sector entities play an important contributing role in that they issue permits, licences, authorizations and concessions and they design the regulatory framework to which the PPP structure must be allied.

Project Vehicle Company

The sponsors and other equity holders in the SPV are responsible for meeting their contractual obligations, which include:

- producing and delivering the defined services to the required standard;
- designing and building or upgrading the infrastructure asset;
- raising funds for the capital needs of the project;
- focusing on government's objectives, while responding in cooperation with the public procurer to variations in the project environment;
- returning the assets in the specified condition at the end of the contract.

Financiers

Under either of the two structures outlined earlier, an SPV is formed in which one or more of the bank, constructor, and operator may have a share.

Arrangements for financing the SPV will usually be entered into at the same time as the contract and subcontracts are concluded. A precondition for this to happen is a revenue stream that will provide security for the financing institutions and encourage equity participation. In short, a corporate entity must be created that can represent itself as an acceptable credit risk. A benchmark figure for the finance would be, say, 90 per cent debt, comprising either senior bank debt or bonds, plus 10 per cent equity provided by the investors in the SPV. Subordinated debt is also used, which is akin to equity in that the rights of holders of this debt are subordinated to other creditors (except shareholders). All financial obligations must be serviced within the life of the contract.

Because the major costs of constructing the facility are funded by non-recourse debt, the private debt markets must commit to significant sums of debt up front. PPP structures are useful for facilitating capital intensive infrastructure transactions because the spreading of project risk among a number of participants creates a sense of mutual interest – everyone stands to lose if the project fails. As a result, financiers are assured that the participants are likely to work together to resolve issues that may otherwise stall the project.

Subcontractors

The project company's obligations and responsibilities to the public procurer are delivered through specialized subcontractors, who in the traditional model are often equity investors in the SPV. Functions that are usually subcontracted out by the SPV are construction, equipment supply, and operation and maintenance, with a separate agreement for each.

Advisers

The advisers provide financial, legal, technical and other advice to both the public and private sectors in structuring PPPs. Governments rely on their advisers to implement and provide an independent check on each PPP-type transaction, and add value to the public procurement. The sponsors use outside advisers or their in-house team to bid for projects. Usually the financiers rely on their own advisory group or occasionally outside advisers to assess the financial viability of a project and the risks attached to the revenue stream providing security for the finance.

Rating Agencies

When projects are financed through the public issue of bonds, rating agencies are consulted to provide credit ratings for the underlying debt. These agencies are typically involved at very early stages of project formulation so that credit concerns can be addressed and a new structure developed (e.g. altering the extent of equity in the SPV). Insurers may also be used to provide credit enhancement.

Insurers

Insurers provide risk enhancement in project financing irrespective of whether the risks are commercial or political. Typically, they work closely with project sponsors and lenders, so as to produce an insurance package that limits risk at an achievable price. There is a relatively new sub-sector of insurers that cover credit risk of debt issues (normally bonds). These 'monoline' insurers are involved in credit risk arbitrage that often creates value for project financing in circumstances where the market generally would tend to overestimate the risks.

CASE STUDIES

Earlier in this chapter we argued that PPPs can provide for private sector involvement in infrastructure-related services at a number of levels. Also, we said that there were two different approaches to the structure of PPP contractual relationship: the 'traditional' consortium joint venture model involving contractors, facilities managers, and so on, and the 'financier-led' model that has come to the fore in Australia recently. In this section we give two examples of PPPs. One case study relates to 'full services' DCMF prison facilities in the UK under the traditional approach, and the other is a 'limited services' hospital project in Australia, utilizing the 'financier-led' arrangement.

Bridgend and Fazakerley Prisons[6]

In 1995, there were around 130 prisons in the United Kingdom with a considerable number of them dating back to Victorian times. New facilities were needed to help to counteract overcrowding in prisons and accommodate the expected growth in the prison population in areas where there is continued pressure on available prison places. Until then, prisons in the UK had been procured against designs approved in detail by HM Prison Service. Contracts for the design, construction, management and financing for two prisons at Bridgend and Fazakerley, concluded in 1995, were the first two PPP prison transactions in the United Kingdom. These DCMF prisons were a progression from privately operated facilities which existed in four prisons across the UK, including HMP Doncaster and Wolds Remand Prison. These original private prisons are still operating successfully showing 'significant cost benefits' over comparisons with existing public sector best performers.[7]

An extra 1400 places were sought from the two new facilities: an 800-place prison at Bridgend, South Wales and a 600-place prison at Fazakerley, Merseyside. These were to be designed to accommodate prisoners on remand, awaiting sentence, serving short sentences or awaiting transfer to another prison (Category B prisoners) and also for a small number of Category A (maximum security) prisoners. In all, for the two prisons, the Prison Service received 60 expressions of interest in response to their required notice of the tender in the *Official Journal of the European Communities* (OJEC). Of these, five were invited to submit bids. Following the end of a 17-month process the contracts to design, build, finance, operate and maintain the prisons were awarded in 1995 to Securicor/Costain/Skanska for Bridgend and Group 4/Tarmac for Fazakerley.

The construction phase was completed ahead of schedule (five months for Bridgend, four months for Fazakerley), and much faster than in other prison projects. In both cases, the contracts are for a period of 25 years, at the end of which the prisons revert to Crown ownership. The private sector consortia have taken on the full responsibility for prison design, construction and subsequent management, and they are also providing a custodial service and ancillary services, such as catering, prisoner education and onsite medical facilities, over a 25-year period after the assets are built. While HM Prison Service is using an alternative method to obtain the custodial and correctional services, it is not delegating any responsibility relating to the procedures controlling the length of time each inmate remains in custody.

A core requirement for the private sector was defined as the provision of a specified number of prisoner places. What this meant was that the prison as a whole and each cell had to be built and maintained to specified standards. As well, the prison regime and the operation of the prison had to be in accordance with prison rules and other standards relating to the prison and the control, health and general well-being of prisoners. In general, however, the supplier was free to meet these specified standards in whatever way it chose.

Some other features of the contract specification are as follows. The contracts transferred the risk of time and cost overruns to the contractors. No payment was made until the prisons were operational. Contractors are paid for availability rather than actual usage. The contract price contains a fixed element relating to construction costs, some operating costs (non-salary costs) were fixed in real terms, and further costs (relating to salaries) are indexed to 2 per cent above the RPI (retail price index). In addition, the contractual conditions allows for some risk-sharing of cost increases beyond the contractors' control, some benefit sharing if contractors' profits are higher than anticipated, and additional fees are payable if the specified number of prisoners is exceeded. These risk-sharing arrangements turned out to be controversial, in view of the financing relationships.

When bids were received they were assessed by HM Prison Service on the basis of deliverability, price, quality and innovation. A weighting was applied to both the quality and innovation scoring based on the following factors in order of importance: keeping prisoners in custody; providing decent condi-tions and meeting prisoners' needs; providing adequate management systems; providing a positive regime to address prisoners' offences; helping prisoners prepare for their return to the community and demonstrating sensitivity to the local environment.

In terms of value for money, the economic appraisal indicated a minimum 10 per cent saving for the two DCMF prisons over a 25-year operational period against a comparison with a realistic public sector comparator (the basis of this comparison is explained in the next chapter). But all this saving was due to Bridgend. The NAO estimated that in net present value terms Bridgend is expected to cost £266 million over its contract life (against £319 million in the public sector), while Fazakerley is expected to cost £247 million (against £248 million). Notably, the Fazakerley Prison contract did not go to the lowest bidder, again Securicor/Costain/Skanska, but instead went to the Group4/Tarmac consortium. This was due to the Prison Service's concerns about the capability of one contractor simultaneously to undertake two prison projects using a prototype design. Although not the lowest bidder, the Group4/Tarmac consortium had come first in quality evaluations and second to Securicor/Costain/Skanska in innovation assessment for both prisons.

As we have said, in the end, a consortium of Group 4 and Tarmac was awarded the contract for the provision of 600 prisoner places at Fazakerley and the Securicor, Siefert and WS Atkins consortium together with joint venture construction partners Costain and Skanska, was awarded the contract for 800 prisoner places at the Bridgend project. Figure 5.4 shows the contrac-tual relationships for the consortium of the more successful Bridgend transac-tion. It is typical of a PPP project and shows the complexity of the private sector arrangements. In addition, from the government side, the procurement was steered by an external project manager (from Coopers & Lybrand) appointed at the outset of the process, who worked with a team of HM Prison Service staff, supported by HM Treasury solicitors, legal advisers (Freshfields), and financial advisers (Lazards). A member of the Private Finance Panel Executive served as an independent observer to the evaluation panel and acted as an intermediary between the public and private sectors during the contract negotiations.

Financial arrangements for the two prisons are set out in Table 5.3. Again, these are fairly normal with the level of equity/subordinated debt *vis-à-vis* project finance at 10–15 per cent, reflecting a sensible allocation of risk. What is perhaps unusual is the low level of 'true' equity; in the Bridgend project this is only £250 million. One reason is the low level of demand risk

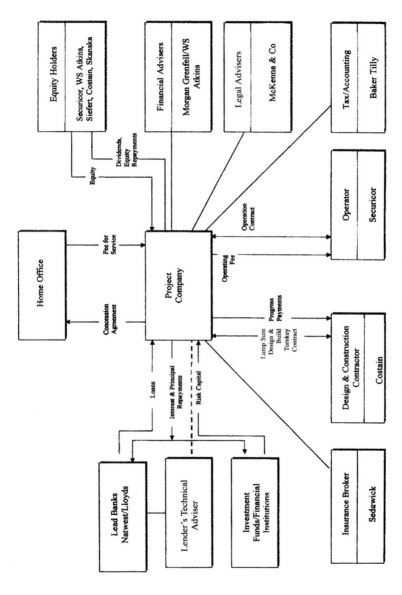

Figure 5.4 Contractual arrangements in the Bridgend Prison project

– prison occupancy was forecast to be 100 per cent! Moreover, payments are linked to availability criteria and not demand except to the extent that occupancy exceeds 100 per cent. Senior debt was repayable over roughly 18 years. Subordinated debt is effectively between debt and equity ('mezzanine finance'). This is more flexible than senior debt, having limited security, usually longer payback periods and tax-deductibility of interest.

These financing terms were fairly typical of PFI projects at that time, and the projects really mark the beginning of the market. With the expansion of the PPP market, and under competitive pressures operating in the capital market generally, terms for senior debt have lengthened considerably (up to 40 years) and margins *vis-à-vis* LIBOR have fallen from 1.5 per cent to 1 per cent or less. Also, cover ratios have fallen, with ADSCR (annual debt service cover ratios) below 1.20, which has allowed higher gearing ratios (greater than 90/10), with lower dividends reflecting downward pressure on equity markets. All in all, as the PPP market has matured, financing is now much cheaper than it was earlier.

Fazakerley PFI prison was later the subject of a special NAO report (NAO, 2000). The companies which were part of the deal caused some controversy by refinancing their debts, associated with the projected savings of £9.7 million after the prisons opened. This saving was added to the direct gains of £3.4 million from opening the prisons ahead of schedule,[8] only £1 million of which was returned to the public sector. This 'windfall' allowed the firms to increase their projected rate of return from the 12.8 per cent shown in Table 5.3 to 39 per cent, and led to calls by the NAO and the OGC for a cost-sharing formula (the OGC recommended 50/50) to apply for windfall gains from refinancing in new contracts. HM Prison Service argued the importance of not removing the opportunities for the private firms to benefit substantially from successful risk-taking. The Fazakerley consortium was able to refinance the project because of its success in delivering the project ahead of time and establishing a track record of operations. From the perspective of the capital markets, the significant saving on financing costs can be attributed to the decline in perceived risk of PFI-backed bond and debt issues as construction ended and operations began. In effect, the PFI prison model had been 'road-tested', and perceived and actual risk factors removed.

Another contentious feature was that the government acted as insurers of last resort of the Fazakerley and Bridgend prisons if the operators could not obtain commercial insurance. Follow-up projects have encountered some difficulties due to the government's refusal to repeat this experience, with insurers then being concerned about payouts for riots and disturbances. HM Prison Service felt that the success of Fazakerley and Bridgend meant they could transfer greater risks in forthcoming projects. Their argument was that commercial insurance would give operators the incentive to maintain an

Table 5.3 Financing arrangements for the Bridgend and Fazakerley prison projects[a]

Type of finance	Amount (£m)	Interest rate	Term
Bridgend			
Base loan facility	72.0	9.6235% to date of operation, 9.4735% first five years and 9.5735% for remainder	15 Nov 2013
Standby loan commitments	5.0	LIBOR+1.65% until operational, LIBOR+1.5% first five years and LIBOR+1.6% for remainder	15 Nov 2013
Equity/subordinated debt	15.6	Projected 19.4% after tax	
Fazakerley			
Base loan facility	92.5	£82.6 million at 9.05945% until operational, 9.5945% until15 Dec 2015 and LIBOR+1.5% thereafter Balance: LIBOR+1% until operational, LIBOR+1% thereafter	15 Dec 2015
Working capital facility	3.0	LIBOR +1.5%	15 Dec 2015
Equity/subordinated debt	8.1	Projected 12.8% after tax	

Note: [a]At the inception of the project. Debt was later refinanced. (See text).

Sources: National Audit Office (1997), Pollitt (2002).

exemplary record when it came to discipline, as no-claims bonuses could be earned.

But why have the projects been successful? The projected efficiency savings would appear to have resulted from two features. First, the prison projects are 'full' DCMF models where all the operation and management of the public service is part of the contract. There is no separation of ancillary and core services, which enables the contractor to integrate thoroughly the design and build of the prison with its operation and make productivity gains through the way it manages the single most important input in any public service – the workforce. Prisons may be a special case, to some extent, in that there are longstanding staffing problems in some conventionally procured and managed prisons. This may be true, but in fact in the case of Bridgend, the Prison Service estimated that the bidder's approach to design reduced the cost by approximately 30 per cent (cost savings were attributed to fewer buildings, smaller perimeter, less unused space, appointments for visits, cook/chill catering and so on). A second key feature would seem to be the clarity of the contractual model in prison PFI projects. The Prison Service is the sole purchaser and has over time built up expertise in contracting.

In the Bridgend case, which was clearly the more successful of the two, the main contributors to value for money, ranked in order, were:

1. optimal risk transfer, and the incentives so introduced in terms of completion time and financing structure;
2. innovations in design; and
3. efficiencies in delivering services.

Subsequent projects have drawn on this experience and have introduced more innovative features. For example, in the case of HMP Dovegate, 200 of the places within this 800 person PFI prison form a therapeutic community with its own director, with the aim of sharing the risks associated with meeting the needs of those prisoners in the therapeutic community with the prison service. The contract itself includes a number of unique elements:

- For the first time, the contract includes a performance bonus that is linked to the reconviction rates of prisoners from the therapeutic community after release.
- The operator is to be penalized if a prisoner does not complete a 12-month treatment programme or does not have the opportunity to complete a resettlement programme after therapy.
- The contractor must also contract with a suitable organization for a research programme into the effectiveness of the therapeutic community's programme, comparing this with another therapeutic prison run

by the public sector. (Commission on Public Private Partnerships, 2001, p. 129).

The Berwick Hospital Project[9]

In May 2001, the Victorian government announced the development of a new 229-bed public community hospital at Berwick in the State of Victoria, Australia to provide comprehensive primary, secondary and tertiary health care services to people in the south-eastern suburbs of metropolitan Melbourne. This 25-year project is a partnership between the public sector (represented by the Department of Human Services and Southern Health and advised by PricewaterhouseCoopers) responsible for operating the hospital, and the private sector (represented by the Progress Health consortium, involving ABN-AMRO and Multiplex) responsible for building, financing and maintaining the hospital. The project is of interest because of the division between 'core' and other related services, and because it is 'financier-led'. Berwick Hospital is one of four recent PPP projects in Australia that have involved the 'financier-led' model (the others are the Victoria County Court, the Spencer Street Station redevelopment project, both of which were mentioned earlier, and the NSW Schools project).

Under the contract, the operation of the hospital is to be undertaken by Southern Health, the public sector body, which is responsible for the provision of all clinical, diagnostic and medical support services at the hospital along with most 'soft' facilities management activities such as cleaning, bedding, laundry, catering, waste management and health and safety. Progress Health, the private sector SPV, is to provide hospital accommodation services, specified information technology systems and their maintenance, general maintenance of physical buildings and grounds, car parking and security operational services. In order to provide these services to Southern Health, the private sector entity needs to build, own, finance and maintain the hospital infrastructure and car park in return for payments based on specified performance requirements. Construction commenced in November 2002 and is expected to be completed by mid-2004.

As well as securing the design, construction and completion of the project infrastructure within an acceptable period, Progress Health must provide defined information systems hardware and network including data cabling and connectivity to other networks, and supply the energy systems infrastructure (i.e. gas, electricity, water) and maintain it. Progress Health worked closely with Southern Health to provide a design solution and physical facilities of an adequate standard to meet Southern Health's service delivery requirements, while retaining the flexibility to address ongoing changes in medical and health care practices, to accommodate demands for the future development of new services, and to maximise the opportunities for greater integration of in-patient care with ambulance and community-based services.

A unitary payment is made by the government to Progress Health to cover the provision of services to agreed standards, and the entire payment is at risk under the principle of 'no available, satisfactory hospital facilities, no fee'. Within that one payment stream, there are two features. One (a service payment abatement regime) is performance-linked to the services, and related to specified service output criteria including facility/room availability, temperature and humidity control, access for Southern Health, and meeting health and safety standards. If the standard of the accommodation falls below the required levels (as set out in the payment mechanism) then the State may be entitled to a deduction from the unitary payment. The other part is a quality element linked to the maintenance, car parking and security services provided by the private sector. Again, if the delivery of services falls below the required standards, the State may be entitled to a deduction from the unitary payment.

The need for the new hospital facility on a greenfield site in the area was first identified in 1996 and procurement began in 1997 under the previous government with the project as a BOOT (inclusive of private sector delivery of medical services), not a PPP. However, it had a difficult development period, including the withdrawal of a preferred bidder late in 1999. On recommencement, but this time as a PPP, the project moved from invitation of expressions of interest to contract execution in a little under 12 months. It is the first hospital project to be delivered under the Victorian Government's 'Partnerships Victoria' policy, as well as being the first hospital PPP project brought to financial close in Australia.

According to an independent review of the project, published in 2004, what appears to be a sound level of community consultation has been undertaken. Various rights are recognized in a public interest test and protected through provisions of the contract. It also appears to offer good value for money. The government's contractual arrangements involve commitments to make payments over the 25-year contract life of an estimated Aus$378 million in nominal terms (Department of Treasury and Finance, 2003), including adjustments for forecast inflation. This payment stream is equivalent to a net present cost of $115 million (discounted at 8.65 per cent, nominal pre-tax) at June 2003. The cost was calculated as being a 9 per cent saving against the net present risk-adjusted cost of the Public Sector Comparator (Fitzgerald, 2004). This saving may be different under the new discount rates being used for value for money comparisons (see Chapter 6 for a discussion of the new discounting regime).

Part of the reason for the cost effectiveness of what can be seen as a 'plain vanilla' project with a relatively routine level of services comes from the integrated bidding process under the 'financier-led' approach, and the associated financing arrangements. ABN-AMRO as the financier and supplier of equity to Progress Health, and manager of the bidding process, sought to achieve a strong investment grade rating for the venture as a consequence of a satisfactory risk transfer from the public sector to the private sector when coupled with low construction risk, low probability of post-completion service failure despite a complex key performance indicator (KPI) regime, and high gearing and low credit margins to keep down the cost of capital. The efficiency of the design solution for the building also contributed to the project's cost effectiveness.

Figure 5.5 sets out the contractual arrangements for the project, with Progress Health as the project vehicle company. Given the past failure of the hospital procurement process, time to financial close was a key concern for the government, while for the consortium time after financial close was crucial to maintain a competitive bid. ABN-AMRO had confidence in Progress Health's project management and design team of Multiplex Constructions as the builders and Silver Thomas Hanley as architects. It also had a positive view of the interface with Southern Health. Southern Health retains responsibility for core services such as clinical, cleaning, waste management and laundry, and

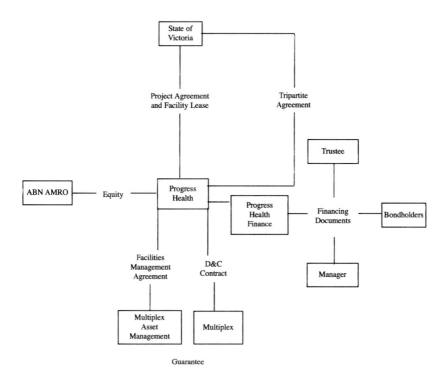

Figure 5.5   Contractual arrangements in the Berwick Hospital project

so on, while all other facility services and additional equipment have been subcontracted to Multiplex Asset Management (MAM), an emerging facility management company in Australia born out of the PPP process and a subsidiary of Multiplex.

Financing comprises $7 million of structured equity (including subordinated debt) and $87 million of senior debt. The senior debt consists of fixed rate index-linked annuity (amortizing) bonds with a 26-year term. Interest payments involve quarterly coupons, and the index-linked feature means that the principal value rises with inflation. Senior debt is to be serviced out of the services payment received quarterly from the Department of Health (the creditworthiness of which is guaranteed by the State Government of Victoria), and accrues from the start of the operating phase, subject to the provision of facilities maintenance services, rendering the bonds fully amortizing over the term. Bondholders also have the benefit of an ABN-AMRO Construction Letter of Credit, so that underlying construction risk is not a consideration for debt holders. Excess coverage is provided by the equity yield from the services payment plus public car-parking revenue. The ADSCR is estimated as approximately 1.14, which is seen as a sound level.

Because of the proven track record of Multiplex and the simplicity of the construction method, construction risk is considered to be low, providing some assurance to ABN-AMRO that the letter of credit risk is commensurately low. Facilities management risk is also seen to be low as the services comprise typical building responsibilities, external cleaning, grounds maintenance and pest control, helpdesk and training, and car parking. Under the contract for facilities management, there are a number of features whereby the facilities managers MAM are to reimburse Progress Health for any losses due to abatement. Progress Health's first recourse is to MAM's fee; MAM has provided performance security for its obligations, and MAM's obligations are in turn guaranteed by Multiplex. While MAM and its staff are experienced in these types of operations, there is the additional capacity to replace MAM in the event of serious failure, relying on finding a replacement from the wide market of alternative service providers.

Overall, the Berwick Hospital project can be seen as a low-risk, relatively straightforward PPP. It has been argued in a number of circles (e.g. HM Treasury, 2003b) that such relatively routine projects are not suited to PPPs, which are better left for dealing with large, complex one-off infrastructure transactions. However, this case does illustrate that a PPP can offer value for money in a 'plain vanilla' deal when there is appropriate interaction between the parties and there can be the benefit of lower transactions costs due to the single entity-led consortium. It also shows that the public sector and private sector are more than capable of rapid execution when the political will exists to get the project moving.

The financier-led approach is still in its early days and it remains to be seen how well control over the project vehicle can be aligned with the risk-taking and the longer-term objectives of the partnership. Under the traditional approach, the extent and proportions of equity investment of each of the contractors (i.e. construction, facilities management, etc.) has been seen as an important protection in terms of demonstrating the long-term marriage of service delivery outcomes and risk allocation with equity control of the project company, and its partnership with the government. This equity commitment is removed under the single entity-led consortium model and replaced by a contractual relationship between the subcontractors and the SPV. For example, there could be concern that the single entity controlling the SPV (in this case the financier) might seek quickly to sell their interests in the project company leaving the risk with the underlying service providers. However, there are controls in the PPP contracts restricting change in ownership of equity. These controls essentially prevent sell down to other parties unless it can be demonstrated that the acquiring party is a fit and proper person and has a standing equal to the selling party by reference to the government's original evaluation criteria.

Nonetheless, the issue of who is best placed to run the relationship after financial close remains a question still to be resolved in the Australian PPP market. Despite the apparent success of the financier-led model in four recent significant projects brought to financial close in Australia, the real issue becomes one of what model creates the best partnership on a continuing basis. The financier-led approach amounts to a 'one-stop shop' involving an integrated single entity-led consortium, which offers the potential for low cost by virtue of reduced contracting costs and financing that is tailored precisely to the project and the cashflows it generates . But can the risks be handled satisfactorily for all parties? Also, does this represent the best partnership between the government and the private sector? After all, it is the contractors and the facility managers, not the banks, who ultimately deliver the long-term services and partner with the public sector. It is in this respect that the jury is still out on the financier-led model.

NOTES

1. One such project would seem to be the Mobile Data Network for police and ambulances in the greater Melbourne–Geelong areas, completed in March 2004, which promises an 11 per cent saving to the public procurer against the risk-adjusted public sector comparator.
2. A framework for addressing these three issues is provided in Partnership Victoria (2001).
3. The French programme began in 1987 when, in response to problems of overcrowding in French prisons, the French government developed 'Programme 13,000', a plan for the private sector to build 25 prisons over five years, including four metropolitan prisons and creating 13,000 prison places. The facilities were principally remand prisons and detention centres. In

21 of the institutions, the construction and facilities management (accommodation and catering, health, work, vocation training and maintenance) were provided by the private sector. Security, integration, administration and management remained the responsibility of the French Prison Service and its personnel. In the remaining four institutions, the facilities were entirely managed by the Prison Service and their personnel. For the former group, the 10-year contracts for non-custodial prison services expired between November 2000 and March 2001 and the Ministry of Justice organized a re-tendering process in line with European Community regulations.

4. Thus the Spencer Street Station redevelopment discussed in the previous paragraph has the benefit of locking in a 30-year inflation-adjusted allocation for maintenance of the station, which is something the old station certainly never had.

5. This section has benefited greatly from a report by the American Chamber of Commerce (2002).

6. Information has been obtained from a number of sources including National Audit Office (1997), Allen (2001), Commission on Public Private Partnerships (2001), American Chamber of Commerce (2002) and Pollitt (2002). One of the authors was adviser to one of the projects.

7. Costs per prisoner in four privately managed prisons in 1997–8 were 11 per cent lower on average than in comparable publicly managed prisons and staff costs accounted for all of this difference. The most important element of labour cost savings was reduced staff hours per prisoner, accounting for a third of the total. Available evidence suggests that the quality of privately managed prisons – as measured by the Prison Service's key performance indicators – is similar to that of publicly managed institutions. Further savings from lower levels of absence due to sickness appear to reflect better management of labour, (Andrews, 2000).

8. In the case of the Bridgend prison project, WS Atkins, Securicor and Skanska gained close to £5 million by refinancing a £77.5 million loan at a 400 basis points (4 per cent) lower rate (Allen, 2001, p. 42).

9. Information on the project comes from a number of sources including PricewaterhouseCoopers, ABN-AMRO, and the Fitzgerald Report (2004).

6. Issues in public private partnerships

INTRODUCTION

This chapter examines a number of issues regarding the value-for-money test and the public interest test for PPPs. The questions examined include:

1. Is the fully integrated or 'bundled' PPP structure an efficient solution?
2. Can PPPs be good value for money when the government can always borrow more cheaply than the private sector?
3. What is the basis of the value-for-money test used for implementing PPPs?
4. Should the discount rate used for value-for-money tests be a risk-adjusted rate or a riskless rate?
5. Does the available evidence suggest that PPPs have delivered value for money?
6. How is uncertainty to be handled?
7. In what ways should PPPs be accounted for?
8. Can PPPs adequately provide for the public interest?
9. What factors make for a successful PPP?

Following an examination of these questions, the chapter ends with a case study of a recent PPP/PFI hospital project in the UK that illustrates some of the issues involved in determining whether a PPP offers value for money. But first we look at the development of the business case, for it is at this stage that many of the issues first surface.

THE BUSINESS CASE

Formulating a business case enables the government to form a view on the applicability of a partnership approach before significant resources are spent on developing the detailed specifications of the project. As part of this process, the project is fully appraised and risks and costs are identified to develop a cost–benefit analysis and test the net benefit of the proposal. Evidence of the potential for the private sector to add value requires an analysis of private sector skills and the commercial incentives for the private entities to exercise them. Assessing the associated impacts allows preparation of the public interest test and the identification of other matters about which the government should be aware.

Deciding whether to offer an infrastructure project to the market as a PPP, or to deliver it by traditional procurement, rests on a number of considerations, not least of which is the government's commitment at all levels of the public sector to the idea of private sector involvement in this way, and the ability of the public sector procurer to manage the process. On purely practical grounds, however, the decision necessitates an examination of three main issues. These are: (1) whether private parties have the capacity to deliver the project; (2) whether they have the incentive or motivation to do so; and (3) whether such delivery could constitute value for money.

1. *Capacity.* An assessment of the private sector's delivery capability and reliability focuses on observable strengths and weaknesses of the particular industry sector. Major constraints are likely to come from the public interest test and from any necessity to exercise flexibility over time. A public interest test is designed to ensure that public interest issues are properly documented for consideration in the project approval process, enabling any measures necessary to protect the public interest to be set out later in the project brief and contract, so that bidders are fully aware in advance of specific requirements on these grounds.

2. *Motivation.* Determining the private sector's willingness to participate primarily revolves around two aspects: whether the risks and rewards inherent in providing the required outputs create a genuine business opportunity for the likely participants; and whether the banks and financial markets will support the proposal. These issues, in turn, give rise to a more detailed examination of commercial matters such as whether risks are manageable or insurable, whether accounting and taxation arrangements are an incentive or an impediment to the project, and the state of capital markets and activity levels in the market sector at the time. Some indication of the likely level of competition would also follow.

3. *Value for money.* Ensuring that taxpayers get value for money from an infrastructure project is of the essence in any procurement policy. In the case of procurement by means of a PPP, the project should be able to demonstrate that, on a whole-of-life cycle basis, the cost to the community of the relevant service provided by the private sector is lower than for the same service provided by the public sector, so long as there is a proper allowance for the quality of services, price, time frame, risk apportionment and certainty of process in order to render the two alternatives comparable. A complex trade-off between cost, risk and performance is involved, and the cheapest proposal is not always the most cost-effective one when risks and resulting incentives are taken into account.

Some have argued that PPPs as currently structured can never be good value for money. One argument is that the partnership arrangement bundles together a number of very different functions (design, construction, operations, maintenance, etc.) and that a more cost-effective solution would be to 'unbundle' these aspects into separate contracts. The other argument is that the use of private finance for capital investment projects can never constitute good value for money since the public sector can always borrow funds on better terms than private entities. These two arguments are examined in turn.

BUNDLING

A defining characteristic of PPPs is the integration within a private sector party of all (or most of) the functions of design, building, financing, operating and maintenance of the facility in question, often in the form of a special purpose vehicle (or virtual corporation) created for the specific project. Some writers (e.g. Daniels and Trebilcock, 1996; Trujillo *et al.*, 1998; Hart, 2003; and Quiggin, 2003) have questioned whether this is a cost-effective arrangement.

Consider, first, the analysis by Hart (2003), who develops a theoretical model to examine the economic efficiency of 'bundling' from an 'incomplete' contracting perspective, in which imperfections arise because it is hard to foresee and contract about uncertain future events. PPPs are generally entered into for a lengthy period of time, usually 20 to 30 years, and are developed in an environment of uncertainty. As such they exhibit, as Hart suggests, the characteristics of 'incomplete' contracts, and their usefulness as integrated arrangements hinges on the nature of contracting costs. His model compares a 'bundled' contract for facility construction and service provision with 'unbundled' conventional public procurement in which the government first contracts with a builder to construct the facility and then later contracts with another private sector party to operate and run the facility. The choice between the two alternatives, bundled versus unbundled, turns on whether it is easier to write contracts on service provision than on building provision.

Hart's model leads to a straightforward result. Under the assumed conditions, conventional provision ('unbundling') is better if the quality of the building can be clearly specified, whereas the quality of the service cannot. In contrast, PPP is better if the quality of the service can be well specified in the initial contract (or, more generally, there are good performance indicators that can be used to reward or penalize the service provider), whereas the quality of the building cannot. Hart surmises that schools may fall into the first category. Contracting on the building is relatively simple, while contracting on the service may not be. On the other hand, hospitals may fall into the second category in that although specifying service quality is far from straightforward, it may be easier to come up with reasonable performance measures concerning how patients are treated than it is to specify what may be a very complex building (2003, pp. 73–4).

Quiggin (2003) comes to much the same conclusion, in that he sees merit in a fully integrated (bundled) approach where construction incorporates a particularly innovative special-purpose design, leading to an integration between construction risk and operating risk. But, with most public projects following well-established design principles, such cases are regarded as rare. His particular concern is that in many PPP projects that are 'financier-led', a financial institution devotes substantial resources to putting together a consortium to make a bid, only to 'unbundle' the components as soon as the bid is successful. In these circumstances, Quiggin considers that the government would do better by contracting directly with the private parties that ultimately bear the risk rather than contracting through the financial intermediary. Daniels and Trebilcock (1996) visualize a more limited potential for 'unbundling', with potential gains for the public sector in partly decoupling, say, design from other functions if a consortium with an inferior design but superior construction and other capabilities won the integrated bid. In principle, the government stands to realize efficiency gains from contracting out the design function and, effectively, creating a competition for ideas.

Trujillo *et al.* (1998) explore the potential for 'unbundled mechanisms' in the case of BOT-type projects such as toll roads, although they consider that many other PPPs could be unbundled. Bundling is normally argued for on the grounds of enhancing the potential to realize economies of scale and scope along with innovations in design, pricing and risk-sharing. Usually, however, the BOT concessionaires are joint ventures of a number of private companies which agree in advance to subcontract each of the different activities and take equity stakes in the SPV to cement the relationship. The authors argue that two problems are thereby introduced. First, good constructors may be teamed with less good financiers. Superior knowledge of one activity may not carry over to other activities. Second, competition is limited to those bodies which are part of the group. Companies, especially local entities, with perhaps good technical know-how but poor financial capability are unable to bid because the activities are jointly, rather than separately, auctioned. Transparency and competitiveness in the bidding process are lost, or more correctly traded-off for innovation opportunities, which the authors consider may not always be the best solution.

For these reasons, Trujillo *et al.* (1998) examine the case for unbundling. They recognize that the costs of unbundling (e.g. creating different entities, and monitoring the specifications in the different stages) may be considerable, but may be offset by an improved allocation of risk. There is then the question of how the unbundling is to be done. The authors consider two possibilities.

One is for a public sector agency to play the role of the concessionaire in BOT projects. However, the lack of qualified public sector institutions capable of articulating the project and supervising the private sector participants limits this option. As an alternative, the authors suggest appointing a private company to carry out the job. Subject to the conditions established by the public sponsor, the private agent would subcontract and monitor the arrangements, while simultaneously structuring and launching the joint venture or special purpose vehicle needed for financing. That is, a private company acts as a service company for the project but without assuming the project risks.

In this latter case, it might be argued that this type of 'unbundling' is effectively what happens already under a PPP since the concessionaire rarely assumes all the project risks and many are put out to a range of specialist contractors.[1] Yet there is an important difference between the two situations – incentives are stronger when the supplier is bearing at least some of the risks of supply. The assumption of overall responsibility prior to risk transfer gives the concession winner the appropriate incentives to do the job properly, which may not be present to the same degree when there is a nexus between the principal (the public body) and the agent (the private sector service company coordinating entity).[2] Also, a feature of PPPs is that risks are usually shared between the private sector and the public sector, with the government 'taking back' some risks for which private bodies would charge 'too much'. For this risk allocation process, the public sector entity might find it less costly to negotiate with a single body rather than with a host of individual subcontractors, either directly or by proxy through the coordinating company.

Daniels and Trebilcock (1996), after raising the question of unbundling, and considering it at some length, reach a similar conclusion. They argue that the case for bundling and vertical integration is much the same as that for the existence of firms in economic theory, and rests on the presence not only of contracting costs (examined by Hart), but also information costs and economies of scale and scope.[3] Essentially, the case for integrating design, construction, finance, operations and maintenance is that private firms can coordinate these activities at lower cost than can government, and they are better able to respond to economic incentives.

In our view, the question of the incentive structure is central to the issue of bundling. As Grout (1997) has observed, when contracts are incomplete, and not every eventuality can be covered, incentives pose a particular problem and it is important to get them correct. For instance, there are large information difficulties surrounding construction contracts, and determining the responsibility for cost overruns is a serious source of conflict when there are design changes and other unexpected developments. However, writing the contract in terms of the flow of services from the infrastructure facility rather than the process of construction can change the incentive system. If, for example, the same entity is responsible for both construction and supplying the services, but is remunerated only for the successful provision of services of a suitable quality, it is important for the entity to build the correct facility, get the process of delivery right, and contain costs while not sacrificing quality. Financiers also have incentives to make sure that services are supplied on time and to the requisite standard when the revenue stream that is generated represents the main source for repaying debt. It is the welding of upfront design and financial engineering to downstream management of the construction costs and revenue flow that gives the PPP its distinctive incentive compatibility characteristics.

Without wishing to trivialize the argument, there are some similarities between the 'unbundling' issue and the decision of whether to employ a builder for home construction or subcontract oneself the functions of bricklaying, carpentry, roof construction, plumbing, electrical wiring, and so on. Anyone who has tried to do their own subcontracting would probably agree that it is a difficult route. As in the building trade, there are a host of informal links that bind the subcontractors and the project sponsors together, and these enable the job to be done.

COSTS OF FINANCE

What of the view that public sector finance is always at a lower cost than that obtained by private sector borrowers, and thus PPPs cannot be good value for money? PFI projects, and most PPPs, differ from traditional public procurement by virtue of the requirement that private sector entities finance the projects. Given that the extra cost of private sector funding *vis-à-vis* public borrowing is likely to be between 1 to 3 percentage points, some have argued that PPPs/PFI can never be cost effective. Others, while accepting that they can be value for money because the private sector is able to deliver sufficient cost savings in other aspects of the project (design, operation, management), nevertheless concede that private borrowing costs are higher.

A number of writers consider that the 'lower government borrowing cost' argument is seriously flawed (Kay, 1993; Gilibert and Steinherr, 1994; Grout, 1997; Klein, 1997; Argy *et al.*, 1999; Partnerships Victoria, 2003), and an examination of their arguments serves as a useful preliminary to the next two sections dealing with the value-for-money test and the choice of discount rate, respectively. Both Grout and Klein adopt a position that in some ways is analogous to the famous Modigliani–Miller theorem about the cost of capital. Modigliani and Miller argued that the 'true' value of a firm is governed by the risk characteristics of the underlying stream of returns, and (in the no tax regime case) is independent of how finance is raised. Somewhat analogously,

Grout and also Klein argue that what is important is the 'true' risk of the project, which is independent of whether the public sector or the private sector provides the funding. What differs is that the private provision of finance; that is, the PFI/PPP route, explicitly builds the risk into the cost of funds. By contrast, traditional public procurement masks the risk because the government can fund the project at a risk-free rate independent of the actual risk position. As John Kay has remarked: 'we would lend to the government even if we thought it would burn the money or fire it off into space' (Kay, 1993, p. 63).

But why can government borrow at a risk-free rate of interest? This reflects the fact that (and again we quote John Kay) 'the cost of debt both to governments and to private firms is influenced predominately by the perceived risk of default rather than an assessment of the quality of returns from the specific investment' (1993, p. 63). For private debt there is a risk of default, whereas for government debt there is little or none (at least in the case of governments of most developed countries) because the government can raise the taxes to meet the obligation. The government is risk-free in the eyes of the investor lending funds because the risk is transferred to the taxpayers, who bear the cost through the risk of higher future tax payments and different consumption outcomes. In Klein's words, taxpayers have assumed a contingent liability for which they are not remunerated. They have become, in effect, shadow equity providers. This residual risk imposed on taxpayers is a cost, which ought to enter into any cost–benefit analysis. If this were done, the real cost of government borrowing would be the same as the private sector if the underlying risk of the projects were the same. Taken to its limit, the lower government borrowing cost argument would seem to imply that all activities should be undertaken by government as the cost of capital is so low. Were this to happen, would the debt then still be regarded as riskless?

Obviously, public debt is not riskless. For central government debt there is the risk that debt can be monetized, while at the regional level of government there is the risk of adverse economic performance. Nevertheless, in comparison with private bodies, governments enjoy near risk-free status because they can resort to general taxes and 'inflation' taxation to avoid bankruptcy. The private sector is, however, exposed to this 'taxation risk', an externality that is ignored in risk evaluation but which needs to be built into social risk calculations.

The corollary is that the higher credit rating of governments, and hence their lower borrowing rates, is largely irrelevant to the choice between public and private provision of infrastructure. Argy *et al.* (1999) argue that, subject to three conditions, the cost of capital should be assumed to be the same for both the public and private sectors. These conditions are:

1. that the risks associated with the specific project (variance in returns) are mainly 'commercial' rather than policy-related in character;
2. that the private capital market is reasonably efficient; and
3. that private sector financing transaction costs (being on a smaller scale) are not overwhelmingly large relative to those usually incurred by the public sector.

According to the authors, these three conditions probably do hold for many new infrastructure projects so that, provided the rewards match the risk, reliance on the private sector for provision should not entail any extra capital cost (and indeed if the private sector is more efficient at project design and managing the capital, the capital cost should be lower). This position probably oversimplifies matters – a more complete comparison of public and private borrowing cost has been made by PricewaterhouseCoopers (2002), and we consider this study later in the chapter.

In summary, most PPP/PFI projects involve substantial private sector finance and, in all but very exceptional circumstances, this finance in itself will be more costly than public sector borrowing, although there are many hidden costs in the latter. Clearly, governments are not immune from fiscal difficulties, which can lead to credit rating downgrades and higher project costs, but the main reason why the government's cost of borrowing is low is that it can levy taxation to repay the debt. Due to these taxing powers, lenders to government consider that it is unlikely to default, and so demand a lower interest rate risk premium. But having the true risks hidden and passed on to taxpayers in the form of a contingent liability does not mean that public investments are risk-free. Project risks depend more on the project's design than on the specific financing mechanism (Flemming and Mayer, 1997).

For a long time it was argued that the cost of capital of publicly funded projects is below that of private, not due to lower borrowing costs but because, through the tax base, the government can achieve better risk-sharing and pooling than is possible in the private sector (Arrow and Lind, 1970). This position has been replaced by a new view that the cost of capital of equivalent projects is the same in the private and public sector when account is taken of taxpayers shedding their contingent liability through the capital markets (Brealey *et al.*, 1997).[4] The new orthodoxy sees a project's cost of capital as being set by the cost of bearing the market risk of the project which, according to standard finance theory,[5] can be established by adding to the risk-free rate a risk premium dependent on the extent to which the asset's returns are co-variant with market returns (the asset's 'beta').

There may be grounds for questioning how appropriate a market-based analysis such as the capital asset pricing model (CAPM) is for dealing with projects where there can be a divergence between market and social risks, as a result of externalities and distributional considerations (Flemming and Mayer, 1997). Taxation also drives a wedge into cost of capital calculations, with the private sector evaluating projects at an after-tax cost of capital, and the government at pre-tax costs (Brealey *et al.*, 1997). Some of these issues are taken up again when we examine the question of the appropriate discount rate and the returns to PFI projects.

VALUE FOR MONEY

Value for money has been defined as 'the optimum combination of whole life cost and quality (or fitness for purpose) to meet the user's requirement' (OGC, 2002b, p. 6). Based on experience with PFI projects in the UK, there is an acceptance among public service project managers that there are six main determinants of value for money (Arthur Andersen, 2000); namely, risk transfer; the long-term nature of contracts (including whole-of-life cycle costing); the use of an output specification; competition; performance measurement and incentives; and private sector management skills. Of these, competition and risk are seen to be the most important.

Accordingly, what is required to achieve value for money is that

- projects are awarded in a competitive environment;
- economic appraisal techniques, including proper appreciation of risk, are rigorously applied, and that risk is allocated between the public and private sectors so that the expected value for money is maximized; and
- comparisons between publicly and privately financed options are fair, realistic and comprehensive.

Competition

Competition creates an environment that encourages bidders to be innovative in their design solution and efficient in service delivery. Based on the results of some early (and to some extent, unsatisfactory)[6] PFI contracts in the British health service, it came to be recognized that a considerable degree of competitive tension was needed in the bidding process, so that the private sector provides its most efficient bids. A deep and competitive market of capable bidders is needed to get the benefits of the PPP procurement process, and the market capability tests conducted at the business case stage remain an important pre-condition.

One of the principal PPP benefits is the whole-of-life cycle 'bundled' approach. This integration creates a facility that is not only tailored to the provision of core services but also closely aligned to the requirements of the facilities operator. It results in a design, from both an architectural and an engineering perspective, which aims to maximize service efficiencies in the ancillary services as well as aid maintainability and minimize life cycle costs, for example using better quality materials. Even small changes (e.g. allowing access space for ease of maintenance) have had a large cumulative effect. As Peter Drucker (1984) argues, innovation is often not about grand architectural design but about the cumulative impact of a large number of small changes. Thus in one hospital project in the UK, the contractor was able to cut down on cleaning costs by having window sills at 45 degrees so that people could not put things on the sills and generate extra cleaning costs. In an Australian hospital project, designing dedicated access space in the roof area and allowing access corridors enabled maintenance of the plant and machinery without having to close down ward space. These benefits can be lost in traditional procurement methods due to little or no integration between design, construction and operation of the facility.

It is in this sense that the PPP model can be seen as an incentive contract since the private sector entity is encouraged to think beyond the bounds of the construction phase and build in features that will facilitate operations and maintenance. Despite the arguments considered earlier in this chapter of those who see possible benefits in an 'unbundling' by government of PPP contracts into separate design, construction, operations, and maintenance contracts, vesting the coordination in one private sector entity (or consortium) provides a better set of incentives and a clearer line of accountability.

Risk

The PPP programme has raised awareness of project risks in ways that public procurement has to date not been able to do. The result is that the identification, allocation and management of risks have grown to become an essential part of PPP processes. These processes are examined in Chapter 7.

Value for money is improved by the transfer of appropriate risk as the supplier is able to reduce either the probability that the risk will occur, the financial consequences if it does eventuate, or both. There comes a point, however, when this transfer becomes sub-optimal. If risks that, in fact, cannot be best managed by the private sector continue to be transferred to private bodies, value for money will decline since the premium demanded by the private sector will outweigh the benefit to the public procurer. Optimum, rather than maximum, risk transfer is the objective of the PPP arrangement.

Public Sector Comparator

Competition and risk allocation are pre-conditions but do not guarantee value for money. The possibility of achieving extra value for money by implementing a PPP can be estimated with a twofold analysis. This analysis is conducted prior to the PPP implementation and comprises, first, the calculation of the benchmark cost of providing the specified service under traditional procurement and, second, a comparison of this benchmark cost with the cost of providing the specified service under a PPP scheme.

The benchmark cost of providing the specified service with traditional procurement is known as the public sector comparator (PSC). Policy Statement Number 2 of the UK Treasury Taskforce (1998) guidance material defines a 'Comparator' as 'the benchmark established against which value for money is assessed' (section 1.3.1) and the PSC as 'a cost estimate based on the assumption that assets are acquired through conventional funding expenditure and that the procurer retains significant managerial responsibility and exposure to risk' (section 1.3.2). In effect, the PSC is intended to reflect the full risk-adjusted cost to government of delivering the project through conventional government funding.

In the Partnerships Victoria (2003) Technical Note on the Public Sector Comparator, the PSC is defined as a 'hypothetical risk-adjusted costing', by the public sector as a supplier, to an output specification produced as part of a PPP procurement exercise (p. 6). Features of the PSC calculation are as follows: the results are expressed in net present value terms; estimates are based on the outputs specified for the PPP procurement; they utilize the most recent actual method of providing that output (e.g. a traditional form of contracting such as design and build) including any reasonably foreseeable efficiencies the public sector could make; and the calculations take full account of risks that could be encountered. Nevertheless, the PSC remains a hypothetical estimate, not an actual cost to government.

Figure 6.1 illustrates the value-for-money comparison between a PSC and a PPP bid. Assuming all things equal (i.e. quality and risk allocation), value for money is demonstrated when the total present value cost of private sector supply is less than the net present value of the base cost of the service, adjusted for: the cost of risks to be retained by the government; cost adjustments for transferable risks; and competitive neutrality effects.

- *Base or raw cost* is the cost of providing the services required by the public sector. This is the public sector's estimate of what it would have to spend to build and maintain the infrastructure and provide the associated services over its expected useful life in accordance with the performance specification.
- *Retained risks* are those which, by their nature, always rest with the public sector. The cost of retained risks is usually identical for the PSC and the private supplier. Retained risks are normally those involving changes to the enabling laws or regulations and the demand risk for the

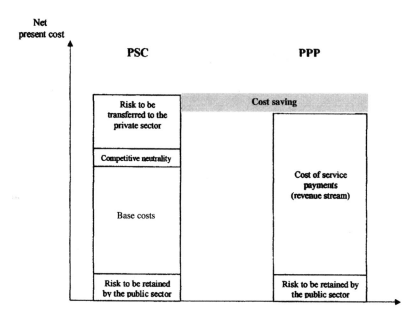

Figure 6.1   PSC and value for money

services where there is no direct charge to the public (for instance long-term demographic changes).

* *Risk adjustments* are made for transferable risks that reflect the probability that services may not be delivered at the cost shown in the base cost projection because of events like cost overruns or technical problems, or that budgets may be maintained, but only at the expense of reductions in service quality.

* *Competitive neutrality* adjustments reflect that the PSC should be competitively neutral with the private sector proposal. Competitive neutrality ensures that the analysis of private sector bids does not lead to preference by reason only of redistributive mechanisms or other policy arrangements affecting either the private or public sectors. Consequently, where applicable, the PSC should incorporate those state and local government taxes, levies or charges that may be payable by the private sector, as well as the cost of insurance that the public sector would otherwise set up through captive insurance arrangements.

THE DISCOUNT RATE ISSUE

The next issue is the discount rate used for the value-for-money test. In preparing the PSC, a financial model of the project is developed that includes forecasts of all the cashflows related to the project, on the assumption that the project is carried out in the public sector. A discount rate is then used to estimate the net present value of the forecast cashflows. What discount rate should be used is a vexed question that has been the subject of considerable discussion globally in the PFI/PPP arena, and there are many different approaches being used. Also, it is an area where policy has changed in recent years.

For example, the UK government has taken the approach that one discount rate should be used for all projects across the public sector. For many years, the discount rate used by the UK government for the economic appraisal of PFI projects was 6 per cent per annum in real terms, although 8 per cent per annum real was used for at least the first four DBFO road projects, that being the rate used for railway investment (NAO, 1998). The rationale for the choice of 6 per cent real was that the discount rate used should reflect the fact that resource expenditure by government has an opportunity cost. Where, as in the case of PFI, government spending choices include options of the purchase of in-house and contracted-out supply, in-house capital needs to be costed in a way that can be compared with private sector supply, ensuring that public investment is as effective at the margin as the alternative private use of resources. Hence the UK government's decision to apply 6 per cent as the low-risk cost of private capital, funded by a mix of debt and equity. But that position has now been revised.

In the 2003 edition of the *Green Book* (HM Treasury, 2003a) a discount rate of 3.5 per cent in real terms was introduced, based on what it regards as social time preference (i.e. the pure time value of money from society's viewpoint).[7] The change in policy was described by the UK Treasury as follows:

Instead of reflecting risk in a risk premium on capital, Government investment decisions reflect risk by calculating the present value capital sum it regards as the necessary contingency for the risks inherent in a project. For example, when deciding between procurement options, project managers calculate an expected value of all risks for each option, and consider how exposed each option is to future uncertainty. They then discount the cost of these options in future years at 3.5 per cent per year to a present value, which purely reflects society's preference for consumption now over consumption in the future, rather than discounting the value of project cash flows at a higher rate to make a compensation for risk . . . Risks are therefore priced individually for each project option. The discounted costs of these risk-adjusted options can then be compared with each other, or with the cost of a PFI project, in a PSC, to determine which procurement option represents best value for money taking account of risk and uncertainty. This approach is consistent with the fact that in conventional procurement the public sector pays for risk not in its borrowing – which for the public sector is at non-risk rates – but when risks crystallize and must be covered in publicly funded projects. (HM Treasury, 2003b, p. 42)

The treatment in the *Green Book* itself goes on to explain about the additional adjustment for 'the cost of variability in outcomes':

> In estimating the future costs and benefits associated with particular proposals, there will inevitably be variation between these estimates and the actual costs and benefits realized. This will be over and above the impact of optimism bias, and will be as a result of random factors unforeseen at the time of appraisal.
>
> For the public sector as a whole, such random factors will tend to cancel out, taking all proposals together. But in some cases, this would not be expected to happen. Some projects – for example, transport use – will tend to have appraisal risks that are systematically related to the overall performance of the economy. Because the majority or all of such projects will be affected by the same factor, appraisal errors will not cancel out between projects.
>
> A decision-maker who is risk averse cares about this potential variability in outcomes, and is willing to pay a sum in exchange for certainty (or willing to put up with variability on receipt of compensation). This compensation is the cost of variability, and should be included in appraisal when it is considered appropriate. (Annex 4, paras 33–5)

Partnerships Victoria when introduced in 2001 also used a discount rate of 6 per cent real, and that rate too changed in 2003 but in a different direction to the UK one. The Partnerships Victoria position remains that the discount rate methodology used to calculate the PSC needs to be consistent with that used by the government to assess bids and that, in the general case, the government should apply a common discount rate to bids and the PSC for assessment purposes (Partnerships Victoria, 2003). In the new Partnerships Victoria guidance material, this is recommended to be a rate indicative of the project risk, on the grounds (as we argued earlier) that the cost of capital or discount rate is specific to each project and is a function of the risks for the particular project in question. Nevertheless, for most projects the discount rate employed is based on an *a priori* risk classification in which projects are categorized, according to type, into very low, low or medium risk bands.[8]

While these approaches seem to be opposed to one another, the theoretical principles that underlie them are not, in fact, different at all. The discounted cash flow analysis usually involves discounting the expected cash flows associated with a project to produce a risk adjusted present value figure that takes into account all financially measurable benefits, costs and risks for the project. With respect to risk adjustment, there are two main approaches in the theoretical literature. The first and probably more common method is to adjust for risk in the discount rate through the addition of a risk margin to an appropriate risk-free rate. An alternative approach is to value risk in the cashflows so that a risk-free discount rate can be applied to cashflow forecasts that have been adjusted from their risky form to what are called in the literature 'certainty-equivalent' cashflows.

Consider, for example, the treatment by Brealey and Myers (2003, pp. 339–40) who establish the equivalence of

... two ways to value a risky cash flow C_1:

Method 1: Discount the risky cash flow at a *risk-adjusted discount rate r* that is greater than r_f [the risk-free interest rate]. The risk-adjusted discount rate adjusts for both time and risk.

Method 2: Find the certainty-equivalent cash flow and discount at the risk-free interest rate r_f. When you use this method, you need to ask, What is the smallest *certain* payoff for which I would exchange the risky cash flow C_1?

This is called the *certainty equivalent* of C_1 denoted by CEQ_1. Since CEQ_1 is the value equivalent of a safe cash flow, it is discounted at the risk-free rate. The certainty-equivalent method makes *separate* adjustments for risk and time.

We now have two identical expressions for PV:

$$PV = \frac{C_1}{1+r} = \frac{CEQ_1}{1+r_f}$$

In the figure accompanying this derivation, the certainty-equivalent method is depicted as involving two steps, first a 'haircut for risk' (the reduction of the cashflow from its forecasted value to its certainty equivalents) and then, second, a discount for the time value for money. It is also shown that the 'certainty-equivalent' cashflow CEQ_1 can be calculated directly from the capital asset pricing model using the covariance between the risk cashflow and the market return.[9]

Essentially, in one approach risk is allowed for in the denominator; in the other method risk adjustment is made in the numerator. Despite the formal equivalence of the two, it is easy to understand how the process of putting theory into practice could result in differences arising. If the risk-adjusted interest rate method is used, there is agreement that the risk margin added to the risk-free rate should reflect systematic risk rather than idiosyncratic project risk (as advocated in the new Partnerships Victoria guidelines). The underlying rationale for this principle is straightforward. Whereas idiosyncratic risk can be pooled and diversified in such a way that no one individual bears any significant risk, systematic risks are highly correlated, and pooling and diversification have little effect other than to redistribute a given risk across the community. Since non-systematic risk can be eliminated at virtually no cost (by diversifying), there is no reward for bearing it, whereas under the 'Systematic Risk Principle' (Ross *et al.*, 2002), the reward for bearing risk depends only on the systematic risk of an investment.[10] But CAPM, from which this result derives, is likely to provide only a broad range of appropriate discount rates, because of the difficulty of collecting sufficient relevant and objective data for the estimation of beta with similar attributes to the project in question.[11] Also, there may be many individual risk factors that only have a downside, often large relative to the cashflows from the project, and the presence of non-normality in returns suggests further why CAPM may not be an appropriate basis for determining returns. Practitioners may have to fall back on an intuitive approach to estimating discount rates, based on precedents and judgement rather than market information.

On the other hand, if the risk-free discount rate approach is adopted then it is necessary for risks in the cashflow forecasts to be adjusted using the certainty-equivalence method (or 'the cost of variability in outcomes' as defined in the *Green Book*). This involves estimating what the government would be willing to pay in order to know that its outlay under the procurement will be the expected cashflow payment.[12] While private parties may have an idea or policy about their risk aversion, governments really need a social welfare function showing society's overall level of risk aversion to implement this approach. It is also difficult to price systemic risk as a cashflow, because available market data for this may be even less relevant, and there is little in the way of extra guidance available from existing theory as to how this calculation is to be made. Practitioners largely are left to make their own assessment of the value of risk for a specific set of expected cashflows (e.g. using predictions of insurance premiums required to avoid risk or CAPM-based formulae to estimate separate adjustment factors for each key cashflow element, based on individual beta estimates for each cashflow factor). Although the idea of using a risk-free discount rate appears to have appeal, the rest of the exercise seems particularly difficult to carry through, and as a consequence the extent of risk in the cashflows may be underestimated.

A related issue is whether the discount rate used to assess public provision should be the same as that used to assess a PPP. There is a tendency for governments to use the same discount rate for a project whether it is publicly provided or is to be provided to the government by the private sector through a PPP. (Here we are thinking of a risk-adjusted rate like the old 6 per cent real. The same issue arises with certainty-equivalence but with respect to cashflows.) Grout (2003) argues that the standard practice of using the same discount rate in tests between public sector provision and PPPs is inappropriate because it prejudices private sector provision and leads to excessive reliance on public procurement. His argument runs as follows. When public sector provision is being valued a discount rate is applied to a cost cashflow. This cashflow represents the cost of building the facility if it is done in the public sector. In contrast, for valuing the private sector provision a discount rate is applied to a stream that constitutes an outlay for the public sector but is a revenue item to the private entity and is being valued from the revenue side. With a PPP this revenue stream is not the equivalent cost of building the facility – it is instead the cashflow associated with the flow of benefits valued at the price in the contract – and there is no reason to suppose that the risk characteristics are equivalent for these two cashflows. Indeed, Grout argues that there is every reason to suppose that they are not, because in general costs are less risky than revenues (particularly when the revenues depend on services of a suitable quality being provided). Under what appear to be plausible conditions, he contends that a higher discount rate should be used for the PPP than for the public sector equivalent. Failure to do so will suggest that private provision is less efficient than public since the present value of private provision will be overestimated relative to public procurement.

There is a final point that needs to be made on the discount rate issue. Those who adhere to Knight's (1921) distinction between risk and uncertainty would contend that 'true' uncertainty is overlooked. Uncertainty is mentioned in the *Green Book* in a number of places, for example (HM Treasury, 2003a, p. 32):

> An expected value is a useful starting point for understanding the impact of risk between different options. But however well risks are identified and analysed the future is inherently uncertain. So it is also essential to consider how future uncertainties can affect the choice between options.

Yet in the one practical illustration provided of allowing for uncertainty in an analysis of costs (Box 4.5), reference is made to the 'probability distributions specified for each variable' indicating that it is 'risk' rather than 'true' uncertainty that is being discussed.

Situations of uncertainty can be distinguished sharply from those of risk, despite the fact that in both instances the actual future outcome is not predictable with certainty. For example: 'A *risky* situation is one in which the probability distribution of outcomes is known; an *uncertain* situation is one in which even this information is totally lacking' (Marglin, 1967, p. 71). And in the words of Keynes (1936), 'the outstanding fact is the extreme precariousness of the basis of knowledge'. Marglin then goes on to note:

> uncertainty presents a more formidable problem precisely because our knowledge is based only on hunch and insight . . .
> the fact that the world invariably presents situations that lie between the two extremes does not render the dichotomy useless . . .
> The effects of technological change, changes in tastes, deviations from planned levels of investment, and changes in international conditions on investment benefits can at best be seen 'through a glass, darkly,' and to attempt to analyse these sources of uncertainty in terms of probability distributions appropriate to risky situations is at best premature. (pp. 71–1)

Blatt (1983) argues that moderate deviations from estimated cashflows, in either direction, are bound to occur and these can, and should, be handled by means of using 'certainty-equivalent' cashflow estimates rather than the 'most probable' estimates. However, he considers that this type of adjustment has nothing to do with the horizon of uncertainty, which refers to truly uncertain, unpredictable, future contingencies which may befall any project. Such 'disasters' and other consequences for a project are not incorporated into the procedure of deriving 'certainty-equivalent' cashflows. This particular calculation allows for different degrees of risk, and the risk in question is, in effect, that associated with the variance of actual cashflows from predicted ones in the absence of disaster and other non-quantifiable elements. This is a potentially important point, and we return to it in the next section.

Quite clearly, this whole area is one in which there is a considerable evolution of thinking at present, and at the time of writing no consensus has emerged on the correct approach, let alone how to put it into practice. Nevertheless, despite (or perhaps because of) these differences, the PPP and PSC comparison should not be treated as a 'pass–fail' test. Rather, any PPP proposal needs to be subjected to a sensitivity analysis to see whether different assumptions, for example about different forms of risk allocation, would significantly alter the value-for-money assessment. This process is examined in the next chapter. It is also true that PPP procurement relies to a considerable extent on judgement, skill and experience. In the majority of cases, the difference between the PSC and the private sector proposal will be relatively narrow and this becomes apparent in the case study later in this chapter. Consequently, the agency will need to make professional judgements as to the value for money to be derived from contracting with the private sector and the risks which that route involves, while not ignoring that there are also large risks in the public procurement route (and the new UK guidelines in the *Green Book* include an explicit adjustment procedure for the 'optimism bias' that we documented earlier).

Notwithstanding all these difficulties, the development of the PSC remains a valuable discipline on public sector procurement in assisting those involved to understand the project, the risks involved and how to deal with them contractually. For the PSC to provide a meaningful value-for-money test against the bids, it must include a comprehensive and realistic pricing of all quantifiable and material risks. In our view these risks tend to be underestimated by government bodies as demonstrated in the Mott MacDonald (2002) study in the UK (denial about what actually happens, insufficient data, and the paradox in maintenance that even the budgeted number is often not the amount necessary to keep the assets fit for purpose over their life). The risk analysis required for the PSC should be seen not as a stand-alone exercise, but as part of the broader process of risk identification, allocation and management within the project.

EVIDENCE OF VALUE FOR MONEY

The most complete evidence on the value for money of PPP-type approaches comes from the Private Finance Initiative (PFI), the UK government programme to increase the involvement of the private sector in the provision of public services. Introduced by the Conservative government in November 1992, it continued under Labour in 1997. As of July 2003, 451 PFI projects had completed construction and were in operation, including 34 hospitals, and 119 other health schemes, 239 new and refurbished schools, 23 new transport projects, 34 new fire and police stations, 13 new prisons and secure training centres, 12 waste and water projects, and 167 other projects in sectors such as defence, leisure, culture, housing and IT. The PFI scheme has been widely discussed and extensively examined, and two types of evidence are considered in this section. First, we report summaries of PPP–PSC value-for-money comparisons for individual projects. Second, we examine evidence of the rates of return on PFI projects.

Value-for-Money Tests

It is difficult to draw inferences from individual episodes. Inevitably in a market environment not all PPPs will go to plan, and there is a tendency in some quarters to treat every failure of a PPP as evidence that PPPs are fundamentally flawed. A judgement as to whether a PPP has worked needs to be made against a realistic assessment of what can be achieved by public procurement, rather than some idealized conception of government performance. After all, not every traditional procurement goes to plan, and government failure is very real and cannot be overlooked. In order to evaluate whether PPPs have something to offer, it is important to look at available evidence as to the overall success or failure of the PFI *vis-à-vis* conventional procurement.

Earlier in Chapter 4 (see Table 4.3) we reported the evidence assembled by the UK Treasury and the NAO to the effect that the overwhelming majority of PFI projects were delivered on or ahead of time, and that almost all were within budget. This evidence contrasts sharply with an earlier survey of traditional government procurement of infrastructure, where projects were mostly over budget and over time. These results are also consistent with the Mott MacDonald (2002) survey, where 'optimism bias' seemed to be less for PFI projects than for other procurement methods.

There have also been independent assessments made of projects in terms of value-for-money tests. A review, commissioned by the Treasury Taskforce and published jointly by the London School of Economics and Arthur Andersen in January 2000, analysed 29 public sector projects that used the PFI and it was calculated that on average the predicted saving, compared with conventional procurement, was 17 per cent (Arthur Andersen, 2000). In its own separate analysis, the National Audit Office has produced value-for-money reports on 15 projects, 7 of which (including a hospital project) were evaluated for value for money against a public sector comparator for traditional public procurement. Overall, the total cost savings of these projects was 20 per cent (NAO, 2001).

These estimates of projected savings are arrived at by comparing the cost of the PFI project with its public sector comparator, and thus refer to long-term projects that by definition are not yet complete – the actual outcomes will not be known for many years. In addition, Allen (2001) argues that such averages conceal considerable differences across PFI types, with road and prison projects achieving 'reasonable efficiency gains', while those for schools and hospitals show 'minimal gains' (p. 32). This difference is attributed to two factors. The first is that for road and prison projects, there is no partitioning of core and ancillary services, enabling the private contractor to make design and build innovations in the knowledge that they will also be responsible for operating and maintenance services. In PFI health projects, core and ancillary services remain segmented, perhaps reducing some of the potential for innovation. The other reason is that for roads and prisons there is a single, central government agency handling the contracting, whereas with health and education private sponsors must deal with a number of bodies such as local education authorities and school governing councils.

There is another point that needs to be borne in mind with respect to health and schooling – both of these continue to be highly charged political areas in the UK. Health, in particular, is the sector about which critics of PFI have been most vocal (e.g. Mayston, 1999; Pollock *et al.*, 1997; Pollock, 2000). However, the dilemma that cannot be avoided is that public funding has not kept up with advances in medical technology, and this has led to a budgetary crisis in the system. In such an environment, if PFI can deliver genuine cost savings or efficiency gains then the experiment would seem worthwhile. Yet PFI cannot overcome the basic issue of 'affordability', which arises because the 'Trust's expectations exceed the realities of their budgets' (Grimsey and Graham, 1997, p. 220).

Rates of Return Test

A very different test was undertaken by Pricewaterhouse Coopers (PwC) (2002), commissioned by the Office of Government Commerce. It analysed the projected rates of return on a sample of PFI projects to ascertain whether the returns that the private sector expected to earn for managing and bearing risk were excessive or in line with what might be anticipated from a competitive market among bidders. We noted earlier in this chapter that a high degree of competition is needed in the bidding market for PPP/PFI to guarantee that the private sector entities will submit their most competitive bids and offer good value for money to government. The report takes as its starting point the fact that, with competition, project internal rates of return should reflect exactly the returns required by diversified investors, as indicated by the weighted average cost of capital.

In order to examine whether this is the case, a sample of 64 PFI projects was selected, covering a wide range of activities to which PFI has been applied, and representing about 23 per cent of all PFI projects in terms of construction value. As the measure of expected private sector return, the report uses the nominal post-tax internal rate of return as projected at financial close. The project return is compared with the weighted average cost of capital, and is the return that should be expected from a project by a diversified investor, according to the project's risk. It is derived from publicly available information for businesses with broadly comparable activities, principally in the regulated utility sector, using CAPM to derive the appropriate cost of equity, and adopting the cost of debt from the financial model for each project to produce a weighted average cost of capital. CAPM hypothesizes that equity investors demand a premium above the risk-free rate of interest to compensate them for the risk associated with the investment in hand, where the risk premium is a function of the systematic risk of the investment under consideration.

Across all projects in the sample, the internal rate of return is found to average 7.7 per cent per annum. By comparison, the average weighted average cost of capital is estimated to be 5.3 per cent per annum. Thus the 'spread', the amount by which the average project internal rate of return is higher than the cost of capital, is 2.4 per cent per annum. This spread is described as an estimate of the total excess projected return on PFI projects above the cost of finance. Note that the equity returns and project returns are expected returns (*ex ante*). The projects will not necessarily earn this return over their lifetime project (*ex post*) because things might go better or worse than expected. Indeed, while most projects have been successful, a number have led to investors losing money rather than making their expected returns.

Nevertheless, the PwC report contends that even if the projected returns are earned, only part of the spread represents excess returns to the investors, for two reasons. First, between 0.7 per cent and 1.3 per cent (average 1 per cent) may be accounted for by bid costs. The costs of bidding under PFI are higher than in other types of procurement. Overall projects bidders must be expected to recover all their costs – including those on unsuccessful bids – before making a return. For the projects in the sample, the costs incurred before a preferred bidder is announced average about £1 million. The average bidder succeeds in one bid out of three or four, yet the financial projections for individual projects that provide the basis of the PwC study only show the costs of bidding for the particular project that has been won. Thus they do not explicitly reflect costs of other unsuccessful bids, which have to be recovered at least in part through the equity return. Second, under the 25–30 year contracts of the PFI, bidders may price their target returns over a fixed rate such as the swap rate rather than the gilt rate, as assumed in the conventional CAPM. The use of swap rates rather than the gilt rate as the risk-free rate in the cost of equity would increase the average cost of capital from 5.3 per cent to between 5.75 per cent and 6.25 per cent.

Consequently, of the 'spread' of 2.4 per cent per annum, 1.7 per cent is thought to be accounted for by two factors:

- unrecovered bid costs on other projects (about 1 per cent);
- the higher cost of underlying rates for private sector borrowing compared with public sector borrowing, primarily caused by the cost of swaps compared with gilts (about 0.7 per cent).

After taking account of these two factors, the excess projected return to project investors is therefore estimated as being about 0.7 per cent. These excess returns are attributed to 'structural issues' that in the past have limited competition in the PFI market. For instance, the length of PFI procurements and the level of bid costs incurred by the private sector are thought still to create barriers to entry to the market.

We do not disagree with the PwC report as to the significance of a competitive PFI market – market capacity and competitive pressures in the bidding process are essential ingredients in generating value for money. But we are also aware that there is a missing piece of the jigsaw, and that is 'true' uncertainty, and we now consider the possible implications of this distinction for PPP projects.

RISK AND UNCERTAINTY

Frank Knight, we recall, differentiated 'risk' from 'uncertainty'. In both cases, the actual future outcome is not certain, but in the case of risk, the probabilities of the various future outcomes are known (either exactly mathematically, or from past experience of similar situations). In the case of uncertainty, the probabilities of the various future outcomes are merely 'wild guesses' because

> the 'instance' in question is so entirely unique that there are no others or not a sufficient number to make it possible to tabulate enough like it to form a basis for any inference of value about any real probability in the case we are interested in. (Knight, 1921, p. 226)

On what basis, for instance, would one have assigned a probability distribution to September 11 and its impact on world tourism?

From the viewpoint of the preceding analysis, the relevant questions would seem to be, first, do firms take account of uncertainty and second, how do firms allow for uncertainty in their decision-making?

The answer to the first question is straightforward. Firms ignore uncertainty at their peril. Shackle (1955) argues that 'true' uncertainty involves not only unique events but also typically crucial ones.

Crucialness is the real and important source of uniqueness in any occasion of choosing: and far from being unusual, it is all-pervasive. (p. 63)

By a crucial experiment I mean one where the person concerned cannot exclude from his mind the possibility that the very act of performing the experiment may destroy for ever the circumstances in which it was performed. (p. 6)
For a business man, the possibility of a crippling loss of capital implies a large-scale operation, and perhaps we can say, typically either the founding of a new enterprise or a large extension of plant for an existing one. It is, indeed, in the field of investment-decisions (in the economist's sense of the word 'investment'), that personal uniqueness of the occasion mainly occurs. (p. 86)

The large sunk costs would suggest that infrastructure is a crucial investment, while the network effects, externalities and other characteristics identified in Chapter 2 would indicate that there is a degree of uniqueness to every venture.

The UK *Green Book* urges public sector project appraisers to 'consider how future uncertainties can affect the choice between options' (HM Treasury, 2003a, p. 32), and recommends sensitivity analysis, Monte Carlo analysis and scenario planning (creating detailed models of future states of the world). Sensitivity analysis and Monte Carlo analysis are considered in the next chapter, and both are standard tools for dealing with risk (rather than 'true' uncertainty). It is interesting to note that the old US *Green Book* (United States Government, 1958) suggested three ways of dealing with uncertainty. One was conservatism in estimating costs and benefits; a second was a conservative estimate of the economic life of projects; and the third was an addition of a premium to the discount rate that varied directly with the lack of confidence in benefit and cost estimates. Marglin (1967, pp. 97–8) criticized this last approach in what is essentially an early statement of the 'old' view owing to Arrow and Lind (1970) that we discussed earlier based on the government's diversification capacity.

The fact that the failure or below par performance of some projects may be balanced by an unexpected degree of success of others allows a government to concentrate more on expected values, and to worry less about the dispersion of outcomes, of individual projects than private investors can afford to do.

However, Marglin points out that 'conservatism is an appropriate counter-measure for the invariably optimistic bias of the technicians who estimate benefits and costs' (p. 73). Obviously, 'optimism bias' is not a new problem in public sector procurement.

The private sector firm engaged in infrastructure investment faces a very different scenario, and cannot overlook what Marglin describes as the 'nonactuarial nature of uncertainty' (p. 73). As Blatt (1983) puts it:

> the threat of disaster, i.e. bankruptcy, is a very important factor. The future is too uncertain to predict at all well, but a businessman wants to have a reasonable chance of avoiding disaster, not merely for the next project, but for his entire expected time before retirement. He must, therefore, choose between projects available right now in a sufficiently conservative fashion so that he retains a fair chance of not sitting in the poorhouse or the debtors' prison at retirement age . . . The precise meaning of 'disaster' can vary considerably: to a businessman, it is a loss so great that it drives him bankrupt; to a manager, employed by a firm, a much smaller loss than that can result in his being dismissed, without much of a chance of finding alternative employment as a manager. (pp. 279–80)

How then is uncertainty likely to be taken into account? There are many, as we noted earlier, who consider that probability analysis cannot help. In Shackle's words:

> we might say without further ado that frequency-ratio probability has nothing to do with true uncertainty. (p. 26)
>
> To [the mathematical probability theorist] we simply multiply the frequency-ratio of each contingent profit by the amount of that profit and by one thousand, and add together all the answers. The result is what is called the mathematical expectation. This impressive name may mislead us into thinking that the mathematician has performed a miracle, has got something out of his calculating machine that he did not put into it, and has changed the enterpriser's situation from essential uncertainty to certainty. But he has not . . . the frequency-ratios tell us nothing about the individual throws of the dice, or the individual and particular business ventures. (p. 84)
>
> It is because in the text-book examples of drawing from an urn, and in the games of chance, factors whose existence and nature are unknown are excluded by the rules of the game, that these examples and games are irrelevant to reality. (p. 39)

It is the uniqueness and crucialness that creates the problem: 'Napoleon could not repeat the battle of Waterloo a hundred times in the hope that, in a certain proportion of cases, the Prussians would arrive too late' (p. 25).

From the viewpoint of infrastructure, whether probability analysis will suffice turns on two questions. Is there a sufficiently large number of projects that are similar, statistically speaking, to each other and to those in the past to enable reliable probability distributions to be formed? Or, are the infrastructure ventures sufficiently different (unique, crucial) that we are dealing with projects that cannot be treated as if off a production line? Some routine PPP projects involving schools and accommodation may be able to be replicated in adequate numbers, in the appropriate sense, but for many other projects this would not be so, especially if PPPs are seen as particularly valuable for major, complex, innovative and largely one-off projects.

If, then, standard probability analysis based on known probabilities cannot deal with true uncertainty, what can? At a theoretical level, the main approach to the analysis of uncertainty is in terms of state preference theory which represents the random events facing an individual in terms of a set of mutually exclusive and exhaustive states of nature or states of the world.[13] At an empirical level, a not uncommon approach is to recognize the distinction between risk and uncertainty, and then treat both as risk. For example, Lessard and Miller (2001) do this, but at the same time emphasize that risks are multi-dimensional, and can combine and interact to create turbulence so that projects become 'ungovernable' (p. 8). They also argue the importance of creating options for subsequent choices within a real options framework. Real options theory (Dixit and Pindyck, 1995) presumes that decision-making is sequential and that decision-makers may benefit from choosing options that may seem suboptimal today but which increase flexibility at later times, leading to better decision-making when more is known about the project. There is some affinity in this accumulation of information with Bayesian decision theory, which is the third approach to uncertainty that we would mention.

Bayesian theory starts with incomplete knowledge of the prior distribution and is based on the formation of subjective probabilities derived from preferences over risky options that are updated in the light of new information.[14] Many argue that the Bayesian approach to learning by experiment provides a logical framework for quantifying partial belief that brings uncertainty within the fold of probability analysis and decision-making under risk, rendering redundant the distinction that Knight made between risk and uncertainty (LeRoy and Singell, 1987; Hirschleifer and Riley, 1992). However, not everyone agrees that the distinction between risk and 'true' uncertainty can be discarded (Kelsey and Quiggin, 1992; Runde, 1995). Implementation of the Bayesian decision rule is far from simple (Kirman and Salmon, 1995): it is computationally complex, may be unable to cope with 'radical' uncertainty (Casson, 2000b, Chapter 4), and relies on a process of trial and error that the decision-maker in infrastructure projects cannot pursue.

Among the authors cited earlier there is consensus that 'ineradicable uncertainty' cannot be handled by frequency distributions and calculations of mathematical expectation, and must be tackled by a different line of thought, but there is less agreement thereafter. Firms may be forced to fall back on simple expediencies such as allowing a margin for error to be on the safe side (Shackle, 1955, p. 83), or employ a simple decision rule like the payback limit rule; that is, whether the cumulative net revenue from a project will cover the original investment within a specified period of time (Blatt, 1983, p. 286). Firms may take into account both the 'best possible' and the 'worst possible' outcome of each course of action (the former the highest hope from the project, the latter the worst fear), and make these pairs of outcomes the basis of the decision, having in mind an upper limit for the loss that can be contemplated and whether the worst-case scenario could be survived (Shackle, 1955, p. 89). Blatt argues for the adoption of a risk-adjusted, time-dependent cost of capital, not just one with a constant risk margin, for which businessmen (or businesswomen) would set their maximum allowable risk differently and have different subjective estimates of the horizon of uncertainty. This time-dependency, he notes (1983, p. 285), explains why there is so much controversy over the determination of the appropriate value of the risk-adjusted discount rate. In his view, no appropriate value exists!

Despite these different ideas about coping with uncertainty, there is agreement at least among the latter writers that, in the face of true uncertainty, firms will adopt a conservative 'safety-first' approach in which the objective seems clear.

> The business management has to see each project it starts to its conclusion, and its policy must be such that it retains a reasonable chance of surviving in business for longer than just the very next project. (Blatt, 1983, p. 261)

The same can be said of specialist equity investors and others drawn into the venture. Any sensible bidder for a PPP project would want to allow some measure for uncertainty. How exactly this is done is not clear but it would seem apparent that the 'ineluctable, irreducible uncertainties that everywhere confront us in this life' (Shackle, 1955, p. 16) will not go away by assuming them away, and that firms with an instinct for survival will allow for true uncertainty in one way or another.

If we are correct, then there are obvious implications for the 'missing' 0.7 per cent in the PricewaterhouseCoopers rate of return study, which they attribute to structural weaknesses in the PPP market but which we would see in some measure as linked with uncertainty. But uncertainty also has implications for value-for-money tests. Earlier we referred to the analysis of Grout (1997) who argued that the riskiness of PPP cashflows is higher than that for PSC cashflows, warranting a higher rate for the PPP discounting than for the PSC. The fact that uncertainty exists and will be priced into the PPP cashflows reinforces this point.

ACCOUNTABILITY

Accountability is a requirement for any organizational structure, public or private. Those in charge of economic resources must give account of their stewardship, irrespective of whether the transactions and resources in question are those of a government organization or a private sector entity (Grimsey and Lewis, 2002b). This stewardship function has been a regular feature of organized human activity from the earliest times (Brown, 1905; Brown, 1962; Stone, 1969). Originally at the level of the individual property owner, nowadays accountability would be described in terms of an accounting by management (either public or private) to assist in the efficient allocation of resources by providing information, either for *ex post* monitoring of performance or for *ex ante* decision-making by those responsible for making investment decisions (Whittington, 1992). Yet accountability also has broader economic and social purposes and objectives because of the many other groups that have a legitimate interest in knowing about the activities and operations. Their interests need to be recognized in PPPs.

The taxpayers' objective remains one of achieving effective and efficient 'value for money'; that is, with identifying the most cost-efficient way of securing a high quality service (Commission on Public Private Partnerships, 2001). Value for money can be achieved in a number of ways: by establishing a competitive and contestable market for infrastructure projects; from private sector innovation and skills in asset design, construction techniques and operational practices; and from transferring key risks in design, construction delays, costs overruns and finance and insurance to private sector entities for them to manage. Risk allocation is needed for project success, and value for money is a key facet of it. If sufficient risk cannot be transferred to private parties, it is unlikely that a PPP will deliver value for money.

The significance of this last point becomes apparent when we consider one of the most common criticisms of PPPs. Government bodies in both Australia and the United Kingdom have been accused of having a predisposition to PPP-type arrangements because they represent 'back door' financing (Commission on Public Private Partnerships, 2001; Walker and Walker, 2000). Some of the reasons why public sector entities might be attracted to PPPs involve the potential to get off-balance sheet status. This motivation presumably is similar to those of other enterprises engaged in off-the-balance sheet financing (despite the government bodies not producing commercial-style accounts), namely to expand activities beyond balance sheet restrictions while preserving credit standing (Lewis, 1992). As off-balance sheet undertakings, payments under the PPP agreement would be shown as revenue charges in the year to which they relate, rather than as an asset, and a corresponding liability, to be accounted for when the project is entered into.

Most of the accounting issues have been thrashed out in the literature (our own contribution is Grimsey and Lewis, 2002b), and we do not want to go through them here in part because matters have moved on. It is true that the pivotal issue with respect to the accounting treatment revolves around where the risks lie, and judgements about the relative importance of different kinds of risk are likely to be paramount, for example, the balance between construction risk, design risk, demand risk and residual value risk (Heald, 2003). However, the real issue is not so much one of whether or not the PPP undertaking is off-balance sheet, and thus whether the arrangement constitutes borrowing in another name, but whether it represents good value for money. This is the real prerequisite for evaluating the PPP route. The UK Treasury Taskforce guidance on PFI accounting specifically countenanced against sacrificing value for money in the search to obtain off-balance sheet accounting treatment:

> The objective of PFI procurement is to provide high quality public services that represent value for money for the taxpayer. It is therefore value for money, and not the accounting treatment, which is the key determinant of whether a project should go ahead or not. Purchasers should focus on how procurement can achieve risk transfer in a way that optimizes value for money and must not transfer risks to the operator at the expense of value for money. (Treasury Taskforce, 1999, para 1.8)

The current position is summarized by the UK Treasury in its July 2003 review of PFI:

> The decision to undertake PFI investment is taken on value for money grounds alone, and whether it is on or off balance sheet is a subsequent decision taken by independent auditors and is not relevant to the choice of procurement route. Almost 60 per cent of PFI projects by value are on balance sheet. (HM Treasury, 2003b, p. 1)

This last quotation brings out the point that value-for-money considerations are *ex ante*. The accounting decision is made *ex post*, looking at matters after the event.

A major reason why accounting has proven to be such a controversial aspect of PPPs is because the scope of these arrangements strains design boundaries and commercial concepts envisaged by the existing leasing standards. Leasing standards pre-date the emergence of PPP models for involving the private sector in the delivery of services (dependent on infrastructure assets). When the leasing standards were drafted they did not contemplate the more complex and interwoven risk transfers that characterize many PPP service delivery models. Development of an international standard on PPPs still appears some way off, and in the meantime there seems to be a recognition in the industry that the UK approach, in particular Financial Report Standard 5 (FRS 5), constitutes the best available.[15]

Accounting principles distinguish property, an asset, from services, accounted for as current expenditure. In the case of a PPP, the issue is whether to regard the resulting property as an asset of the government or to record the stream of unitary charge payments as expenditure in the year in which they occur. Whether a party has 'an asset of the structure or property' will depend on whether it has access to the benefits, and exposure to the risks, normally associated with ownership of that property. FRS 5 methods seek to resolve this fundamental question by employing a standard set of tests to measure the quantum of key risks for the type of property (assets) involved, and then estimate which party bears the overall majority of the risks. An example might be where a building or other facility is needed to fulfil a contract for services, and there is a need to determine which party has an asset of that property, and recognize the identified assets and corresponding liabilities.

A starting point of the accounting analysis under FRS 5 is to determine if the contract is separable; that is, whether the commercial effect is that individual elements of the contract payments operate independently from each other. 'Operate independently' means that the elements behave differently and can therefore be separately identified. The more integral the asset is to the provision of the service, the more likely the asset will not be separable. If the contract is not separable down to any underlying amounts, FRS 5 methods will directly apply. Should the contract be separable, and can be reduced down to the supply of an asset, leasing rules can be used to determine whether the arrangement is a finance lease (on balance sheet) or an operating lease (off balance sheet) by reference to the payment stream for the asset.

Once separability has been assessed, the essential principles of FRS 5 as applied to PPPs can be summarized as follows:

- if property is necessary to fulfil a serviced contract, the party which has an asset of the property must be determined;
- a party will have an asset of the property when they have access to the benefits and exposure to the risks inherent in the benefits;
- the purchaser should recognize an asset and a liability to pay for the asset where the commercial effect of the contract is that the purchaser bears a greater percentage of the risks associated with the potential variations in property profits/losses;
- where the components of the contract payments are separable, those components relating entirely to services are not relevant to determining who has the asset of the property; and
- once separable service elements have been excluded, any remaining elements are either payments for the property, in which case lease accounting applies, or other contracts where FRS 5 applies directly.

In determining who bears most of the risk of the property for the overall contract, it is necessary to weigh up the risks, and determine their relative importance. The UK experience is that it is very rare that one party will clearly show that they hold all the risks and benefits associated with a property. At a minimum, a qualitative assessment of the risks, plus an assessment of non-quantifiable risks, is required before drawing a preliminary conclusion as to who bears the risks associated with the property. For example, in the majority of cases for social infrastructure projects, demand risk and residual value risk will remain with the concession provider. However, if this division is not straightforward, it will be necessary to quantify, to the extent possible, the importance of each risk and the relative allocation of risks between the concession provider and the concession operator.

THE PUBLIC INTEREST

Suppose that it is adjudged that a PPP represents good value for money. How do we know that the wider public interest is being served? In short, how are PPPs to be made accountable in the community? Under the traditional 'Westminster' model, public service providers are ultimately answerable through the ballot box, since public servants are accountable to ministers, who are themselves accountable to Parliament, while Parliament is accountable to the people. The system revolves around verification of the official use of public monies, drawn from the public account. Budget bills are presented to Parliament for debate and review for the expenditure of funds raised from general revenues. For some PPPs this scrutiny may never happen because the income stream comes from tolls and other charges rather than expenditures from the budget, while for others the off-balance sheet status removes the disciplines imposed on public borrowings. Yet, at the same time, the market constraints operating on commercial enterprises do not apply either, for no privatization is involved.

There are encouraging signs that this apparent vacuum is rapidly being filled. In the United Kingdom, the Commission on Public Private Partnerships (2001, Chapter 10) has come up with a set of principles against which any system of public accountability should be judged: transparency, responsibility and responsiveness. *Transparency* means that organizations delivering public services are required to disclose key information, making their decisions open to public scrutiny. *Responsibility* means that there is clarity as to the organization or individual that is answerable for particular decisions and courses of action. *Responsiveness* means that services are able to adapt to reflect citizens' needs, priorities, and expectations and give quick redress to individuals when things go wrong. In this way accountability is a vital mechanism for improving service quality.

So too is probity. Probity refers to uprightness, honesty, proper and ethical conduct and propriety in dealings. In the context of government tendering, these things are protected by 'due process'. Such due process is one in which clear procedures, consistent with the government's objectives and the legitimate interest of bidders, are established, understood and observed from the outset. All bidders need to be treated equitably and decisions taken in a transparent manner that allows them to be subsequently understood and justified. Probity management rests on a well-constructed plan that fosters an appropriate culture and sets out proper procedures to apply between bidders and the public sector bodies. Nevertheless, probity should not rule out interaction between the parties during the tender process, for such contact is often necessary if project objectives and value for money are to be achieved.

In many markets PPPs are not yet at the stage where the government and the private sector agree on all risk allocation issues, and there are still significant commercial issues where the two parties are quite some way apart. Sometimes it is difficult for the market place to really understand government's objectives for a project. It is therefore valuable if the government maintains a dialogue with the market throughout a PPP project – continually checking market appetite, marketing the project and discussing specific issues on a regular basis. Clearly this type of interaction needs to be consistent with principles of fair and proper conduct, but at the same time probity considerations should not in any way preclude such contact and restrict dialogue between parties that are attempting to enter into a long-term partnership.

Development of a unified approach across the range of public sector bodies would help to establish a common set of standards for the management of probity and governing principles for probity advisers and auditors, confidentiality and disclosure, and conflicts of interest. Such an approach is needed because government agencies are accountable for the efficient management of public resources, and probity standards help to deliver a clear and open process in which taxpayers can have confidence. They also provide the government's existing and prospective partners in the business community with the reassurance that they will be treated fairly and consistently in their dealings with the public sector. This in turn encourages a wider field of bids, increased competition and better value for money.

Finally, there is the question of the wider public interest, for government has particular responsibilities and democratic accountabilities with respect to the delivery of services to the community. Quite clearly, the use of taxpayers' money to pay for the services necessitates that there be checks and balances to ensure that money is spent wisely. It is ultimately Parliament's right to determine how revenue is raised and spent, and it has created the statutory position of Auditor-General to verify that proper financial standards are being maintained by the executive branch of government. In Britain and in the Australian states that have implemented PPPs, the Auditors-General have played a central role in reporting on PPP arrangements, and it seems desirable that this function should be strengthened. However, governments are responsible for more than using taxes appropriately. People need to be treated in a fair and equitable manner, and government has a special duty of care to those citizens disadvantaged by personal and economic circumstances. For PPPs the issue that has to be addressed is whether public functions can be delegated to private sector entities without losing sight of the expectation of citizens that public services ought to be more than seller–buyer, customer–provider exchanges and serve a larger social purpose (Watson, 2003). Accountability needs to cover equity, probity and access as well as financially responsible behaviour. Behn in his book *Rethinking Democratic Accountability* (2001) talks about accountability in four senses: accountability for finances, accountability for fairness, accountability for performance and accountability for personal probity (p. 24).

Under a PPP agenda, protection of the public interest can be considered in terms of a number of elements, and a 'best practice' framework would allow for a checklist of questions to be answered in the bidding process, constituting a public interest test.[16] These are:

- Is the project effective in meeting government objectives?
- Do the partnership arrangements ensure that the community can be well informed about the obligations of government and the private sector partner, and that these can be overseen by the public auditor?
- Have those affected by the project been able to contribute effectively at the planning stages, and are their rights protected through fair appeals processes and other conflict resolution mechanisms?
- Are there adequate arrangements to ensure that disadvantaged groups can effectively use the infrastructure or access the related service?
- Does the project provide sufficient safeguards for consumers, particularly those for whom government has a high level of duty of care, and/or those in the community who are the most vulnerable?
- Are there safeguards that ensure ongoing public access to essential infrastructure particularly if there is a breach in the contract?
- Does the project provide assurance that community health and safety will be secured?
- Does the project provide adequate protection of users' rights to privacy?

While there may be a concern that private provision will inherently result in a lesser consideration of public interest matters than may occur under public provision, we would contend that, in fact, PPPs offer an opportunity to expand the level of public interest protection. The traditional model of accountability derives from a particular approach to public administration that emphasizes the divide between the public sector and the private sector and puts the stress on political control via a chain of relationships through which authority flows from citizens to MPs, MPs to ministers, ministers to civil servants, and civil servants to service providers. Too frequently in practice, however, the line between policy and administration has been blurred; administrative coordination has been flawed; decisions made have often been in secret and not disclosed. What is needed instead is a new framework, which enshrines the highest standards of accountability in line with accepted standards of probity. PPPs, with their deliberate, step-by-step approach to decision-making, are a good vehicle for bringing this about.

CONDITIONS FOR SUCCESSFUL PPPS

Accountability and a regard for the public interest are important for the success of a PPP project because, as Berg *et al.* (2002) emphasize, 'legitimacy' is an important aspect when institutional frameworks are being designed for sectors of the economy like infrastructure. Legitimacy is of significance on a number of scores. First, consumers of the infrastructure services must be convinced that they are paying appropriate prices for services received. Second, if there are government subsidies for services, taxpayers must view these as contributing to social objectives. Third, those who receive and value the services need to accept the public and private arrangements that are brought together to attract and allocate resources for infrastructure activities. Without such acceptance, it will be difficult to raise the private finance on which the project depends.

Obviously, there are many other considerations that must be taken into account in designing a successful PPP, and a number of bodies have outlined what they consider to be the main factors. We have already noted the six key 'drivers' of successful PFI projects identified in the report (Arthur Andersen, 2000) commissioned by the Treasury Task Force: risk transfer, long-term contracting, output-based project specification, competition, performance measurement and private sector management skills. Also recommended was greater centralized monitoring of PFI project performance, transfer of experienced staff between government departments, use of ongoing benchmarking to ensure continuing value for money from existing projects, and more careful assessment of the value of risks transferred to the private sector.

From its own parallel evaluation of 15 PFI projects, the National Audit Office highlighted four key aspects of successful PFI projects: clear objectives, application of proper procurement processes, getting high-quality bids and ensuring that the final deal either makes sense or is dropped or re-tendered (NAO, 2001).

Berg *et al.* (2002) conclude their examination of private sector initiatives in infrastructure by arguing that a proper mechanism for private sector involvement must be designed, which should include a number of criteria. They single out four elements in particular: incentive compatibility, governance, credibility and transparency. The arrangements have to provide incentives for the private sector to bear risks, and the contract should clarify responsibilities and roles in a clear and transparent way if it is to be governed in a correct fashion. Credibility is seen to be especially important for developing countries, since foreign investors and multinational enterprises are likely to be major participants in projects and they face various political as well as country risks. Without credibility in the arrangements it will be difficult to attract investment for infrastructure projects. This issue is taken up in Chapter 9.

Our own view is that PPPs do provide such a 'proper mechanism' for private sector involvement, but they have to be managed to bring about good outcomes. From our knowledge the factors that need to be put in place are as follows:

- Government bodies must view the transaction as the purchase of a service and not the acquisition of the underlying asset (with payment made when the service is provided satisfactorily, not when the asset is built).
- Both parties must accept that the transaction is not a purchaser–supplier contract but is a partnership in which there is a sharing of risks and responsibilities.
- It is necessary to establish that both sides have the capabilities to fulfil and carry out their side of the bargain. The private party has to have the abilities and motivation. The government agency must understand the market and have the capacity to formulate the business plan and manage the contract.
- Interaction is essential during the tendering process, and the negotiations for contract fulfilment need to be managed with cooperation and forbearance. Competitive tensions will inevitably surface and they must be recognized and dealt with in the right spirit.
- Careful preparation work has been undertaken with respect to:

  - definition of outputs
  - consensus among participating bodies
  - a clear approval process
  - allocation of ownership rights
  - identification of rights and responsibilities
  - a valid comparator for value for money
  - a clear business model.

- Timelines need to be established that are realistic and take into account other commitments.
- The PPP contract should be sufficiently flexible to take account of any new targets and future monitoring and reporting requirements that may develop over the lifetime of the project.
- Risk allocation has to be cost-effective so that risks are allocated to the party best able to manage them and respond to the incentives they offer.

This last factor is essential for maximizing efficiency. Only by transferring risk can there be certainty that the private sector has the incentives to price and produce efficiently. The risk allocation in PPPs is the topic of the next chapter when we consider the nature of the risks and the 'tools' available for allocating risks between the participating parties. But first we outline a case study of a recent hospital project in the UK with particular focus on the reasons for going ahead with the deal. The type of incentives just mentioned featured prominently in the decision.

THE WEST MIDDLESEX UNIVERSITY HOSPITAL PROJECT[17]

The West Middlesex University Hospital Project was chosen as a case study for two reasons. First, it is a recent example of the conventional NHS approach to PFI, which reached financial close on 30 January 2001 and came on-stream in April 2003. Second, the case study illustrates the considerations that are involved in determining whether a PPP/PFI project offers value for money. But we begin by outlining the background to the project.

As many of the old hospital buildings dated back to Victorian times and were in bad condition, the Trust, the local Health Authorities and the NHS London Regional Office (LRO) all considered that a redevelopment of the West Middlesex hospital site was essential and long overdue. The 35-year PFI deal for the redevelopment of the West Middlesex Hospital is for new buildings along with facilities management and maintenance services for all of the buildings on the site. This particular project is the culmination of a series of plans to improve the site that have been circulating since the 1970s, and its aim is to alleviate the problems created by the sprawling layout of services and the poor, unsafe condition of some of the buildings. Much of the building stock on the site is over 100 years old and in recent inspections the site as a whole has failed to meet statutory fire and health and safety requirements. The general layout and conditions make the site unsuitable for modern, high quality healthcare.

In fact, the PFI procurement process, which was well advanced, was stopped in 1997 when the Department decided to make it a priority to complete the existing schemes. West Middlesex Hospital was fourteenth on a list of urgent projects, the first 13 of which went ahead. The project was included in the next wave of PFI hospital projects brought forward in 1998. LRO indicated that the project remained a priority and it would have been taken forward through conventional procurement if a PFI solution was not deemed appropriate. Thus the decision to proceed with the PFI route was not undertaken because PFI was 'the only game in town'.

The West Middlesex University Hospital NHS Trust let the PFI contract to a private consortium called Bywest. Figure 6.2 sets out the contractual arrangements for the project, which requires Bywest to redevelop the Trust's site at Isleworth, West London and then to provide ongoing maintenance and facilities services. The project involves demolition and replacement of the most dilapidated Victorian buildings. Bywest will also carry out extensive refurbishment of newer, existing buildings. This work will be funded from land sales, rather than by unitary payments under the PFI deal. Contractors to the Bywest consortium comprised Bouygues for construction and Ecovert, part of the same group, for facilities management. This linkage provided a unified approach to bidding. Competitive bidding was also aided by the financing arrangements. Both bond financing and bank loans were examined for the project, but bank financing was chosen. Abbey National seemed keen to be involved in the financing of PFI hospital deals and offered finance at very competitive terms, according to the Trust's advisers.

Advisers to the NHS Trust were appointed after a competitive tendering process which saw KPMG selected as the financial advisers, MacFarlanes as the legal advisers and James Nisbet and Partners as the chartered surveyors. In its report, the NAO (2002) adjudged the financial advisers as having 'extensive experience of hospital PFI deals', the legal group as having 'extensive knowledge of the Trust', and the chartered surveyors as providing 'excellent analysis of the bidders' proposals' (p. 14). This is just as well because, in total, the cost of the advice amounted to £2.3 million.

In line with other NHS PFI projects, Bywest is responsible for design, redevelopment, building, financing and operating the hospital facilities for 35 years, with the possibility of extending the term to 60 years. Support services are also to be provided, such as catering, portering, security, cleaning, maintenance and provision of supplies. For its part, the Trust continues to manage the hospital, fund its financial obligations from public sector resources and supply health care services such as nursing, clinical staff, drugs, treatment, diagnostic services, and so on. These health care services are free to individual users (all UK citizens).

When the contract was put out to tender there were 39 expressions of interest, generating a 'longlist' of nine entities, and a 'shortlist' of six. Three

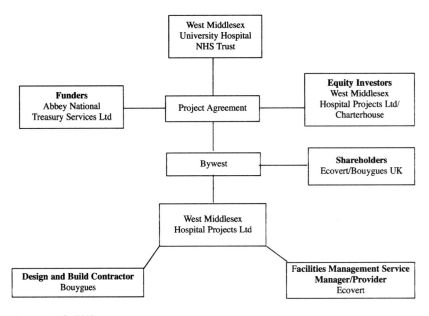

Source: NAO (2002).

Figure 6.2   Contractual arrangements for the West Middlesex University Hospital project

bidders were given a final invitation to negotiate. In order to save time and costs, the Trust elected to go from three bidders straight to a single preferred bidder without an intermediary step involving two final bidders. The Trust chose Bywest in February 2000 and reached financial close nearly a year later on 30 January 2001. Bywest offered a slightly lower price than the other bidders, and the Trust concluded that the bid offered the best value for money with perceived strengths in design, proposed timetable and personnel issues.

Some features of the PFI transaction are given in Table 6.1, with costs based on an annual unitary payment of £9.8 million that did not commence until April 2003 when the Trust began to operate from the new hospital. The payment mechanism is geared towards ensuring that the Trust receives the services agreed in the contract to meet its business needs. Bywest has the incentive that if the level of service provided falls below that required by the Trust, the Trust will make deductions from the unitary payment. For example, should one of the six operating theatres be unavailable for 24 hours (one week-day), the payment deduction on the contractor is approximately £1400. Provisions are contained in the contract for regular monitoring to ensure the contractor is delivering the required level of service. The Trust is emphasizing

Table 6.1 Key features of the West Middlesex University Hospital project

	PFI deal as contracted	Conventional procurement alternative
Final deal cost at 2001 prices (discounted over 35 years to April 2001 and excluding clinical costs)	£125 million – 35 years £130 million – 60 years (Based on annual unitary payment of some £10 million)	£130 million – 35 years £140 million – 60 years (Risk adjusted)
Cost profiles	Annual unitary charge of some £10 million plus refurbishment costs of £12 million under separate arrangements	Full capital construction and refurbishment costs of some £62 million (cash estimate) over first four years, followed by ongoing maintenance and ancillary services
Risk allocation • Remaining with public sector	• Clinical service provision • Change in Trust requirements • NHS specific regulatory/legislative changes	Most risks retained by the public sector
• Passed on to private sector	• Construction design (except changes due to external NHS requirements) • Meeting specified performance standards and operating cost risk • Non-NHS specific regulatory/legislative changes	
Cost of advisers used in procurement (actual prices)	£2.3 million	The Department has suggested a range of between 2 to 4% of capital value for schemes over £20 million. This would give between £1.2 million and £2.4 million in this case
Original estimate of deal cost (based on 30 year contract): • Invitation to negotiate (1998/99 prices)	£91 million	£93 million
• Selection of preferred bidder (February 2000 prices)	£95 million	£98 million

Trust's assessment of additional benefits of its chosen procurement over conventional procurement		
	Greater price certainty	Cost overruns passed to public body
	Incentivizes contractor to complete development on time as full payment only starts once the building is ready for use and occupied	
	Payment linked to delivery of service which incentivizes the PFI contractor to deliver the quality of service which is specified over the contract period	Only recourse for poor performance is to terminate the contract which can also lead to payments from the Trust
	Same contractor designs, maintains and operates building under one contract and is therefore incentivized to adopt whole-life costing	Design, maintenance and operation of building is dealt with under separate contracts

Source: NAO (2002).

a partnership approach to making this project work over the next 35 years, with the Trust and Bywest establishing a PFI Monitoring Group, including user representatives, that will meet regularly to assess performance. The key objectives of the group will be to ensure delivery of agreed quality standards and to resolve issues that may prevent this from happening.

In line with PFI guidelines, the Trust undertook a prior financial comparison of the costs of the PFI bid as against the estimated costs of providing the same level of service using conventional procurement. It compared the net present value (NPV) of the unitary payments under the PFI deal to a public sector comparator (PSC), adjusted for risks transferred under the contract. The final comparison showed that the estimated cost of the PFI deal is slightly lower than the PSC, as set out in Table 6.2. In NPV terms, the pre-risk adjusted NPV of the unitary payments is £123.8 million as against the PSC of £129.3 million.

Obviously, the comparison covers a 35-year period so there are inevitable uncertainties in forecasting future values; for example, costs of construction and service provision and changes in design or service requirements. The estimates of the value of risks transferred under the deal are especially subject to unpredictabilities and involve a lot of judgement when estimating the likelihood of a chance risk event occurring over the life of the deal in order to put a money value on these risks. This is significant in this case since the final comparison is clearly dependent on the estimated value of the risk transfer assessment.

Table 6.2   Value-for-money test for the West Middlesex University Hospital project[a,b]

	PFI deal (£ million NPV)		Public sector comparator (£ million NPV)
35 year pre-risk adjusted	984.1		976.5
Risks transferred	–0.6		12.5
Total risk adjusted	983.5		989.0
Total difference		5.5	

Notes:

[a] Financial comparison of PFI deal and PSC by the NHS Trust in January, 2001.

[b] Clinical services are outside the scope of the deal, but the Trust included identical clinical costs on each side of the calculation in line with the Department's guidance. The pre-risk adjusted NPV of the unitary payments for the project over 35 years is the £123.8 million. The public sector comparator was £129.3 million.

Source: NAO (2002).

In point of fact, for this project the Trust's initial comparison showed the PFI price slightly higher than the cost of conventional procurement. According to the NAO, both the Trust and its financial advisers were convinced of the overall value for money of the deal, taking all factors into account. But there were doubts about the accuracy of this initial financial comparison, and going forward to the Department of Health with an estimate showing the PSC cheaper than the PFI deal might well have jeopardized the case. Because the risk analysis was seen as incomplete, the figures were revisited. Risk work-shops were held and adjustments to cost and risk estimates were completed before seeking Departmental approval, which resulted in the PSC becoming slightly higher than the PFI price. The final calculations showed a risk-adjusted saving from using the PFI of £5.5 million compared with a PSC, including project costs and clinical costs, of £989 million over 35 years (net present values). The reassessed cost comparison therefore reinforced the value-for-money case for the PFI deal, without in itself constituting conclusive evidence.

It is important not to forget that the exercise of assessing the PFI relative to the PSC calculation is not one that compares like with like. The PSC calculation is a hypothetical one of what the project might cost using the public procurement route, with many uncertainties attached to the costings, particularly with respect to the evaluation and treatment of risks and the likelihood of cost overruns resulting. By comparison, the PFI figure is actually a firm bid, put on the table by a consortium willing, able and ready to do the job and with a desire to start delivering the infrastructure services as quickly as possible in order for the revenue flows to begin. Also, in this case, the bid was supported by confirmation in writing from Bywest at the selection of preferred bidder stage that it would hold its proposed price, assuming that the specification remained unchanged. As is normal in such cases, some specifications and other elements related to the site buildings did change, but the 'deal drift' was, in the view of the Trust and the NAO, 'controlled', and the annual price in the event increased by less than 10 per cent during this period, mainly due to infla-tion and the decision to use land sale proceeds to fund other work (NAO, 2002, p. 16).

In view of the uncertainties inherent in such cost estimation, particularly in respect of the PSC, it is probably fair to conclude, as the NAO does, that 'there was little to choose between the PFI and the traditionally procured options in terms of the financial comparison alone' (p. 22). Somewhat ironically, in view of the concerns of the Trust's advisers on this point, the Department told the NAO that it would not necessarily withhold approval for a PFI project that appeared slightly more expensive than conventional procurement if there were convincing value-for-money reasons for proceeding with the deal. Indeed, as the NAO noted, the attention given by the Trust to the juxtaposition of the figures in the value-for-money comparison may have diverted attention away from the wider benefits that the PFI approach was expected to secure. These benefits are summarized at the foot of Table 6.1 and relate to (1) the incentives given to the contractor to finish on time and within budget, (2) the incentives built into the payment mechanism for services to be of the appropriate quality, and (3) incentives for the designer and contractor to take account of whole-life costing implications. Other important considerations for the Trust were the certainty of pricing and the transfer of responsibility for the assets, enabling it to focus on the delivery of core services.

Of course, there are also possible 'disbenefits' in the Trust tying its hands by entering into such a long-term service delivery contract. Business needs change over time, so there is the risk that the contract may become unsuitable for these changing circumstances during the contract life. There is some allowance for this event in the contract which has some inbuilt flexibility to accommodate such uncertainties. Up to six additional wards (170 beds) can be provided or alternatively bed numbers could be decreased. The Trust believes the contract provides sufficient leeway to address future changes in long-term health care.

Overall, this case illustrates a situation that may be typical of many large, complex PPP/PFI projects in that the financial comparison between the PFI transaction and the public sector comparator was not clear cut, but this comparison did not take account of many of the potential benefits and costs associated with a long-term PFI contract. These other elements must be harnessed and managed effectively to ensure that the deal offers value for money. The Trust believes it has managed the potential disbenefits and risks effectively in the West Middlesex University Hospital contract, while there are benefits from doing the project as a PFI because of the incentives to the private sector to deliver the project on time, and to provide continuing infrastructure services at a fixed price and to a satisfactory quality.

NOTES

1. In this way, the operation of PPPs can be seen as paralleling the growth of networking and 'virtual corporations' formed by creating groups of contracting partners and taking advantage of digital technology (see Lewis, 2003).
2. In general, the separation between principal and agent gives rise to problems of asymmetric information and hidden actions. Effectively, the principal does not know how good the agent is, and cannot easily observe the agent's actions. Sappington (1991) provides a relatively recent survey.
3. See, for example, Oliver Williamson (1996) and Mark Casson (2000, Chapter 5) for analyses of the role of transactions costs and information costs. Economies of scale and scope are examined by Alfred Chandler (1990), as is indicated by his title *Scale and Scope*.
4. In the words of Brealey *et al.* (1997): 'in the presence of complete capital markets, in which the pay-offs to all projects are spanned by existing securities, taxpayers can shed any risk that accrues from the undertaking of a project by the government by trading in the capital

markets. The risk premium demanded by the capital markets is the cost of shedding this risk. It is therefore the risk premium demanded for both public and private sector projects' (p. 23).

5. The standard references are Brealey and Myers (2003) and Copeland and Weston (1988).

6. PFI had mixed results when it was first introduced to the NHS, as it was then mandatory for all capital schemes over a certain value to be market tested. This resulted in a banking-up of incomplete deals, a number of which were, in hindsight, either inappropriate to tackle under PFI, or unaffordable for the NHS. Also, many of the schemes coming to the market faced the following issues: their focus tended to be on acquiring an asset rather than providing a service; some key stakeholders did not fully accept or understand the PFI concept; and risk allocation was sub-optimal – either too much or too little risk was transferred to the private sector. The UK Labour government has applied the PFI model much more selectively by devoting the resources needed to make the selected PFI schemes a success; addressing the way PFI projects were structured; moving towards optimizing risk and value; seeking to place risk with the party best able to manage it; and tight project management to ensure the investment required by both public and private sectors is kept at an acceptable level.

7. According to the *Green Book*, social time preference is defined as the value society attaches to present, as opposed to future, consumption. The social time preference rate is a rate used for discounting future benefits and costs, and is based on comparisons of utility across different points in time or different generations. It has two components. The first is the rate at which individuals discount future consumption over present consumption, on the assumption that no change in per capita consumption is expected. Second, there is an additional element, if per capita consumption is expected to grow over time, reflecting the fact that these circumstances imply future consumption will be plentiful relative to the current position and thus have lower marginal utility. This effect is represented by the product of the annual growth in per capita consumption and the elasticity of marginal utility of consumption with respect to utility. With the first component estimated at 1.5 per cent per annum, and the second at 2 per cent per annum, the social time preference is valued at 3.5 per cent per annum in real terms.

8. Exceptions are where projects exceed $500 million in value, making it worthwhile to calculate an idiosyncratic project risk discount rate, or when the systematic risk profile is an unusual one. See Partnerships Victoria (2003).

9. Brealey and Myers establish the linkage as follows: 'CEQ_1 can be calculated directly from the capital asset pricing model. The certainty-equivalent form of the CAPM states that the certainty equivalent value of the cash flow, C_1, is $PV = C_1 - \lambda \, cov \, (\hat{C}_1, \check{r}_m)$. Cov $(\hat{C}_1, \check{r}_m)$.is the covariance between the uncertain cash flow, $\hat{C}_1$, and the return on the market, $\check{r}_m$. Lambda λ, is a measure of the market price of risk. It is defined as $(r_m - r_f)/\sigma_m^2$. For example, if $r_m - r_f = .08$ and the standard deviation of market returns is $\sigma_m = .20$, then $\lambda = .08/.20^2 = 2$' (p. 240, n. 24).

10. Systematic risk is a measure of the extent with which a particular project's returns are likely to move when compared to the 'market portfolio', i.e. fluctuations in the economy. The measurement of systematic risk is known as beta and the beta of a project or asset determines the returns that an investor would require to invest in such a venture. Where beta is equal to one the project will move the same as the market portfolio. Where it exceeds one the project is more risky than the market, and conversely it is less risky if its beta is below one.

11. One attempt to estimate benchmark betas for PFI projects using observable market data for regulated utilities in the UK was undertaken by PricewaterhouseCoopers (2002) in a report discussed later in this chapter.

12. An example may illustrate the calculation required. Suppose a cashflow outlay where there are three possible outcomes: a budget outcome where the cost is, say, $1000, a downside case where the cost is, say, $1600 and an upside case where the cost is, say, $800. If we assume that both the downside and the upside cases each have a probability of 25 per cent, then we can calculate the expected value of the cash flow to be equal to

$$\$1000 + 25 \text{ per cent x } (\$800 - \$1000)$$
$$+ 25 \text{ per cent x } (\$1600 - \$1000) = \$1100.$$

However, this figure merely provides an estimate of the weighted average or expected cash-flow outcome. To determine the value of the risk for the PSC, it is necessary to estimate what the government would be willing to pay in order to know with certainty that the outcome would be $1100. In other words, if the government, by giving up the possibility of the outcome being $800 or $1000, could ensure that it would not be $1600, what would it be willing to pay over and above the additional expected $100 cost above that 'budgeted'? If this figure were assumed to be $80, that is, the government would be willing to pay $80 in order to ensure that the realized cost is $1100, the risk-adjusted PSC cost would be equal to $1000 + $100 + $80 = $1180. This is the value which ought to be incorporated into PSC cashflows which are being discounted at a risk-free rate.

13. The main contributions to state preference theory came from Arrow (1965), Hirschleifer (1970) and Karni (1985). While this model has enabled economists to examine choice under uncertainty, most have continued to focus on the analysis of risk. This focus on risk has the advantage of being able to draw on the modern theory of probability in which the conse-quences of economic entities' actions are alternative well-defined probability distributions over the random variables that they face (Machina, 1987).

14. Bayesian decision theory is a branch of statistical decision theory, and thus is concerned with the problem of making optimal decisions under uncertainty. Unlike orthodox statistics, which views probabilities as long run frequencies of repeatable events, Bayesian theory adopts a subjectivist view of probabilities in which probabilities may describe degrees of belief or states of partial knowledge. Bayes's theorem describes how we learn or, more correctly, how we ought to learn and says how our beliefs, expressed in terms of prior prob-abilities, should be modified by information, combining prior information with sample observations into a probability distribution (Lindley, 1985, p. 102). Bayesian decision theory consequently commences with information about the states of nature that is initially incom-plete. From this state of 'prior ignorance' or little prior knowledge, decision-makers form subjective probabilities about uncertain events. Over time, these subjective probabilities are tested and improved in a learning process until they approach asymptotically the true prob-abilities associated with the relevant events. For a recent exposition of Bayesian theory, see Bernando and Smith (2000).

15. For the UK accounting approach, the key base reference documents include:

   - UK Accounting Standards Board – *Financial Reporting Standard 5 – Reporting the Substance of Transactions* (FRS 5);
   - UK Accounting Standards Board – Application Note F, *Private Finance Initiatives and Similar Contracts* (AN F); and,
   - HM Treasury Taskforce Technical Note 1, *(Revised) How to Account for PFI Transactions* (TN 1).

16. Such a public interest test features in the Partnerships Victoria guidelines for practitioners.
17. Information is drawn from the National Audit Office report on the project (NAO, 2002).

7. Risk management

RISKS OF PPPS

This chapter analyses the risks of PPP arrangements from the perspectives of the various parties. For the public procurer, there is an obvious need to ensure that value for money has been achieved with public funds. To the project sponsors, such ventures are characterized by low equity in the project vehicle and a reliance on direct revenues to cover operating and capital costs, and service debt finance provided by banks and other financiers. Risk evaluation requires not only the analysis of risk from these different perspectives but also intimate knowledge of the project. To this end, as well as considering the general principles involved, we draw on practical experience of evaluating such projects to present a framework for assessing the risks, using as illustration a case study which is typical of many PPP projects.[1]

The project concerned is the Almond Valley and Seafield (AV&S) project involving the construction and operation of a water treatment facility for East of Scotland Water (ESW), with a services contract over 30 years between ESW (the public procurer) and Stirling Water. There is also a separate operating agreement between Stirling Water and Thames Water, the private sector operator of the works. The project reached financial close in March 1999 and Figure 7.1 sets out the links and key contractual arrangements between the parties involved. This brings out the point that a major infrastructure venture such as this is complex in terms of documentation, financing, taxation, technical details, sub-agreements, and so on. In many ways, it has to be complex to handle adequately the large number of risks inherent in such projects.

The public procurer seeks an effective use of public funds which, in the case of a PPP, can come from incentives created by the integration of asset design, construction techniques and operational practices, and by the transfer of key risks in design, construction delays, cost overruns and finance and insurance to private sector entities. For the project sponsors, PPP (and PFI) is essentially project financing, characterized by the formation of a highly geared special purpose company for the project and using project revenues to pay for operating costs and cover debt financing while giving the desired return on risk capital. A project must meet the public sector's value-for-money test and the private sector's need for robust revenue streams to support the financing arrangements (Grimsey and Graham, 1997).

The possibility that the predicted revenues do not materialize poses the greatest risk to the commercial viability of a project. This risk largely is borne by those providing finance or financial guarantees. Straight equity participation is generally low, only 5 per cent of the total funding (£4.95 million out of funding of £99 million pounds) in the case of the AV&S project. This situation is more starkly illustrated by the case considered earlier in Chapter 5 of a design-construct-manage-finance (DCMF) of a PFI private prison currently operating in Bridgend, South Wales which was funded with only £250,000 of equity constituting 0.3 per cent of the total funding of £83.5 million. Subordinated debt is often regarded as the equivalent of equity and is favoured in the UK because it enables the sponsors to extract cash from the project vehicle, where dividends would be restricted by the profit and loss account, and also because the interest is tax deductible. But in the AV&S project, subordinated debt comprised only a further 14 per cent of funds invested. A financial structure needs to be 'engineered' with as little recourse as possible to the sponsors while at the same time providing sufficient credit support so that the lenders are satisfied with the credit risks.

What are the risks? At least nine categories of risk face any infrastructure project (Chapman and Ward, 1997; Kerzner, 1989; Smith and Walter, 1990; and Thobani, 1998). These include:

- technical risk, due to engineering and design failures;
- construction risk, because of faulty construction techniques and cost escalation and delays in construction;
- operating risk, as a result of higher operating costs and maintenance costs;
- revenue risk, e.g. because of traffic shortfall or failure to extract resources, the volatility of prices and demand for products and services sold (e.g. minerals, office space, etc.) leading to revenue deficiency;
- financial risks arising from inadequate hedging of revenue streams and financing costs;
- *force majeure* risk, involving war and other calamities and acts of God.
- regulatory/political risks, resulting from planning changes, legal changes and unsupportive government policies;
- environmental risks, because of adverse environmental impacts and hazards;
- project default, as a result of failure of the project from a combination of any of the above.

Successful project design requires expert analysis of all these risks and the

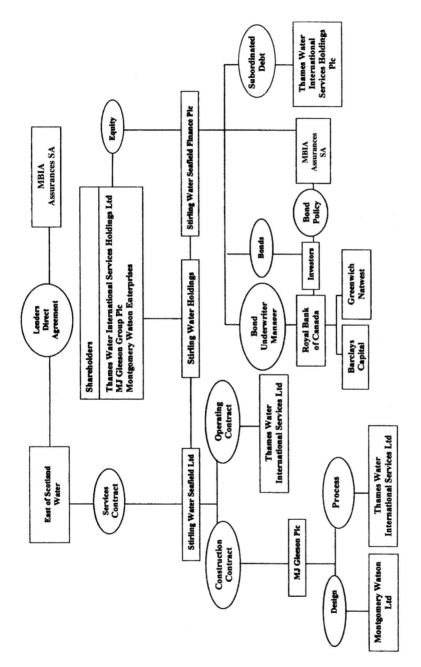

Figure 7.1   Contractual arrangements in a PFI/PPP project

design of contractual arrangements prior to competitive tendering that allocate risk burdens appropriately. With such a long list, it is important 'not to lose sight of the wood for the trees'. Many risks alter over the duration of the project; for example, the construction phase will give rise to different risks from those during the operation phase. Some technical design risks diminish once the engineering work is done. Planning risks change after the necessary procedures are met. Other risks, such as market-related ones, may continue over the life cycle of the project, and some risks may lie outside anyone's control.

For these reasons, some writers have sought to provide a taxonomy of risks according to type. Merna and Smith (1996) categorize risks as 'global' or 'elemental'. Global risks are those that are normally allocated through the project agreement and typically include political, legal, commercial and environmental risks, whereas elemental risks are those associated with the construction, operation, finance and revenue generation components of the project. Miller and Lessard (2001) classify risks into three categories. 'Market-related' risks derive from the markets for revenues (e.g. demand for road use) and financial markets (interest rates, exchange rates). 'Completion' risks come from technical designs or technologies employed, construction cost and time overruns, and operational problems. Finally, 'institutional risks' arise from laws and regulations, opposition from environmental and local groups, and government bodies wanting to renegotiate contracts. These classifications are designed to give some broad idea of the different sources of risk. Based on a study by Millar and Lessard of 60 large engineering projects around the world, managers ranked market-related risks as dominant in 42 per cent of projects, followed by technical risks (38 per cent) and institutional risks (20 per cent).

Most of these risks are common to any project-financing activity, and apply with more or less force depending on the project concerned. With some PPP agreements, revenue risk might be low, indeed negligible. For example, the revenue from a toll bridge might be more assured than that of an oilfield, while a private prison is likely to operate with a higher occupancy rate (e.g. 100 per cent) than a luxury hotel! At the same time, however, there is clearly the risk of losses arising from a changing political climate toward the provision of public services by the private sector, while the prices charged for many public sector services are politically sensitive and may be regulated or price-capped in some way.

Nevertheless, in principle, the risks of PPP projects seem little different from those of some other project financing activities, and can be evaluated using much the same basic techniques. The critical question, as always, is whether revenue streams can cover operating costs, service debt finance and provide returns to risk capital.

Consider the case of infrastructure in the form of a power plant. Sponsors of the power project borrow money to build a generation plant. The sponsors contract to supply power to utilities, projecting that the contract revenues will suffice to pay debt service and generate profits. But risks abound. Will the plant actually be built on time? Will the plant work? And will the market value of the contracts enable participants to avoid an income shortfall? Can rates be raised to levels that more or less equal the utility's costs for providing electricity, an activity that has historically been regulated by government? None of these questions can sensibly be dodged or ignored in project evaluation.

In fact, Lessard and Miller (2001) describe large engineering projects (and many PPPs are that) as being 'high-stake games' that are characterized by 'substantial irreversible commitments, skewed reward structures in case of success, and high probabilities of failure'. They go on:

> Once built, projects have little use beyond the original intended purpose. Potential returns can be good but they are often truncated. The journey to the period of revenue generation takes 10 years on average. Substantial front-end expenditures prior to committing large capital costs have to be carried. During the ramp-up period, market estimates are tested and the true worth of the project appears; sponsors may find that it is much lower than expected. (p. 2)

Ultimately, because of the high gearing, the 'bottom line' (i.e. project default risk) is borne by the financiers if debt cannot be repaid, although significant costs fall on the government if it has to 'step in' to guarantee continuity of services, which is why the public procurer must concern itself with the risks facing the private body and not simply home in on the lowest bid. When considering this default scenario, possible future cashflows can be thought of as falling into two categories:

1. Moderate (and perhaps not so moderate) deviations from estimated cashflow projections, resulting from fluctuating prices, costs, timing delays, minor technical problems, etc.
2. Disasters to a project, resulting from a major cost overrun, downturn in the economy, change in legal rulings, alteration to the political climate, environmental disaster etc., which could lead to project failure and bankruptcy.

This difference (according to Blatt, 1983) is not simply one of scale, but reflects the Knightian distinction between 'risk' and 'uncertainty' that we examined at length in the previous chapter. Blatt argues that the 'moderate deviations' can be described in statistical terms and handled by risk analysis. But 'disaster scenarios' cannot for they represent situations of true uncertainty where actual probabilities cannot be assigned to the possible occurrences because the potential outcomes and causal forces are not fully understood.

Knight considered that the main function of the 'entrepreneur' is to bear the brunt of uncertainty. The profits of enterprise ('pure profits' over and above interest payments on debt capital and/or dividend payments to shareholders) are a reward for facing this uncertainty. Sometimes, however, the reality in the financing of projects is often quite different to that envisaged by Knight. For example, developers who put up blocks of offices or flats for future sale commonly set up a new limited company for each new building. This company borrows money and/or sells equity shares. If the building fails to make a profit, this particular company goes bankrupt, but the sponsor may survive. The successful entrepreneur is often one who knows how to shift the burden of uncertainty onto others in such a way that he himself will survive, waiting for a more opportune time for others to again be persuaded to take chances with their money. As Blatt (1983) puts it, the prudent entrepreneur reacts to true uncertainty by attempting to make others bear the consequences. In many instances, investors, financiers and other creditors are at risk.[2] In other cases, the risk is to the pockets of taxpayers.

Clearly, in these circumstances, an analysis of the nature of the risks – and who bears them – is vital. As is the case with the theory of taxation, the distinction between the initial incidence and the final incidence must be borne in mind, and a detailed study of the project structure is important. Also the evaluation of projects requires the use of several risk analysis techniques tailored to suit the interests of the various parties to the project.[3] Nevertheless, the Knightian distinction remains. At least in theory, risk can be evaluated, calculated with different probabilities, hedged or transferred, pooled and diversified, transformed or insured against, but true uncertainty or a disaster scenario is something else again. How are risks handled in practice in PPPs? To answer this question we will look first at the risk allocation 'tools' and then consider risk analysis in the particular case of the AV&S project.

RISK ALLOCATION STRATEGIES

Under conventional procurement policies, risk taken on by government in owning and operating infrastructure typically carries substantial, and often unvalued, cost. Transferring some of the risk to a private party which can manage it at less cost can reduce the overall cost to government, although it is not cost-effective to transfer all risks. A PPP seeks to achieve the 'best' allocation. Basically, the risk allocation between the government and the private party in a PPP project is governed by three things:

1. specified service obligations;
2. the payment/pricing structure; and
3. express contractual provisions adjusting the risk allocation implicit in the basic structure.

These elements together allocate risk between the parties.

Service Obligations

As we have reiterated, the public sector aim under a PPP is not to procure assets, but to receive services (e.g. hospital and courtroom accommodation services). A clear services/output specification reflecting government policy objectives is a pre-condition to the successful realization of government aims for a partnership project, including achieving a desired level of risk transfer. Both the quantity and the quality of the service must be capable of being measured and compared with key performance indicators.

Service delivery specifications have to be drafted in a manner that accurately and clearly communicates government's output requirements, while neglecting as far as possible any prescription as to how the service is to be delivered or the asset maintained. This encourages innovation among the bids concerning the range of service delivery options and pricing proposals, which should in turn provide government with value for money. The actual technical/engineering method of service delivery and estimate of costs required to construct and maintain the asset and deliver the service ought to be matters entirely for the private party – at its own risk. Government's only concerns are, first, to be satisfied that the engineering solution is sufficiently robust to sustainably deliver the required services/output; and second, if the asset is to return to government with a useful life beyond the contract term, that it is suitably maintained during the contract term. If government attempts to define how the services are to be delivered (as opposed to simply specifying output specifications), it may unwittingly take back risk that would otherwise have been borne by the private party.

Payments Mechanisms

Development of a robust payment mechanism is needed for two reasons: first, to establish the necessary degree of risk allocation in a project; and, second, to induce appropriate performance by the private sector. The second outcome is particularly important. Unless payment mechanisms are in tune with government objectives for a project, the private party will not have the incentive to pursue actions geared to revenue flow which accord with public sector project objectives.

Depending on the project, features of the payment mechanism may include:

- service-based mechanisms with payments based on a combination of availability of the service and service performance levels;
- transaction- or usage-based elements for which payment is made per transaction unit; and
- benefits-based incentives where payment is linked to improvements in the business or organizational environment, such as safety or efficiency improvements.

Service-based payments are particularly suited to accommodation services, from which government may deliver core services, where usage may be variable but availability is a pre-requisite. Usage alone is a relatively crude basis for payment, although to some extent it may be a measure of consumer attraction and implicitly may indicate service quality. In the case of information technology services, the number of transactions may reflect the speed of the service which is in turn performance-related. Benefits-based elements can be valuable where improvements in safety, efficiency and natural or business environments are important and government objectives for a project are measurable.

Normally, given the range of government objectives involved in PPP projects, payment mechanisms include at least the first two, and perhaps all three, of the features described above. For example, in the case of the PPP to provide non-core accommodation-type services for the Victoria County Court, payment is made on the basis of the availability of courtrooms (involving both physical and functional availability to specified performance standards) in combination with actual usage.[4] But the general idea of the payment mechanism is simple enough and rests on the principle that the transfer of risk to the private sector gives it the correct incentives. Having some or all of the revenue stream at risk due to lack of availability means that there are no incentives to reduce the quality of services, while there is every incentive to build into the design of the facilities features that help maintain service quality.

Risk Take-back

This was discussed earlier in general terms. In theory, the conception of risk allocation is straightforward. The government frees itself entirely from asset-based risk (including design, construction, operation and residual value risk), and becomes the purchaser of long-term risk-free services with reduced payments made or compensation received if they are not provided at the right time or to a satisfactory quality. In practice, risk allocation in a PPP is more complicated than that. Rather than shifting all risk to the private sector, the aim is to allocate risk to the party best able to bear it. The government may agree to assume some risks, in effect 'take back' certain risks, for which the private party would charge too much if the risk transfer to the private party were to remain complete. Generally, a risk matrix is employed as an organizing framework for the allocation of risk.

A standardized risk matrix framework is set out in Table 7.1. Its purpose is to illustrate how a more detailed risk matrix can be constructed to show the range of risks that may apply to each project phase and, broadly, to set out the possible public sector position on allocation. When prepared and used wisely, a risk matrix can be a useful tool to both government practitioners and the private sector.[5] Optimal risk allocation aims to minimize both the chances of project risks materializing and the consequences if they do. It has two elements: (1) optimal risk management and impetus to achieve it; and (2) value for money. The first of these is based on the view that the party best able to control a risk should be allocated that risk. The second element – value for money – is related to the first, in that the party best able to manage a risk should also be able to manage it at least cost.

Although many risks are in the control of each party, to some degree certain risks are completely outside the control of both parties. If neither party is in a position of full control, the risk allocation should reflect how the private party 'prices' the risk and whether it is reasonable for government to pay that price, taking into account the likelihood of the risk eventuating, the cost to government if it retained that risk, and government's ability to mitigate any consequences if the risk materializes. Alternatively, the parties may share the risk through various risk-sharing mechanisms.

Essentially, in risk allocation, nothing is free. When bidding for a project, the private party estimates the project risks and their potential impacts on project revenues, and in effect sets premiums to insulate itself from the financial results of materialized risks. The premiums are then averaged across the project or all projects in which the private party is involved and are weighted according to the probability and consequences of various kinds of events. In this way, the risk premium calculated can be visualized as a form of self-insurance. Nevertheless, the financial consequences of some risk, either in full or in part, may be transferred explicitly to others, including insurance providers.

Private parties accept most risks, provided the premium paid suffices. The question for government is whether the risk premium is good value for money or whether it is more cost-effective to accept the risk itself, taking into account the likelihood of a particular risk occurring and how government bodies may be able to mitigate the impacts. For this purpose, a risk management plan is needed which involves the following elements:

Table 7.1 Risk matrix for public sector/private sector infrastructure investments

Type of risk	Source of risk	Risk taken by
Site risks		
Site conditions	Ground conditions, supporting structures	Construction contractor
Site preparation	Site redemption, tenure, pollution/discharge, obtaining permits, community liaison	Operating company/project company
Land use	Pre-existing liability	Government
	Native title, cultural heritage	Government
Technical risks	Fault in tender specifications	Government
	Contractor design fault	Design contractor
Construction risks		
Cost overrun	Inefficient work practices and wastage of materials	Construction contractor
	Changes in law, delays in approval etc.	Project company/investors
Delay in completion	Lack of coordination of contractors, failure to obtain standard planning approvals	Construction contractor
	Insured *force majeure* events	Insurer
Failure to meet performance criteria	Quality shortfall/defects in construction/commissioning tests failure	Construction contractor/project company

Operating risks		
Operating cost overrun	Project company request for change in practice	Project company/investors
	Industrial relations, repairs, occupational health and safety, maintenance, other costs	Operator
	Government change to output specifications	Government
	Operator fault	Operator
Delays or interruption in operation	Government delays in granting or renewing approvals, providing contracted inputs	Government
	Operator fault	Operator
Shortfall in service quality	Project company fault	Project company/investors
	Contractual violations by government-owned support network	Government
	Contractual violations by private supplier	Private supplier
	Other	Project company/investors
Revenue risks		
Increase in input prices	Fall in revenue	Project company/investors
Change in taxes, tariffs		Project company/investors
Demand for output	Decreased demand	Project company/investors

Table 7.1 continued

Type of risk	Source of risk	Risk taken by
Financial risks		
Interest rates	Fluctuations with insufficient hedging	Project company/government
Inflation	Payments eroded by inflation	Project company/government
Force majeure risk	Floods, earthquake, riots, strikes	Shared
Regulatory/political risks		
Changes in law	Construction period	Construction contractor
	Operating period	Project company, with government compensation as per contract
Political interference	Breach/cancellation of licence	Government
	Expropriation	Insurer, project company/investor
	Failure to renew approvals, discriminatory taxes, import restrictions	Government
Project default risks	Combination of risks	Equity investors followed by banks, bondholders and institutional lenders
	Sponsor suitability risk	Government
Asset risks	Technical obsolescence	Project company
	Termination	Project company/operator
	Residual transfer value	Government, with compensation for maintenance obligations

- identify all the project risks. These include the general risks which feature in the risk matrix and the project specific risks (for example, the risk to public health in a water project);
- determine the core services which are to be provided by government and for which the risk cannot be transferred to the private party;
- examine each risk and identify those which government is best placed to manage as a result of the level of control it exercises and those which it may otherwise not be optimal to leave with the private party. These should in each instance be taken back by government;
- ascertain whether any of the remaining risks should be shared because of market convention or specific factors relating to the project; and
- adjust the risk allocation inherent in the basic PPP adjustment structure and use the contract to reflect that adjustment and allow for any power imbalance between the parties arising from special government powers.

On practical grounds, the government must identify, on a project-by-project basis, the risks that it will take back before it puts the project to the market. Generally speaking, those risks assumed by government are likely to include factors such as the risk of legislation or of a policy change discriminating against the project, the risk of government wishing to change (e.g. increase) the service standards or volumes, some elements of antiquities or indigenous title risk and some elements of pre-existing latent defect and contamination risk. Table 7.2 illustrates how an allocation might work out in practice, the example being that of a PPP for a privately operated prison project under the 'serviced infrastructure' model. A more detailed case study of risk management procedures follows.

RISK ANALYSIS IN PRACTICE – A CASE STUDY

The Project

The AV&S project constituted a major initiative undertaken by ESW (East of Scotland Water, which is now amalgamated with the other Scottish water authorities) to improve the quality of the water within the River Almond and the Firth of Forth and to implement an alternative to the disposal of sewage sludge at sea. The project was driven by the authority's need to comply with its obligations under the Urban Water Treatment (Scotland) Regulations 1994. The project was one of around ten PFI schemes implemented in Scotland in order to comply with the new regulatory standards.

Table 7.2   Risk allocation in a PPP prison project

Government risks	Private sector risks	Shared risks
Site approvals	Site conditions	Technology
Specifications/cell design functionallty	Contractor design fault	Custodial best practice
	Cost overrun	*Force majeure*
Contractual land use rights	Construction delay	
Change to licence conditions	Building maintenance/service cost overrun	
Government delays, e.g. granting approvals	Shortfall in quality	
Demand	Performance-availability of accommodation at required standards	
Political/sovereign		
Discriminatory change in law	Prisoner mix within bands, i.e. flexibility to respond to change	
	Changes in general taxes and tariffs	
	Interest rates	
	Non-discriminatory change in law	
	Environmental risks	

Following a long procurement process of over two years, on March 1999 ESW entered into the 30-year services contract with Stirling Water pursuant to which Stirling Water agreed to upgrade and improve the treatment of wastewater from the feeding catchments of Almond Valley and Seafield and to provide new arrangements as an alternative to the disposal of sewage sludge at sea. The main parties to the project and an indication of their connecting relationships were shown in Figure 7.1, but in summary:

- ESW is the procuring entity and the authority responsible for providing water, collecting and treating wastewater and disposing of sewage sludges within its region;
- Stirling Water is the special purpose company set up for the purpose of financing, constructing and operating the AV&S project;
- Thames Water, MJ Gleeson and Montgomery Watson are the project sponsors providing risk capital and acting respectively as the operator, contractor and designer to Stirling Water; and

- MBIA is providing the credit enhancement insurance policy so that the project can attain a credit rating of AAA. While institutional investors purchased the bonds, the MBIA policy unconditionally and irrevocably guarantees scheduled repayments of principal and interest under the bonds issued and therefore MBIA effectively assumed the role of senior lender.

Considering the financial arrangements of the contract, Stirling Water funded the £99 million project from:

- £79.217 million of 27.5-year AAA rated credit – enhanced bonds paying a fixed coupon of 5.822 per cent;
- £14.835 million of subordinated debt provided by Thames Water. The subordinated debt has the same term as the bonds and a similar interest rate; and
- £4.95 million of equity split between Thames Water (49 per cent), MJ Gleeson (41 per cent) and Montgomery Watson (10 per cent). The internal rate of return (IRR) on the equity was projected to be 16.56 per cent nominal and 12.5 per cent real at financial close.

Project Risks

Stirling Water as the project vehicle took on certain construction and operating risks over the contract period but allocated away contractually many of these risks to the construction contractor and the operator, as is usual under such arrangements. It retained the risk that projected maintenance costs are exceeded, such as those arising from shorter than anticipated asset life-spans, increased inflation on specific items of plant and machinery or the requirement to carry out unexpected repairs.

After the plants were commissioned Stirling Water received payment based on the volume of wastewater treated. The payment mechanism is the key to the risk apportionment and is not like other PFI deals where the operator is paid on making the facility available. The contract borrows the idea of shadow tolls paid within payment bands (ie. defined levels of traffic volume) from the UK's DBFO programme for roads, discussed in Chapter 3 (pp. 60–62). The aim of such a structure is to allocate a sufficient element of volume risk to the service company and also to limit the authority's exposure to an increase in payments arising from a greater than anticipated volume of wastewater delivered. The AV&S payment bands are as follows:

- The first band for wastewater treatment is for between 0 and 90,000 cubic metres per annum and pays 13.883p. This band is designed to generate sufficient revenue to cover fixed operating and maintenance costs and outstanding amounts due under the bond issue;

- The second band for wastewater treatment is for between 90,000 and 101,000 m^3 pa and pays 9.2555p. This band is designed to provide sufficient revenue to meet payments under the subordinated debt; and
- The third band for wastewater treatment is for between 101,000 and 107,000 m^3 pa and pays 4.628p. This band is designed to meet the shareholders' target investment returns.
- The fourth band for wastewater treatment is for flows in excess of 107,000 m^3 pa and is free of charge. This band is designed to cap the payments to be made by ESW.

Payment above the third band effectively is capped, thereby limiting ESW's exposure to payments under the contract, while there is a separate rate for the treatment and disposal of imported sludge. The contract provides for payment to be subject to performance-related adjustments geared to any breaches in environmental discharge consent standards set by the Scottish environmental protection agency. A major concern for Stirling Water is the impact of the quality of the wastewater delivered to the works by ESW on the operator's ability to treat this wastewater to a standard which results in the discharged wastewater and sludge complying with the required consents. For this reason the contract contains a list of influent concentration levels. In the event that these are exceeded and that as a result Stirling Water is unable to treat the wastewater to the required standard, then Stirling Water will nevertheless be entitled to payment in full.

Stirling Water is protected through the contract against circumstances influenced by ESW that would impact on the volume of wastewater such as the issuing of trade effluent discharge consents, the introduction of water metering or greatly increased capital investment in the sewerage infrastructure leading to a reduction of water infiltration to the sewers. However, under the payment mechanism, failure to achieve forecast levels of volume throughput or suffering larger than expected deductions for poor performance would result in lower than forecast revenues, which would impact on the equity return and may adversely effect Stirling Water's ability to make repayments of subordinated debt and even coupons on the bonds.

The proportion of the tariff indexed to the retail prices index (RPI) is 65 per cent, applied to all three revenue-generating bands. The remaining 35 per cent of the tariff is not subject to indexation but is fixed for the contract term. Proportionally this division approximates to the percentage of the nominal cashflow used to service the bond financing. However, it is possible that there will not be a precise match between Stirling Water's revenues and costs, resulting in costs rising faster than revenue arising under the contract and this risk is borne by Stirling Water and its shareholders.

The risk of any adverse changes in law is an important element and on the

AV&S project the risk is shared between ESW and Stirling Water over the first ten years of the contract. After this time, the risk is borne by ESW.

Risk Analysis

Having sketched the key risks inherent in the project it is important to look at the nature and quantum of risk from the different perspectives of the main parties to the project. As a guide to the methodology employed, Figure 7.2 provides a flow chart of the analytical approach. For each of the three major groups of entities, it summarizes their risk perspective, the key variables, the major risks they face, and the risk analysis that is appropriate. There are several risk analysis techniques available ranging in complexity from simple expected cost analysis through sensitivity analysis and on to more complex probabilistic techniques involving computer-aided statistical sampling. The technique that should be used, as indicated, is largely dependent on the exposure of the party to the risk and the nature of the return expected by the party.

Procurer
ESW, as the procurer, was mainly interested in the expected costs in the form of the payments they would have to make under the contract. In accordance with government guidelines the projected payments to each of the bidders were discounted at 6 per cent real (the then specified discount rate) and summed to derive the net present value (NPV) of each of the bids. From ESW's perspective, the risk analysis centred on establishing equality of treatment between bidders for bid evaluation and to facilitate a comparison with the public sector comparator in order to demonstrate value for money in NPV terms. Part of the value-for-money analysis involves a comparison of the project against a traditional public sector procurement and operation route in the form of the public sector comparator (as discussed in the previous chapter). The main risks analysed from this perspective concerned the following issues:

- The contract was conditional on obtaining planning consent and a risk-sharing mechanism was agreed whereby ESW would pay for a proportion of the planning change costs through an adjustment to the tariffs.
- Stirling Water had qualified their bid in relation to passing the risk of costs resulting from finds such as antiquities being uncovered during the construction phase of the project back to ESW.
- Bidders were also asked to calculate the impact of delay to the programmed contract signing date in terms of the acceleration costs necessary still to achieve the commencement date for the main period for wastewater treatment of January 2001. ESW and its advisers made an assessment of the likely delay and adjusted the bids accordingly.

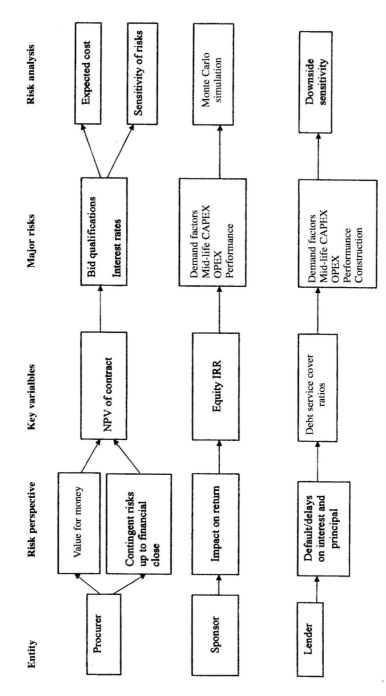

Figure 7.2   Flow chart of analytical approach

The risks were analysed by establishing their expected cost to ESW and adjusting the NPV of the bid. In the case of Stirling Water this resulted in approximately a 1 per cent increase in the NPV of the bid. When compared with the competitors, this led to the conclusion that their bid provided ESW with the most economically advantageous proposal relative to the other bidders.

Under the Project Development Agreement, ESW also retained the risk of movements in the underlying interest rates up to financial close, a practice common to such projects. In this case, the specific risk is that any increase in the level of interest rates, and thus of the financing costs for the project, prior to financial close will result in a higher tariff being levied, while the discount rate used in the analysis is fixed at 6 per cent real. Interest rate risk is generally difficult to quantify with any real precision. To get a feel for the likely impact of this risk, sensitivity analysis[6] was carried out on the financial model that yielded the results shown in Table 7.3. This analysis indicates that ESW was reasonably well protected against movements in the underlying interest rate, with a moderate rate increase of 1 per cent leading to an increase in the NPV of the cost stream of the project of 3.6 per cent (the approximate gradient of the interest rate sensitivity relationship).

ESW also carry inflation rate risk to the extent that RPI deviates from that projected in the financial model. While it is generally accepted that there is a link between interest rates and inflation the analysis looked at these independently since inflation rates may not be reflected fully in the inflation premia built into interest rates.[7] Like interest rates, inflation is difficult to predict and sensitivity techniques were again used. Table 7.4 shows the variation in the NPVs at inflation assumptions ranging from 2 per cent to 6 per cent. The NPVs are reduced at higher inflation rates partly because the debt element of the financing being serviced by the revenue stream of the project has not been

Table 7.3 Procurer: interest rate sensitivity

Interest rate (%)	% increase/decrease in NPV of expected cost stream from base case
Base case −1	−3.3
Base case −0.5	−1.7
Base case	Base case NPV
Base case +0.5	+1.8
Base case +1	+3.6
Base case +1.5	+5.4
Base case +2	+7.5

indexed. The effect of discounting an element of the project's revenue stream fixed in nominal terms at a fixed discount rate of 6 per cent real will lower the NPV of the debt element of the revenue stream at higher inflation rates and therefore lower the overall NPVs. The analysis demonstrates that ESW is well protected against the risk that inflation will increase in the future.

It is widely acknowledged that sensitivity analysis is limited to indicating the potential effects on an outcome, in this case the NPV, if a movement in the variable occurs. Critics of this form of analysis argue that it is not of much use unless some indication is given of how likely it is that a quantified movement will occur. This argument ignores the fact that some important economic variables cannot easily be quantified in terms of likelihood and extent of change. Who in the UK, for example, during the late 1970s could have reasonably predicted that inflation would be 3 per cent or less in the late 1990s, a period of only 20 years – that is, ten years less than the contract term in this case study? In such circumstances, sensitivity analysis provides a useful tool for analysing these risks in terms of bid evaluation.

Sponsors

From the sponsors' perspective, the risk analysis centres around establishing the potential impact on the equity return. For the purpose of this exercise, the distinction between subordinated debt and equity is ignored because the degree of subordination gives subordinated debt virtually the same characteristics as equity. In order to review Stirling Water's financial proposals from the sponsors' perspective an analysis of the impact of the equity risks on the financial model had to take account of potential upside as well as downside risk.

A simulation exercise was therefore carried out using the following methodology. First, a realistic downside (and upside) case for each risk was defined by ESW's technical adviser Halcrow Crouch to establish a triangular risk distribution for each risk. The relevant risks for this analysis were:

Table 7.4   Procurer: inflation sensitivity

RPI assumption (%)	% increase/decrease in NPV of expected cost stream from base case
2	+4.79
3	+1.47
3.5	Base Case NPV
4	−1.36
5	−3.79
6	−5.90

- volume risk;
- the risk of mid-life capital expenditure and asset management costs being greater than forecast;
- operating cost; and
- operating performance.

While construction delay is an important project risk it was not included. This was because the analysis looked at the risks from the project sponsors' perspective as equity investors in Stirling Water. For them, delay risk is dealt with contractually through liquidated damages contained in the construction contract and also business interruption insurance. Effectively, therefore, the risk resides with the construction contractor and the insurer and not with the project sponsors.

Second, having delineated the relevant risks for examination, a simulation exercise was carried out using the @RISK computer software package to determine the distribution of the relevant risks overall. Then, third, from this analysis an assessment was made of the impact on the blended equity/ subordinated debt IRR.

The @RISK software package uses a Monte Carlo simulation process to perform a risk analysis.[8] Simulation in this sense refers to a method whereby the distribution of possible outcomes is generated by letting the computer recalculate the financial model over and over again, each time using different randomly selected sets of values for the probability distributions contained in the spreadsheet model. In effect, the computer is trying all valid combinations of the values of input variables to simulate all possible outcomes.

A summary of the results of the quantitative risk analysis on the Stirling Water financial model is shown in Table 7.5. This analysis suggests, perhaps surprisingly, that the sponsors are unlikely to achieve the base level rates of

Table 7.5   Sponsors: equity/subordinated debt risk analysis

Simulation	Decrease in blended equity IRR
Minimum simulation result	Base case − 7.17%
5% probability of returns being less than:	Base case − 5.48%
25% probability of the returns being less than:	Base case − 3.9%
50% probability of the returns being less than:	Base case − 2.52%
75% probability of the returns being less than:	Base case − 1.47%
95% probability of returns being less than:	Base case − 0.57%
Maximum simulation result	Base case − 0.06%

return, yet they are taking a reasonable amount of financial risk commensurate with risk capital investments in such projects. Although the relevant risks modelled contained upside potential, the analysis also indicates that there is, overall, no likely financial upside for the sponsors. The main opportunity for financial upside comes from increased wastewater volumes, but the payments made by ESW are capped as described earlier. It is perhaps worth noting that the procurer in this case was in a strong bargaining position; England and France have some of the largest water companies in the world and they were vying for a foothold in the relatively small Scottish market.

Senior lenders

For senior lenders the nature of non-recourse or limited recourse funding clearly carries a rather different risk or credit assessment than a conventional full recourse loan where the enforcement of security by the lender is additional to its ability to sue the borrower, and the lender can assess the value of the assets used as collateral. With project financing, the facilities often do not have a capital worth, in terms of a wide market, to which lenders would wish to attribute value. Lenders, of course, insist on having the opportunity to step in and rescue a failing project but they cannot simply sell off the asset to realize value. In contracts such as AV&S, the asset effectively takes the form of the contract with the procuring authority, it is therefore understandable that senior lenders tend to take a pessimistic view where risk analysis is concerned. The key difference between the senior lenders and the sponsors is that for the senior lender holding debt rather than equity there is never any potential upside gain in the project, only downside risk that could reduce the ability of the borrower to make principal and interest payments under the loan agreement.

Senior lenders therefore focus on cover to the income stream over the term of the loan and analyse risk to establish robustness by reference to cover ratios. The most important of these ratios are the loan life cover ratio (LLCR) and the annual debt service cover ratio (ADSCR). The LLCR provides a snapshot on a given date of the NPV of the projected cashflows from that date until retirement of the loan relative to the loan outstanding on that particular date. The ADSCR is a historic ratio that measures the cashflow for the previous year in relation to the amount of loan principal and interest payable for that period.

The sensitivities tested from the lenders' perspective are intended to capture the risks left with the service company rather than the project as a whole, taking account of the fact that it will seek to mitigate key risks by allocating them away contractually. The main instruments used for allocating risk are:

- the design and construction (D&C) contract which mitigates the service company's exposure to design risk and construction cost and time over-run risk; and
- the operation and maintenance (O&M) contract which mitigates the service company's exposure to performance risk and operations and maintenance cost risk.

It is therefore crucial to the financial robustness of bids, given the highly geared financing structure envisaged, that these risks should be allocated away from the service company under strong contracts to suitable counter-parties. However, even when risk is transferred contractually, some residual risk will remain with the service company. For instance, if the operating costs turned out to be significantly greater than originally forecast it is conceivable that the service company could decide that it was in its best interests to share the pain with the O&M contractor by agreeing to a price increase to absorb some of the increased cost, rather than running the risk of the O&M contractor abandoning the contract. The operating expenditure (OPEX) and capital expenditure (CAPEX) sensitivities tested are intended to reflect this residual risk.

Table 7.6 displays the results of the robustness analysis on Stirling Water's financial model. The ADSCR and LLCR (see earlier definitions of these cover ratios) only fall below the minimum requirement (ADSCR of 1.15 and LLCR of 1.15) under the OPEX, flow, and combined scenarios. However, in no case does the ADSCR or LLCR fall below 1.0, which would indicate a default under the loan agreement. This analysis indicates to the senior lenders that the Stirling Water financing plan is reasonably robust to support the level of funding anticipated.

Table 7.6 Senior lenders: robustness analysis of cashflows

Sensitivity	Change*	ADSCR	LLCR
Base case financial model	–	1.26	1.32
Construction cost	+3%	1.26	1.32
OPEX	+12.5%	1.08	1.15
Downside flow		1.07	1.12
Mid-life CAPEX	+10%	1.24	1.29
Operational performance	–2%	1.20	1.26
Combined downside: downside flow plus mid-life CAPEX		1.04	1.10

Note: *As defined by ESW's technical adviser (see text).

Overall, the combination of risk analysis techniques used on the AV&S project demonstrated that:

- To the procuring entity ESW the project delivers value for money and satisfies the main government criteria for investing in capital projects.
- For the project sponsors the project has reasonable levels of return anticipated in the base case and they are also taking a reasonable amount of financial risk commensurate with such investments.
- From the viewpoint of lenders the downside sensitivity testing suggests that the project is sufficiently robust and financially stable.

Conclusion

Project finance and PPP/PFI arrangements are founded on the transfer of risk from the public to the private sector in circumstances where the private sector is best placed to manage the risk. The general principles are common to all public sectors insofar as the projects seek to shift risk from the public sector to the supplier and offer a profit incentive to the private sector in return. However, the principal aim for the public sector is to achieve value for money in the services provided while ensuring that the private sector entities meet their contractual obligations properly and efficiently.

Having satisfied value-for-money and risk transfer principles, fundamentally PPP projects are viable only if a robust, long-term revenue stream, over the period of the concession, can be established. A framework for investigating and carrying out an analysis of the risks has been outlined in this chapter that systematically views project risk from the perspectives of the procuring entity, the project sponsors and the senior lenders. For a project to be successful, the differing (and conflicting) needs of these parties must be met in the risk allocation process, and this would seem to have been achieved in the wastewater treatment project used as a case study to illustrate the application of the framework.

Nevertheless, value-for-money calculations revolve around prospective forecasts of the returns. For these to eventuate, the contractual obligations must be realized. This is the topic of the next chapter.

NOTES

1. This chapter draws extensively on Grimsey and Lewis (2002a).
2. Banks learnt this lesson, to their cost, during the real estate lending sagas of the late 1980s and during the Asian financial crisis (see Lewis, 1994; Bentick and Lewis, 2004). The other example offered by Blatt is of interest in view of our earlier discussion of private sector involvement in infrastructure investment in the nineteenth century. We reproduce his comments here.

> The expansion of the US railway system in the mid-nineteenth century was a highly risky proposition, and plenty of people got stung; but not the promoters of the major railway companies. It was common practice to form two companies: (1) a railway company proper, which issued and sold shares, mostly in London, and (2) a railway construction company, in which the shares were closely held by the promoters. The railway company, having raised capital in London, commissioned the railway construction company to construct a railroad. By no accident at all, the construction turned out to be extremely expensive, so the railway company paid out huge sums to the railway construction company. In due course, the railway company went bankrupt, the shares were worthless, the English investors had lost their money; the American promoters had their railroad and the money. (Blatt, 1983, p. 268)

3. There is a large number of studies examining risk analysis techniques. In addition to references cited earlier, the World Bank (1997) and Uher and Toakley (1997) consider development project risks. Miller and Lessard (2001) consider large engineering projects, while Fender *et al.* (2001) review the stress testing employed by financial institutions.
4. The Victorian County Court project was the first infrastructure project delivered under the Victorian Government's 'Partnerships Victoria' policy and, consistent with that policy, involves the sharing of systematic risks by the government and private providers. The government required the private sector to take the long-term ownership risk of the new Court facility. The private sector was also required to undertake the financing, design, construction and specified ancillary service delivery. The government indicated that it was prepared to enter into a 20-year contract with the private sector entity to provide accommodation and specified ancillary services. Beyond providing support for planning and other approval processes, it was not the intention of the government to accept project risks, which it is not in a position to manage. As part of the ordinary commercial arrangements, the government's objective was to minimize the extent of its risk exposure. The underlying commercial arrangements for the new facility reflect the government's view that it is in the business of providing core court services, not providing the underlying asset.
5. The risk matrix in Table 7.1 is based on Grimsey and Lewis (1999).
6. Sensitivity analysis is described in the UK *Green Book* in the following terms:

> Sensitivity analysis is fundamental to appraisal . It is used to test the vulnerability of options to unavoidable future uncertainties. Spurious accuracy should be avoided, and it is essential to consider how conclusions may alter, given the likely range of values that key variables may take. Therefore, the need for sensitivity analysis should always be considered, and, in practice, dispensed with only in exceptional cases. (HM Treasury, 2003a, p. 32)

7. Reasons why this nominal interest rate may not increase by expected inflation are examined in Lewis and Mizen (2000).
8. According to the UK *Green Book* (HM Treasury, 2003a, p. 33):

> Monte Carlo analysis is a risk modelling technique that presents both the range, as well as the expected value, of the collective impact of various risks. It is useful when there are many variables with significant uncertainties. It can be a useful technique but expert advice is required to ensure it is properly applied, especially when risks are not independent of each other. Before undertaking or commissioning such an analysis, it is useful to know how data will be fed into the model, how the results will be presented, and how decisions may be affected by the information generated.

From the discussion in the two preceding paragraphs, it would seem that these requirements were satisfied in this application of the technique.

8. The governance of partnerships

STAGES OF A PPP TRANSACTION

A number of major steps are involved in a PPP transaction. These are normally divided into the development phase and the realization phase. Figure 8.1 presents a graphical depiction of the two phases. Financial close, the time at which the financing package has been agreed and committed to, marks the end of one and the beginning of the other. Because the financiers commit to financing a project based on a completed contractual framework between the public procurer and the project company, the commercial close, or the signing of the PPP agreement is a defining pre-requisite for reaching financial close. So far in this volume we have concentrated on some of the issues related to reaching this point.

This chapter considers the post-financial close stages, and focuses in particular on contract management. Once the contract has been signed, it then has to be managed by the public sector agency which is responsible for monitoring and implementing the contract. Our aim here is to outline a contractual management and reporting regime to aid this function, indicating the degree to which project objectives are being achieved and providing an early warning of potential problems. Special emphasis is given to establishing, first, key reporting requirements for the meeting of performance quality standards and, second, a performance monitoring system for assessing the 'health' of the contracting enterprise and the risk of default – an important factor when government is unable to walk away from providing the core services.

Almost invariably, the contracting private sector enterprise is an SPV, established as a separate legal entity to undertake the defined activity. The SPV will enter into subcontracts with one or more organizations for the execution of these activities, and agreements for financing the SPV will typically be concluded at the same time. As explained in Chapter 5, SPVs are used in PPP projects to enable lending to the project to be non-recourse to the sponsors, to keep the assets and liabilities of the project off the sponsors' balance sheets, and to insulate the project and project returns from a bankruptcy of any of the sponsors. Since most large PPPs involve an SPV, we will assume this to be the case.

Generally, the realization phase is divided into the detailed design, construction and operational stages. During the detailed design stage the SPV

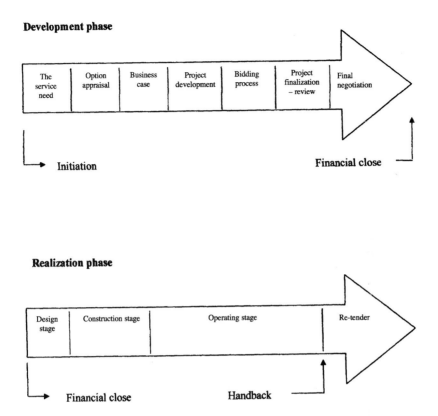

Development phase

| The service need | Option appraisal | Business case | Project development | Bidding process | Project finalization – review | Final negotiation |

Initiation   Financial close

Realization phase

| Design stage | Construction stage | Operating stage | Re-tender |

Financial close   Handback

Figure 8.1   Chronology of a PPP transaction

has the design plans developed, and conducts various planning, organizational, administrative, and set-up functions. Costs incurred by the SPV during this stage are normally met by the equity investors. This early injection of equity gives the other participants confidence about the equity suppliers' commitment to the project. The construction stage is normally the most capital intensive. Costs of construction are covered predominantly by debt and equity.

Once the facility has been commissioned and services are being delivered, the payment flow (or unitary charge) by the public body provides funds that are expected to cover the costs of delivering the services and debt service obligations, while providing a return on risk capital. The unitary charge is generally split between volume and performance criteria (in the case, say, of a new road or sewerage treatment works) and availability in terms of whether the asset is available for use (in terms of buildings). Usually both of these, with the addition of benefits-based incentives geared to safety or efficiency improvements, would apply.

Concession periods can vary, but typically lie in the range of 10 to 50 years. At the end of the concession, the project company is normally required to return the asset to public ownership, under pre-defined handback technical parameters. At this point, the public procurer is left with a choice of re-procuring the operation of the asset by means of a re-tendering process, taking on this function itself, or possibly using the assets for some other purpose including their sale.

This all assumes that nothing goes wrong in the interim, and the government needs to create and maintain a monitoring system to ensure that specified services are supplied to a guaranteed, measurable standard within scheduled payment bands. The contractual performance specifications and the associated incentive payment mechanism are the primary legal means by which the public sector can enforce the project objectives and risk-transfer provisions. The specification sets out the scope and quality of services that need to be provided. In turn, the payment mechanism sets out precisely how the SPV is paid for providing the specified services. Performance regimes and payment mechanisms are central to the success of the project because they provide commercial incentives for the private sector to manage risks properly.

Where contracted standards are not fulfilled, there are mechanisms built into the contract to rectify any underperformance. However, for long-term contracts such as those for a BOT or PPP project 'typically the classical law's remedies simply are not used by the parties' (Campbell and Harris, 1993, p. 168), and disputes are frequently settled without explicit reference to potential contractual legal sanctions. Those authors seek to develop the principles which should govern these exchanges. Their starting point is that efficient long-term contractual behaviour must be understood as consciously cooperative, if only because in practice all long-term contracts are necessarily 'incomplete', involving an element of irreducible uncertainty. Consequently contracts must be interpreted with forbearance and with deference to prevailing customs and practice if a collaborative relationship is to be maintained, and their governance requires an open-ended approach that leaves substantial ground for the variation or complete renegotiation of prior commitments.

Obviously, it is in most parties' interests to seek to avoid disputes, and here we come back to the importance of teamwork and working at the partnership to avoid disagreements. But, inevitably, disputes will arise and when they do a variety of dispute resolution methods are available, ranging from informal negotiations between the parties concerned, through more formal interventions involving third parties, to legal proceedings. These options are listed in Table 8.1. Negotiation is by far the most commonly used approach to resolving disputes, and it is undoubtedly the most effective in terms of cost, call on

Table 8.1   Dispute resolution techniques

Negotiation – the most common form of dispute resolution where the parties themselves attempt to resolve the dispute

Mediation – a private and structured form of negotiation assisted by a third party that is initially non-binding. If settlement is reached it can become a legally binding contract

Conciliation – as mediation, but a conciliator can propose a solution

Neutral evaluation – a private and non-binding technique whereby a third party, usually legally qualified, gives an opinion on the likely outcome at trial as a basis for settlement discussions

Expert determination – a private process involving an independent expert with inquisitorial powers who gives a binding decision

Adjudication – an expert is instructed to rule on a technical issue, primarily used in construction disputes, where awards are binding on the parties at least on an interim basis or until a further process is invoked

Arbitration – a formal, private and binding process where the dispute is resolved by the decision of a nominated third party, the arbitrator or arbitrators

Litigation – the formal process whereby claims are taken through the civil courts and conducted in public. The judgments are binding on parties subject to rights of appeal

---

Source: Office of Government Commerce (2002a).

management resources, speed of resolution, and the maintenance of open lines of communication. These negotiations rely on the cooperative efforts of each of the parties made in good faith so as to realize their joint objectives. In this respect, the contract should be seen not as a stand-alone document but as part of a reciprocated relational web binding the parties together and which is to be kept intact in all but the most acute circumstances. It is in this context that contract management must proceed, with monitoring simply a periodic review of performance to ascertain its conformity with the agreement.

CONTRACT MANAGEMENT

Contract management can be defined as the processes undertaken to maintain the integrity of the contract, and to ensure that the roles and responsibilities contractually demarcated are fully understood and are carried out to the contracted standard. Management procedures need to be established to oversee project delivery, deal with contract variations, monitor the service outputs, and detect any problems at an early stage.

One of the main reasons why government oversight is needed is that the government may become the owner or operator of the facility at some stage, either because the private sector entity has agreed to transfer the facility to the public sector (with or without payment) at the end of the arrangement or because the government may be forced to 'step in' to preserve an essential public service in the face of default by the SPV or non-fulfilment of contractual obligations. However, there are many other contractual risks and issues that need to be assessed and managed by the public sector body (Partnerships Victoria, 2001). These include the following matters.

Service Delivery Problems

The concession agreement will include a specification of what is to be provided and the performance standards to be achieved, along with the warranties required and penalties that might be applied for non-compliance. If services are not provided at the standard required by government, provision would normally allow for an abatement of payment and an obligation to cure the problem. Obviously, the severity of the abatement should reflect the seriousness of the service delivery issue and a distinction between 'major' and 'minor' breaches may be apposite. The private entity would usually be provided with written notice of any service delivery issues and have an opportunity to resolve them within a defined period. Should the service delivery problems not be rectified and continue beyond a reasonable period of time (as defined in the contract), the SPV would have the right to replace the operator before government moves to final termination.

Availability

Since the substance of a PPP is the procurement of a service, the availability of the service is a key issue for government. Failure by the SPV to make services available strikes at the very heart of the project, especially where payment is based (wholly or partly) on availability rather than usage. Projects that involve accommodation-based services (such as the provision of hospital, prison, educational or office space services) are more likely to give rise to availability problems. Availability in this context would usually go beyond basic accommodation services to include properly maintained, cleaned, air-conditioned and well secured court, hospital or office space with fully functioning IT infrastructure.

As part of the contract, there will be a definition of what is meant by a service being available, generally associated with the quantity and quality of the service and the frequency with which it is provided. Payment will usually depend directly on availability, by basing the service charge (or at least part of it) on a measure of available service (for example, in a contract for court accommodation services, the number of courtrooms that are available to service specifications during a particular period) or alternatively the pre-agreed payment may be abated in line with services that are unavailable (for example, payment might be abated in line with the number of courtrooms unavailable). Different weights may be ascribed to different service requirements, so that not all failures to provide a service exactly in terms of the contract will lead to an abatement of the service charge. Other mechanisms (such as step-in and termination) may also be used to redress failures to make contracted services available, but they are generally options of last resort held in reserve.

Public Risk

Government has a duty to insist that facilities are constructed, operated and maintained in accordance with relevant legislation and codes of practice in order to ensure the safety and well-being of consumers and workers. It may need to exercise its rights to 'step in' in order to prevent or mitigate a serious risk to the environment or to public health, or to the safety of people or property, or to guarantee continuity of an essential service or to otherwise discharge its statutory duties. Step-in rights ordinarily exist as part of a package of remedies that the government can take for project company default. They may also need to be exercised simply because the private body is unable to deal with a particular situation appropriately, for example, in an emergency, necessitating government intervention. In certain cases government has a duty to ensure the continuity of the contracted services to the public and needs to retain the ability to assume control of them temporarily if the public interest is jeopardized. This will include stepping in to contracted services on which the quality of its own delivery of core services depends.

Determining the circumstances in which government should exercise its step-in rights involves balancing the private sector's desire to limit step-in instances and government's need to ensure that it has the ability to protect the provision of the contracted services and, where relevant, core public services. Where that balance is struck depends on the nature of the project and the sensitivity of the public service involved. A step-in clause usually includes provisions for a government 'step-out' when the relevant situation has been resolved. That decision also needs careful assessment.

Asset Risk

Most infrastructure facilities have a physical life measured in decades. On

expiry of the concession, the government may be expecting to take possession of an asset that still has a considerable working life at an acceptable
maintenance cost.[1] Asset risk can arise for a number of reasons: the facility
design life or technical life may prove shorter than anticipated; the maintenance and upgrade costs of keeping the facility serviceable might exceed
expectation; the asset may be damaged or destroyed through a *force
majeure* event; the project company may lose the asset through default and
early termination; and the facility may not have the value which the project
financial structure has ascribed to it.

These risks can be mitigated in part through agreed maintenance and
refurbishment schedules, combined with a right to survey the asset and
compel performance if the maintenance obligations are not being met. The
contract may also need to allow for some flexibility to upgrade the infrastructure over time, along with incentives to do so. There may also be some
non-insurable *force majeure* events which come under material change in
circumstances clauses, with some government risk-sharing with the SPV.

Operating Risk

This is the risk that the processes for delivering the contracted services will
be affected in such a way as to prevent the private party from delivering
these services according to the agreed specifications and/or within the
projected costs. Operating risks relate to production and operation procedures, availability and quality of inputs, quality and efficiency of project
management and maintenance and upgrade requirements, with the consequence that the costs of operating the facility will exceed projections and
therefore diminish projected returns so that the facility will not perform to
the required standards. While the structure of a PPP is such that the government frees itself from those operating risks that would attach to itself
owning and operating the facility, operational failure still poses a risk to
government in that it may be left without the services for which it has
contracted. If the contract is breached and the private party is not highly
capitalized, the subcontractors may seek to walk away, limiting government's ability to obtain redress. For this reason, guarantees from the sponsors or the private party's parent companies or performance bonds may be
required to cover performance obligations during the operational phase of
the contract. If the contract is correctly structured and the sponsors have
invested a large amount of capital, the low risk of them walking away may
not warrant the costs to government of requiring operating guarantees.
However, this is not always the case, leaving sponsor risk that has to be
evaluated and managed.

Sponsor Risk

Typically, when a project structure is put together, the SPV that contracts with the government is simply an entity created to act as the legal manifestation of a project consortium, and it has no historical financial or operating record that government bodies can assess. It is supported by external equity contributions often provided by portfolio investors with no relationship to the project beyond their commitment of equity and expectation of financial return. Government therefore relies on the reputation of the consortium members to fulfil the project obligations. Sponsor risk usually arises when the SPV and/or its subcontractors are unable to meet their contractual obligations, and the government is unable to enforce those obligations against the sponsors or recover some form of compensation or remedy from them for the losses sustained by it as a result of the SPV's breach. In addition, it may occur when the sponsor(s) is, for security or other probity reasons, unsuitable to be involved in, or connected with, the delivery of the project, and consequently may harm the project or bring it into disrepute.

Should, after financial close, the SPV not be regarded as adequately capitalized, the government could seek security from the sponsors or parent guarantees or performance bonds, to ensure that the body is fully committed to delivering the required outputs. These sureties are particularly significant in the operational phase when construction guarantees under the construction subcontracts are no longer in place and the sponsor may seek to walk away from the contract rather than address operational difficulties – leaving the SPV to be liquidated in circumstances where it lacks the resources to compensate government for the contract breach. The sponsor may also want to sell its interest in the SPV, and the government needs to make sure that it retains sufficient control over any changes to the ownership of the private party, in order to mitigate sponsor risk.

In some circumstances, parent guarantees may be a poor method of providing security to government, inconsistent with the preference of many sponsors for infrastructure projects to be of a non-recourse or limited recourse nature. It may be more efficient to use performance bonds. One way of keeping down the cost of the guarantees or performance bonds is to have the value at the minimum required to cover necessary costs (such as the cost of installing a new operator). Again, these issues necessitate careful management over time, and may require ongoing tests of probity, continued tests of capability, and topped-up letters of credit or performance bonds to meet claims or to underpin operational performance obligations.

Financial Risk

Under this heading there are a number of risks. First, the financial parameters may change prior to the private party fully committing to the project, adversely affecting price. Second, the financiers (debt and equity) may not continue to provide funding to the project. Third, the financial structure may not be sufficiently robust to provide fair returns to debt and equity over the life of the project, calling into question its continuing viability. In evaluating these risks, the government is mindful of the fact that private sector entities and their financiers must be confident of the stability of the revenue stream, and the continued involvement of the financiers in the project provides some comfort to it that the consortium has incentives to deliver the contracted services.

Nonetheless, many of the problems begin at the outset, and what is needed is for government to undertake a reality check and not to encourage under-bidding. Experience has shown that if the partnership does not work finan-cially for the private sector – where, for example, the consortium has materially underpriced its bid to win the project – it is unlikely that the project will work for the government either. Where a private party drives a bad bargain for itself (the 'winner's curse'), which it may do when under intense competitive pressure or under internal pressure because of the loss of other contracts, the project can set off along a wrong trajectory which is likely to result in continuing difficulty, if not commercial failure. Also to be watched are situations in which the sponsor is dependent on refinancing at more favourable rates to make the contract commercially viable in the longer term. While ordinarily this may be possible when the project enters a lower risk phase, if an event materializes and risk is assessed as remaining at compara-tively high levels, the private party may find itself in an untenable commercial situation, prompting default or walk away.

Default Risk

Default (breach of the contract) occurs when the contracting enterprise is unable to perform its contractual obligations, including the inability to meet deadlines, to perform to a specified standard, and to continue loan repayments. Invariably, the contract will recognize the differing scale and consequences of contractual breaches by accepting some defaults (material defaults) as giving rise to a right of termination, and others (non-material defaults) as attracting an obligation to rectify but not on their own allowing the other party to termi-nate the contract. However, a non-material default may become a material default if it is not rectified within the period allowed and progress is unsatis-factory, or if the default recurs. In these circumstances the remedies available to government may include the right of step-in, as well as a right to terminate the contract. In extreme cases, government can have the underlying infrastructure assets transferred to it, subject to a predefined valuation mechanism.

Before looking to terminate the contract in the event of a default, government generally seeks other avenues of redress (e.g. abatement of service charge). Termination is viewed as an option of last resort, and can have very real ramifications and costs for government (if, for example, it is unable to find alternative services or is unable to deliver its own services). Contracts generally provide for adequate resolution periods and distinguish between – and provide different regimes for – material and non-material defaults. The presence of a reasonable resolution regime for defaults is important for financiers, and one that imposes harsh penalties without a reasonable opportunity to remedy defaults is likely to make the project difficult to finance and increase the cost of finance, leading to a less attractive value-for-money outcome. Good contract management aims to keep the contract in operation for the benefit of both parties, not to seek occasions for it to end, if circumstances are propitious. On the other hand, if the project has little possibility of becoming viable under the present operators, it may be better to cut losses quickly. The real issue becomes one of developing a good monitoring system.

A GOVERNANCE FRAMEWORK

Earlier we outlined the major stages in a PPP contract. Bringing a PPP to financial close involves major investment by all parties to the contract, but it cannot be the end of the matter. Indeed, it is the conversion of the contract into delivery of the outputs that is essential to meeting the overall project objectives. Contract management requires particular skills which need to be put in place before the contract is executed. The contract management team should ideally include people involved throughout the business case, bidding and evaluation processes, as they are well versed about the contract and have had the opportunity to establish working relationships with the key private party personnel. This is important because the length of the contract period makes it virtually impossible to allow contractually for all of the possible changes in circumstances that may arise. In the terminology of Macniel (1974) the contract being managed must be seen as 'relational' rather than 'transactional'

A contract reporting and monitoring framework lies at the heart of contract management. In order to allow sensible control of the project in a dynamic and volatile situation it is important that adequate information on which to base 'control' actions is available. Monitoring of the state of health of a project must therefore be undertaken as an integral part of the overall contract management framework. Essentially, monitoring is an ongoing activity feeding information into an assessment process, which takes place during a review stage and leads to a series of control actions. In the context of a typical PPP project the control actions include:

- decreased payments (abatements for underperformance);
- increased monitoring and/or reporting requirements;
- managerial changes;
- contingency planning for ensuring continuity of services and potential government step-in under the contract; and
- triggering default scenarios and consequent government actions under the contract (such as remedy, e.g. replacement of a specific service provider).

But this process of monitoring information, reporting and subsequent control action can only be truly effective if it is related to a clear picture of what was and is intended; that is, the substance of the contract and the contract operations procedures. From this perspective, control action can then be implemented which it is hoped will draw the project back on track or shift it in some way to ensure better outcomes in the future.

Next we sketch out a model risk and performance monitoring structure detailing the main reporting requirements for providers to the responsible government agency.[2] The contents of the reporting will help enable the agency to assess the contractor's capacity to meet requirements for the short and medium term, and the full life of the project, identifying and managing key business and performance issues. This framework is predicated on the assumption that in most circumstances the government is unable to walk away from the consequences of a PPP contract. Effectively the risk of non-delivery of the service rests with the public sector, although it is also important to note that this is quite different to the financial consequence of such service failure which can be and is usually transferred to the private sector. It is therefore essential that the government agency has access to information that goes beyond the monitoring of service performance standards.

The framework for collecting information operates at two levels:

1. the viability of the business, measured in terms of
   - overall performance (Table 8.2)
   - cash flow management (Table 8.3)
   - risks (Table 8.4)

2. the underlying quality of the project, measured in terms of
   - organizational 'health' (Table 8.5)
   - service performance (Table 8.6)

Business Viability

As a first step, contract managers need to appreciate the business environment and the objectives of the government in entering into the contract. Performance measures are needed for implementing performance management, and the measures should be linked to strategic objectives or to desired outcomes. Understanding the business is the first step in building a performance framework for a PPP project.

So as fully to appraise the business and its operations, the contract manager should consider performance at both a strategic and a project level. Table 8.2 outlines the performance issues to be addressed. Obviously, the information examined will differ depending on the project in question and the structure of the entity being monitored. Each project will vary according to the strategic outcomes and project specific factors. At the project level, the cashflows and the impact of risks are highly idiosyncratic and need to be considered specifically.

Because of their financing structure, PPPs rely on a clearly defined revenue stream to service the underlying cost structure, which comprises operating costs, maintenance costs, finance costs including principal and interest payments on any project debt, insurance premiums, tax liabilities, and equity returns commensurate with the development costs and long-term project risk taken by the investors. Through the use of subcontracts and financial hedging much of the cost base may be relatively fixed, but the same may be true of the revenue side. Anything that reduces the level of income or increases the cost base can eat into profits and potentially damage the ability to service debt. Senior lenders are well aware of this potential, and will focus heavily on the level of cover afforded by the income stream relative to the cost of the loan over three distinct timeframes – the cover in any one period (ADSCR), over the life of the loan (LLCR), and over the life of the whole project (PLCR).

While the government can, to some extent, rely on the performance monitoring standards set by the senior lenders, their interests may not always coincide, and the government may need to be in a position to step in or terminate the contract. For these reasons, the contract manager needs to have a good understanding of how the cashflows work and the sources of the revenue streams. For example, a 'user pays' revenue stream (such as a toll or public transport system) is significantly different to an availability type mechanism (such as a government accommodation project), because the user pays system transfers volume or usage risk to the private sector whereas the availability mechanism transfers performance risk but not usage. Monitoring the cashflow dimensions puts the contract manager in a better position to identify the early warning signs of a project potentially in financial distress. The contract management team would want to consider past performance and projected

Table 8.2 Business analysis

Performance aspects	Tools of analysis	Key issues
Strategic level performance management: the assessment of organizational success in achieving strategic, high-level aims. Strategic performance is concerned with outcomes	*Industry analysis*: review of competitors, substitutes, customers, suppliers, government policy to understand key business features and risks	Is the business strategy robust?
		Are the key stakeholders identified?
	Strategic anaysis: identify external environmental signals and examine the impacts on the projects	Have priorities been established?
		Does the organization have the capability and capacity to deliver?
	Macro-environmental changes: economic conditions, demographic trends, technological changes ,social/cultural factors, legal factors	Has the organization the ability to learn and adopt to change?
	Product/market analysis: analysis of product and/or market growth opportunities	What are the outcomes and are they as planned?
Project-level performance management: performance of the the project and its service providers. At the project level performance is mainly concerned with obtaining desired outputs	*Flow charts*: to fully understand a project, it may be helpful to analyse it in terms of inputs and outputs, and the relationships between them	What are the core products/services being delivered?
		Who are the customers?

Project specific risk matrix: regular monitoring and update of the risk matrix and management plan developed during the procurement phase

What is the capital structure?

Is the project achieving its objectives

Project sector comparator: Updates to the public sector comparator for any variations made to the contract

Are the services being provided at the required quality?

Is there sufficient cashflow?

Performance monitoring: monitoring of performance against the key performance indicators

What security exists for government?

Can the government 'walk away' if things go wrong?

When is the right time to interfere?

209

Table 8.3 Assessment of cashflows

Performance aspects	Tools of analysis	Key issues
Past: analysis of the cashflow performance to date	*Financial model*: the financial model usually required for procurement is a useful starting point for understanding the cashflows (extract forecast from financial model for rolling annual basis and compare actual for forecast)	What are the real sources and uses of cash for the business?
Future: analysis of the projected cashflows		How is revenue likely to change over the project term?
	Project specific risk matrix: regular monitoring and updating of the risk matrix and management plan developed during the procurement phase and application of the quantification techniques to the financial model	What are the revenue determinants?
		Is the underlying cost structure stable?
	Sensitivity analysis: test the effect on the cashflows of changes in value of underlying costs and revenues (and other variables such as risk as appropriate)	What is the underlying capital structure and how appropriate is it?
		What are the risks and are they likely to impact on the cashflows?
	Scenario planning: testing likely combinations of changes in variables to establish downside (and upside) scenarios	At what point are dividends paid/payable?
	'Monte Carlo' analysis: considering the effects of a range of values applied to underlying costs and revenues (and other variables such as risk) using probability distributions and computer aided simulation techniques	Are there constraints on dividends?
		How does the payment mechanism work, including where applicable any abatements for non-performance?

Table 8.4 *Risk analysis*

Performance aspects	Tools of analysis	Key issues
Retained risks	*Project specific risk matrix:* regular monitoring and updating of the risk matrix developed during the procurement phase	What risks have been retained and where is each one likely to have its most significant impact?
	Public sector comparator: regular reviews and updates to the public sector comparator developed during the procurement phase should be carried out to establish the impact of retained risk events that have taken place and also review and update the quantifications of retained risks and any new risks identified	How well can retained risks be quantified?

What are the quantified impacts of retained risks?

Has the risk profile changed? |
| *Transferred risks* | *Project specific risk matrix:* regular monitoring and updating of the risk matrix developed during he procurement phase | What risks have been transferred and where is each one likely to have its most significant impact? |
| | *Organizational chart:* which entities should be monitored depends largely on where the risk resides, for example, it may be pointless monitoring at the level of a special purpose vehicle if government is heavily reliant on the operator and its financial health | Has the risk profile changed?

Where does the risk reside in the project, for example, is it with the contracting entity or does risk get pushed down through the structure to suppliers?

What mechanisms have been used to allocate risk within the service provider's project structure, e.g. service level contracts, parent company guaratees, liquidated damages clauses, letters of credit, etc.? |

performance of each of the elements in the cashflow identified earlier. Table 8.3 outlines the performance areas.

Risk analysis is the next aspect. Successful project design relies on a comprehensive overview of all the risks and the design of contractual arrangements prior to competitive tendering that allocate risk burdens in terms of specified service obligations, the payment (and abatement) mechanism, and specific contractual provisions adjusting the risk allocation implicit in the initial structure. In turn, successful contract management rests on prudent monitoring of all the risks, an analysis of their changing impact on the project, and the formulation of dynamic risk management plans. It is useful to distinguish between those risks that are retained by government and those that have been transferred to the private sector. Table 8.4 gives a possible form to this analysis.

Quality of the Project

A review of the service provider's internal operating environment is an important step towards understanding the underlying creditworthiness (or solvency) of the business. It is through such regular review processes that an awareness of the service provider's strengths and weaknesses is derived. Nevertheless, a single template for organizational health is unlikely to be applicable in each and every circumstance. It is therefore more appropriate to consider a set of questions to assist contract managers in applying a logical thought process to establish and then assess the key reporting requirements for individual projects.

Any review should include issues related to organizational structure and financial position based on a range of 'hard' indicators such as dividend payouts, debt coverage, liquidity, published accounts, and so on. But how well organizations work also depends on management skills and motivation. Calibrating management quality resides firmly in the 'soft' indicator category and is highly subjective. Nevertheless, an experienced contract manager should regularly review and reassess the management quality of the service provider, looking for weaknesses or trends that may provide an early indication of trouble ahead. Table 8.5 thus combines both 'hard' and 'soft' indicators as a basis for evaluating overall organizational strength and vitality.

Finally, there is service performance and its measurement. A PPP contract defines the relationships between, and the rights and obligations of, the government and the service provider throughout the contract life. It follows that both parties in a PPP venture are reliant on the integrity of this contract in terms of how it operates and the services delivered. As the UK Treasury *Green Book* says: 'The likelihood of the benefits being realized will be affected by the contractual terms, and any incentives built in to the contract' (HM

Table 8.5 Measures of organizational 'health'

Performance aspects	Tools of analysis	Key issues
Financial position: an assessment of the creditworthiness or solvency of the organization and/or individual service providers	*Financial reporting requirements*: cashflow monitoring, key debt coverage ratios, working capital requirements and repayments schedules	What strengths or weaknesses emerge from analysis of trends in key financial figures?
		What do the trends in the financial figures indicate about the organization's financial position?
	Dividend monitoring: dividend payments, actual and forecast	What is the rate of return, both achieved to date and projected?
		Have dividends been paid?
	Credit analysis: activity analysis, liquidity, long-term debt solvency, profitability and valuation	Is there an effective cash management system?
		Are capital expenditures appropriate for future operational needs?
	Audited accounts: either for the SPV and/or the underlying service companies covering the last three years	Is the organization knowledgeable and aggressive in tax planning?
	Moodys/S&P ratings (if available)	What person or group constitutes top management?
	Financial performance indicators: cashflow monitoring, key debt coverage ratios, working capital requirements and repayments schedules, etc.	

Table 8.5 continued

Performance aspects	Tools of analysis	Key issues
Quality and quantity of management personnel: an analysis of past, current and future management effectiveness	*Operational reports*: a requirement should be placed on the service provider to give updates on the management structure, including any changes in personnel	What style of management is being used (e.g. autocratic or participative)?
		What influence or control does the board of directors exercise?
	Operational audit: where necessary the government should conduct its own audit of the management structure, including key managerial staff	How long are top management personnel expected to remain in control?
		What is the quality of the middle management and supervisory personnel in terms of planning and controlling work, with regard to meeting schedules, controlling costs, improving quality and performance?
Quantity and quality of operations personnel: an analysis of past, current and future operational effectiveness	*Operational reports*: a requirement should be placed on the service provider to give regular updates on operations personnel, including any changes in staffing	What are the skills and abilities of the work force?
		Are these skills adequate for meeting the need of the contract?

Operational audit: where necessary the government should conduct its own audit of the operations, including where appropriate the uptake of references on operating staff (in accordance with privacy laws and regulations)

What is the general attitude and motivation of employees?

What is the level of employee turnover?

What training has been undertaken or is to be undertaken?

What recruitment, promotion, redundancy or dismissal of any employee and/or any industrial disputes has occurred?

What accidents and health and safety incidents have occurred?

Table 8.6 Indicators of service performance

Performance aspects	Tools of analysis	Key issues
KPIs: key performance indicators provide the essential link between the output specifications and the payment mechanism	*KPI template*: standard approach to measuring and recording KPIs on a project based on service category, e.g. facility maintenance	A starting point in developing KPIs is to assess what level of service existed previously and what is achievable. What the contractor thinks can be achieved and how performance can be practically measured may be very different
	Physical measures: the measurement of quantitative elements within individual specification standards	
	Inspection: physical inspections of operational activities to determine the quality of performance of the service	The KPIs really need to be in place at the point of contract signing. However, as the project progresses and probably very early on in the operational period there should be sufficient flexibility in the contract to amend and review contract KPIs
	Logged failure/rectification time: measuring the time between the government making a request and the service provider attending the incident	
	User feedback: complaints and/or service user interviews	How do KPIs interrelate with the payment mechanism?
	Periodic review & audit: combination of spot check reviews of performance and regular audits of systems	

Performance trends	*Trends analysis:* Graphs showing trends in performance of the services for the payment period in question, compared with performance over each previous payment period – by service/facility	Repeated failure will usually trigger default obligations and/or notifications under the contract
		What is the overall performance of the services across service type and facility?
		What is the performance of each service, service by service, facility by facility, and facility by service

Treasury, 2003a, p. 44). Drawing on the service performance provisions of the project as specified contractually, the contract manager should review at regular intervals the quality of the service as measured against the KPIs and output specifications. Table 8.6 outlines the performance issues to be considered.

Conclusion

This chapter has sought to outline a general reporting regime for project risks and business and service delivery performance for use in PPP infrastructure projects, mindful that the ultimate responsibility for service delivery and performance of essential public services rests with the government. The framework embraces the following constituents:

- measures to assess the ongoing business viability of the contractor to meet requirements for the term of the contract and the major areas of risk;
- suggestions as to how these indicators should be reported, monitored and assessed;
- indicators of reporting quality standards to ensure the contractor is meeting performance requirements;
- aspects that should be periodically audited and/or reviewed; and
- the structure of the reporting requirements.

Earlier in this volume we contrasted PPPs with traditional public procurement of infrastructure, and this basic distinction cannot be ignored. As a consequence of the private sector's ownership of the asset and the complex risk allocation between the parties, the government's performance monitoring processes are likely to be carried out very differently under a PPP arrangement as compared to more traditional procurement. In particular, it is important not to lose sight of the fact that it is the service provider that must have adequate performance monitoring, quality management and management information systems. The contract manager should simply audit these systems by receiving regular planned reports, under a strict timeframe, according to obligations written into the contract, supplemented by undertaking random spot checks to ensure that performance is being measured and reported reliably, accurately and comprehensively.

NOTES

1. This is the general situation. However, with PPPs the design life of assets is often significantly less than that of existing equivalent assets in public ownership. This is because there is generally a closer correlation between design life and the immediate and projected service needs

over the contract term. The exception is for projects where the government specifies the useful life for the asset after transfer on contract expiry or termination.

2. This structure draws on a contractual governance framework developed in Grimsey and Lewis (2004a), an article published in a special issue of the *Journal of Corporate Citizenship* (Issue 15, Autumn 2004) edited by Professor Islami Demirag. The material is reproduced here with the kind permission of the publishers, Greenleaf Publishing U.K.

9. PPPs in emerging markets

INTRODUCTION

Previous chapters have explored the potential benefits of PPPs to infrastructure services delivery in the context of developed countries. Benefits seem likely to come from providing the private sector operator with the appropriate set of incentives. An arrangement in which the private entity is given the responsibility – and the risks – associated with project design, finance, construction, operations and maintenance, but is remunerated only if services are delivered on time and to a satisfactory standard, does this. Under the PPP the private contractor is left free to innovate in project design and to strike an appropriate balance between construction costs and maintenance levels, and the payment and abatement mechanism provides a strong encouragement to minimize lifetime costs, avoid delays in construction and commissioning, and undertake adequate maintenance. Evidence has been presented earlier which shows that such gains appear to have been obtained in many projects, and that the returns being received by project companies are not excessive in view of the risks and uncertainties involved.

Infrastructure investment in developing countries and transition economies[1] takes place in a very different environment. What Miller and Lessard (2001) describe as 'institutional risks' are at their greatest in emerging economies, for in these countries laws and regulations are incomplete and subject to change. The ability to make investments and repay debts depends on law and regulations that govern the appropriability of returns, property rights, and contracts, and while some countries are governed under constitutional frameworks and the rule of law, others are not. Sovereign risks thus loom larger because of the possibility that the government may decide to renegotiate concession agreements or amend property rights. Financing of an infrastructure project in turn becomes a critical resource, and we will accordingly devote a lot of attention in this chapter to the implications for the project financing that has to underpin a PPP project.

Another important factor is the absence of what might be called a PPP culture in emerging markets. This gap reflects in part an unsympathetic legal framework, but it also is an indication that there is not much experience of PPPs. Many of the transition economies, in particular, have emerged from a socialist system under which the idea of private sector involvement in key infrastructure sectors of the economy was anathema. There is the likelihood that sponsors of private infrastructure schemes will face opposition from local groups, economic development agencies, and influential political pressure groups. Other barriers come from an undeveloped domestic market for potential bidders and a poor understanding of PPPs in the public sector, combined with little knowledge of how to organize and manage them. These issues are taken up later in the chapter.

BENEFITS AND PROBLEMS

Given the lack of budgetary resources and the enormous infrastructure needs in emerging markets, public private partnerships (PPPs) remain an attractive policy option. Indeed, the United Nations (2002) describes them as a 'strategic necessity rather than a policy option', representing 'a unique and flexible solution to implement infrastructure projects' (p. 3). Certainly, the UN has become increasingly prominent as an advocate of PPPs on economic, social and environmental grounds as reflected in the Global Compact, the Millennium Summit and Rio+10. Earlier, in January 1996 the United Nations Economic Commission for Europe agreed to establish the Build, Operate, Transfer (BOT) Expert Group, to provide information to its member states on new project finance techniques for countries in central and eastern Europe and the CIS. This information supplements other advice given by international agencies.[2]

Based on experiences elsewhere, PPPs in emerging markets are likely to be concentrated initially in the transport, defence and energy sectors. PPPs can be employed for the construction or development of transport systems, municipal infrastructure such as water, heat distribution, wastewater and sewerage, as well as health, education and prisons (United Nations, 2002; American Chamber of Commerce, 2002). A valuable aspect of a PPP is that it can be designed to achieve social, commercial and environmental goals.

The potential commercial benefits include:

- infrastructure in the shortest possible time from the outset of the PPP contract resulting primarily from the whole-of-life costing principle;
- limiting the risk of delay or stoppage of construction, because the private sector will be determined to finish the works on time as a result of properly constructed incentives;
- value for money, achieved through the efficient allocation of risk between the public and private sectors;
- operational savings arising out of innovative capital build solutions, a

benefit derived from combining the operational and capital phases of
the project;
• projects financed without reliance on public debt;
• public sector skills released from financial constraints and utilized to
maximize efficiency.

In addition, there can also be a set of benefits related to the social gains, such
as:

• ensuring that the PPP facilitates technology transfer from the foreign
investors to the local public sector;
• selecting projects that promote competition and market-based
conduct, skills and innovation;
• having the private sector share its learning experience with the public
sector (perhaps through training sessions); and
• reforming the public sector as a result of gaining new commercial
skills, freeing ideas from capital constraints, and working with the
latest technological know-how.

Environmental considerations add an important third dimension to PPP
projects by taking account of conserving energy, water and other resources,
minimizing waste, enhancing biodiversity, and controlling pollution –
factors important everywhere but especially so in emerging markets where
there are often population pressures and a legacy of poor resource use. There
is a recognition now that PPPs are especially good vehicles for a 'green'
agenda (Office of Government Commerce, 2002b) because of their focus on
the whole-of-life cycle of a project. Under traditional public procurement
there are separate contracts for construction, maintenance and facilities
management, whereas under a PPP these are integrated. Contractors have a
direct pecuniary incentive to consider the interaction between the design of
an asset and its ultimate operating costs, and thus take account of all aspects
of cost, including running and disposal costs, as well as the initial purchase
price of an asset. Extra care devoted to designing a facility may deliver a
much better scheme, reduce waste and meet environmental outcomes, while
not sacrificing value for money. Attention, for example, to those design
features and construction materials that will lower whole-of-life cycle costs
across the length of the contract might mean a contractor choosing to invest
in higher cost design features if those larger initial outlays are offset by
lower maintenance and running costs during the operational life of a contract
(and beyond).

The value of PPPs in promoting environmental sustainability has only
recently come to be appreciated, and emerging market countries can take

advantage of the learning curve through which PPPs have passed in developed countries by building in these elements at an early stage. Often it is simply a case of asking the right questions and raising issues that project developers might not have thought of before. Features that might be borrowed from the UK programme include guidelines to those preparing a PPP proposal that encourages an examination of factors such as:

- minimizing waste, by recycling water and processing waste and recyclables;
- reducing whole-of-life cycle costs, by aligning the balance between initial costs and maintenance and operating costs without compromising user comfort;
- enhancing service delivery, by designing buildings that are well lit and airy, relying on natural light and cooling, with positive effects on users;
- promoting wider social and environmental benefits, by addressing health, safety and environmental concerns of those living and working in the area; and
- encouraging in-built flexibility, by having a facility that can respond efficiently to changing requirements and new technologies particularly those which can conserve resources and reduce waste.

Of course, 'sustainability' in its broadest sense goes beyond an allowance for environmental factors alone and can be viewed as a process for giving greater weight than conventional methods allow to the interest of future generations and by recognizing a wide range of social, environmental, institutional and cultural values.

However, if these potential benefits are to be attained, there are also some problems to overcome, such as:

- potential difficulties in putting together a cost-effective financial package;
- limited financial flexibility of the public sector arising from the long-term commitment of funds under the PPP contract;
- complex, more expensive and time-consuming transactions costs in the development stage, requiring dedicated resources from both public and private sectors;
- the absence of a reliable commercial and legal framework.

These obstacles are examined in this chapter, but first we look at the different forms of private sector involvement in infrastructure in emerging markets.

PRIVATE INVOLVEMENT IN INFRASTRUCTURE

In its 1994 *World Development Report*, the World Bank argued that the causes of poor performance in traditional public sector procurement of infrastructure, and the source of improved performance, lay in the incentives facing providers. On this score it saw that PPPs had promise and that the possibilities for greater private sector engagement in infrastructure should be explored by government and constitute a major component of the development strategy. Private sector involvement is already a feature of infrastructure in a number of emerging economies. This involvement can take several forms, of which the most commonly used are leasing models, BOT/BOO/BOOT arrangements, and concession approaches. A more limited contribution is implied by contracting out and operations and management contracts. At the other end of the scale, there is full privatization.

Institutional arrangements vary for each type of private sector participation.[3] As a general rule, full privatization is considered most appropriate in electricity generation and telecommunications, where there exists competition in the market or from close substitutes. In water supply and electricity transmission and distribution, where competition in the market is more difficult, concessions are popular. If the general regulatory framework is weak, regulation by contract becomes a viable and effective alternative and BOTs are widely employed in transport projects. Service management and lease contracts can be alternatives to full concessions. While most of these arrangements have already been discussed, we now look at them in the particular case of emerging markets.

Lease Contracts

Under a lease contract, a public utility leases the full operation and maintenance of certain facilities to a private operator for a specified period, for example ten years, and grants the operator the right to invoice and collect charges from customers over that time. Remuneration is linked directly to the charges paid by customers, and from these revenues the private operator pays the public utility a rental fee, negotiated in advance, to cover capital costs for the assets employed. In turn, operators holding lease contracts usually finance, prepare, procure, and supervise small plant and equipment renewals, as defined in the contract. Ownership of the assets remains with the public body and it remains responsible for major extensions and upgrades. The operator is consulted on all major works, especially those involving continuity of service, and can participate in tender evaluation or submit its own tender for extension projects. At the termination of the contract, the public utility compensates the operator for works financed, but not fully amortized.

Lease contracts enable the public sector in the emerging market economy to transfer full commercial risk on all operations to the private sector contractor. Because of the remuneration system there are incentives for private operators to update customer files and implement efficient collection procedures to improve the collection ratio from customers, expand the customer base to service more customers and increase the revenue base, reduce operating costs to increase profits, and to undertake regular maintenance to increase the reliability of facilities and postpone their renewal.

BOT, BOO and BOOT Schemes

BOT (build, operate, transfer), BOO (build, own, operate) and BOOT (build, own, operate, transfer) schemes are described by the East Asia Analytical Unit (1998) as essentially adaptations of leasing contracts specifically designed to access private capital for new investments. Briefly, a BOT agreement requires a private sector consortium to finance, design, construct, operate and maintain a facility, for a given period of time, in return for exclusive rights to the revenues obtained from services supplied to municipal or government utilities, or directly to tariff paying customers. Leases on the underlying assets are taken out for a limited period, often 15 to 30 years, and the assets then are given or sold back to the government, depending on the contract. Operational and most construction risk is borne by the private consortium.

From the viewpoint of emerging economies, there are a number of advantages with BOT and BOOT arrangements – they are administratively simple and usually do not involve major sectoral restructuring, so that new facilities can be added to the existing network. In countries with poorly defined regulatory and legal structures and emerging capital markets, the schemes can be implemented quickly and provide important learning experiences. Many BOT schemes act as a useful introduction to private sector discipline, bringing substantial efficiencies in construction costs as well as plant and labour management. They also enable public enterprises to escape budgetary constraints on mobilizing investment funds, because they act as a vehicle, and a relatively quick method, for mobilizing project-based non-recourse finance for new capital investment in a situation where capital markets are poorly developed. However, implementing BOT contracts in an effective way requires attention to the design of tender documents and contract conditions, such as the uptake prices that the public sector utilities pay BOT operators. A lengthy bidding process may be entailed, at least until the government develops a template BOT contract.

Concessions or Franchises

Concession contracts combine elements of operational leases for existing assets and BOT contracts for new investments. Generally, the private sector takes on more market and operational risks than most leases or BOTs since the invest-ment is paid for by user fees. Under concessions, private operators have contrac-tual rights to use infrastructure assets to supply customers directly and obtain the revenue from sales. The operator usually manages and is responsible for all cap-ital extensions and upgrades and normal maintenance. This gives concession-aires more flexibility than BOT operators or lease holders to determine the nature and timing of new investments to augment supply. New assets are handed over to the government when the concession expires. Concession contracts usually run for longer than lease contracts, often 20 to 30 years, so enabling the operator to recover capital and finance costs. In comparison with BOT contracts, concessions provide more incentives to expand the customer base, increase investment, maintain existing assets and, most importantly, reduce technical and non-technical losses within water and electricity distribution networks.

Concessions are important because they are the one truly tried and tested PPP model. As explained in Chapter 3, France has used concessions for over 100 years to supply municipal water. Private water firms provide bulk water treatment and retail water services employing assets which remain municipal government-owned. Public transport, water supply or electricity utilities may operate several concessions concurrently, allowing comparison of concession-aires' prices, service quality and investment performance in meeting commu-nity needs. One advantage of the concession is that it is not an 'add on' to existing facilities, which is often the case with a new BOT project. Concessions can address fundamental operating weaknesses in the existing system. This is discussed further in the last section of this chapter.

Like BOT contracts, concession models are useful in countries where the institutional, legal, regulatory and financial structures have not developed sufficiently to support full scale privatization with independent regulation, or where this route is politically unacceptable. If private firms are to provide risk capital for a genuine concession (or BOT), rather than simply a management contract that leaves risk with government, a number of conditions must be met. These requirements are:

- a clear definition of the scope of the works required;
- an open and transparent tendering process;
- security of access to necessary resources such as land, fuel and other inputs;
- an unequivocal government commitment to enforce the terms of the concession contract;

- assurances that tariffs can be collected at market or near-market levels; and
- the ability to enforce commercial and customer obligations.

FINANCING STRUCTURES

The financial landscape for private investment in developing countries has changed markedly over the years. Prior to World War I, private sector investment in infrastructure projects was made by entrepreneurs willing to put up or draw in risk capital in return for high rewards, and fortunes were made and lost (see Chapter 3). Changes since then have fundamentally altered the source of finance. Private risk capital provided directly by entrepreneurs and individual investors is now extremely rare. Instead, the markets are dominated by institutions which look for a safe investment for their funds.[4] As the project risks increase, such institutions expect higher rates of return from their investments. They are rightly concerned about political risks, currency repatriation risks, exchange rate risks and commercial risks, which are more real and more difficult to assess in the emerging economies. However, it is possible to ameliorate some of these risks by innovative financing techniques. In this respect, in the words of Haley (1992), 'financial engineering instead of civil engineering has become the key to the success of a project' (p. 65).

There are several mechanisms to reduce and spread risks. Governments, international development agencies and local and foreign financial institutions have worked to develop credible techniques to lower infrastructure project risks, and these include:

- structured project finance and credit from specialized financial institutions;
- credit enhancement, including 'mezzanine finance' and debt subordination;
- government guarantees;
- multilateral development bank guarantees and equity contributions; and
- public–private partnerships with direct government equity support.

Structured Project Finance

Structured project financing provides a vehicle for mobilizing equity and debt in infrastructure projects by fashioning the finance to the specific project, with the risks (and returns) borne not by the sponsor alone but by different types of investors (equity holders, debt providers, quasi-equity investors). One criterion of a project's suitability for financing is whether it is able to stand alone as a distinct legal and economic entity, and project assets, project-related contracts, and project cashflows are separated from the sponsor by non-recourse and limited-recourse arrangements. Repayment relies on the cashflow and the assets of the project, but since project assets are highly location, site and jurisdiction specific and embody a high proportion of sunk costs irrevocably committed to the project, they offer only limited security to lenders.

By lending to an SPV set up solely to implement the project, and to which the sponsor contributes equity of 10 to 30 per cent to provide a buffer, lenders obtain security over the potential future income streams. Close attention is given to project financial forecasts and risk profiles, with all cashflows identified and the financing package structured to ensure debt obligations can be met at each project stage. Those participating in the project negotiate complex contracts, subcontracts and guarantees which identify and allocate responsibilities for managing and bearing project risks, while reducing risks for lenders and providing alternative means of redress if the project fails. Contractual parties include the project sponsor, the SPV, the construction company, the eventual project operator, direct commercial and syndicated lenders, other equity holders, those purchasing the output, and the government and state-owned utility contracting with the project service provider. Figure 9.1 depicts the links between them for a resources-based project.

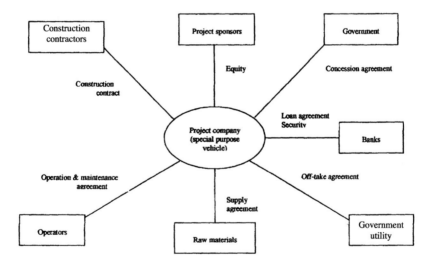

Source: East Asia Analytical Unit (1998).

Figure 9.1   Contractual arrangements in a typical project financing package

Credit Enhancement Mechanisms

Credit enhancement mechanisms can assist in reducing project risks and enhancing lender confidence. Debt subordination instruments, known as mezzanine finance, provide different levels of return on debt in exchange for taking on different preference ordering in paying out liabilities from defaulting companies. Mezzanine finance is so called because it describes the level lying between the 'ground floor' of the structure (equity) and the 'first floor' (senior debt). In a different sense, it also refers to financing that is raised soon after early start-up funding from investors, but prior to floating on the stock exchange after the venture has established an operating track record. Debt is classified into senior and junior levels, with junior level debt receiving higher returns than senior level finance in exchange for absorbing the first losses.

Mezzanine capital effectively adds a third layer of funding, complementing the traditional two-tier debt and equity capital structure of a project. It is distinguished by:

- having a differing priority of claim to cashflow and assets in the event of liquidation, a lower priority than senior debt, but higher than equity;
- often having a conversion option for the holder to transform the instrument from one form, such as debt, to another, such as equity; and
- being most attractive when the spread is significant between expected senior debt and equity returns.

The four principal types of mezzanine financing are subordinated debt, convertible debt, preferred equity, and equity warrants.

Government Guarantees

A national government may provide guarantees to lenders against certain policy risks. Where the guarantees are limited to contractual obligations of government and their utilities, for example power and water purchases or fuel supply by state-owned monopolies, they can be a useful transitional device to promote private sector participation in infrastructure. Governments in emerging market economies may offer minimum or threshold revenue guarantees (to provide reassurance to bankers without increasing public sector risks), special taxation provisions, subordinated royalty or fee payments or bulk purchase and 'off-take' agreements.

The latter are particularly important. Because limited recourse projects are, by definition, funded on the security of the future cashflow, there has to be some form of buyer. Projects fall into two categories: there are those where the identity of the buyer is clear, for example toll roads and some power stations, and those where a physical product is sold, often into a world market. Identifying the off-taker and determining the basic price helps get the project underway, but ought not to become an alternative to sectoral reforms in power, water and other infrastructure sectors that eventually would enable private providers to take appropriate demand, investment and management risks. If required to do so, they would have a revenue-based incentive to minimize their output losses and reduce operational inefficiencies.

Multilateral Development Bank Guarantees

Partial guarantee mechanisms developed by multilateral development banks such as the World Bank and the Asian Development Bank can be extremely effective in addressing sovereign risks faced by private sector infrastructure providers. Rather than directly lending funds to infrastructure projects involving private sector partnerships, the multilateral development banks provide guarantees to the financiers of private project sponsors against host government defaults on the terms of project contracts. Guarantees can be arranged such that commercial risk resides with the private investors. Two types of guarantees are used:

- *Guarantees for project finance.* This is a partial sovereign risk guarantee in that the development bank assumes part of the political risk for a project, thus helping to make the project more financially viable.
- *Guarantees for extending loan maturities.* A partial credit guarantee is designed to extend loan maturities; that is, to extend loan terms beyond those that commercial lenders normally would be willing to offer.

Participation of the multilateral development banks also gives a 'seal of approval' to the projects concerned because of the additional monitoring and project evaluation.

Public Equity Contributions

Another method that governments can use to reduce private sponsors' risk perceptions and assist in obtaining project financing, is to take up equity in joint private–government infrastructure projects, particularly in their high-risk early years. As is the case with multilateral development bank guarantees, government equity participation can provide some assurance to private investors, because governmental participation should reduce sovereign risks arising from adverse policy changes. A joint venture may be preferred if governments are reluctant to promote full private project ownership.

In-kind government subsidies can also assist in getting off the ground financially marginal projects that have significant spillover or public good elements considered to be valuable for the economy, such as toll roads in low income regions that may not be viable for many years. By providing 'seed capital' governments reduce risks for the project sponsor while ensuring the project goes ahead with mostly private finance, and with major commercial risks resting with the operator.

OBSTACLES TO PPPs

Project finance techniques in emerging markets have traditionally been applied mainly in the mining and oil and gas sectors. Such projects rely on large-scale foreign currency financing and are particularly suited to project finance because their output has a global market and is earned in hard currency. Since market risk greatly affects the potential outcome of most projects, project finance tends to be more applicable in industries where the revenue streams can be defined and readily secured. Private sector infrastructure projects under long-term government concession agreements with power purchase agreements that assure a purchaser of the project's output have also been able to attract major project finance flows. There would seem to be no compelling reasons why the techniques cannot be adapted for a range of non-financial sectors, including service projects such as privately operated hospitals and prisons. If so, PPPs in emerging markets would probably echo the experience in developed countries where the market began with 'hard economic' projects and, with accumulated knowledge, spread to soft infrastructure applications.

However, merely opening up areas previously confined to public sector operators to allow private sector participation is not, in itself, sufficient. A number of factors need to be put in place if PPPs are to be developed and successfully implemented. Some of the obstacles are inherent in the concept itself. A PPP is not an easy process to implement. It is complex in terms of the interactions with all the parties involved and in the impact on the public agency. The preparatory work and commissioning process are time consuming, and strong political support is required. Other barriers come from the commercial and legal environment, and these need to be addressed in enabling legislative and policy changes. Some of the major factors are given in the following list.

- *Legal framework.* In many countries there is no legal framework for PPPs. Ideally a robust system of commercial laws needs to be in place. Private sector interests have to be protected under the existing laws. Government agencies have also to facilitate the involvement of the private sector in infrastructure projects or public utilities. Restrictions on public procurement may adversely affect the implementation of PPPs. For example, in Poland, the entering into a public procurement agreement for a period longer than three years requires the prior consent of the President of the Public Procurement Office. A similar approval must be obtained for applying a procedure other than an unlimited tender process in the case of large public procurement contracts (American Chamber of Commerce, 2002). In addition, PPP projects usually require a number of permits, consents and administrative decisions. The partners of the public entity are often foreign companies, the operations of which sometimes face additional restrictions in the host country.

- *Finance*. This has already been discussed and despite the various techniques available to reduce risks, the perception of high riskiness attached to project financing in certain regions is difficult to overcome, and it deters the private commercial banks from lending to the region. Risk is made up of several components (i.e. political, commercial, price, etc.) some of which can be covered by international financial institutions and others by 'take and pay' arrangements. Country credit risk is also an important factor. Private commercial banks are frequently reluctant to enter due to the general legal and regulatory weakness that characterizes some emerging countries. Within the country, global finance limits applied to the amount of indebtedness of state, regional or local government entities may inhibit or even prevent them from incurring the long-term commitments typical of PPPs.

- *Taxation*. A good appreciation of the taxation ramifications is needed in any dealings with private sector entities. The very complexity of PPPs creates many points where an unhelpful taxation system can impose itself. For example, are direct grants from the public sector to pay for a portion of the PPP asset taxable? Is the handback of the asset to the public sector assessed for tax? Is property used in the PPP exempt from taxation? Can infrastructure assets be depreciated for taxation purposes? The existing taxation system, like the legal system, may be ill-equipped to deal with PPPs.

- *Accounting*. Determining the appropriate accounting treatment of PPPs has proven to raise complicated and controversial issues (Grimsey and Lewis, 2002b). The main problem consists of providing a correct answer to the question: in whose books should the assets covered by a given agreement be reported? Recognizing a given asset in the balance sheet also means recognizing a related liability in the accounts. Assets covered by a given agreement should be recognized in the accounting records of the party which is not only exposed to the greatest extent to the economic risk associated with using those assets, but which is also able to make use of related economic benefits to the greatest extent. A detailed analysis of each individual case must be conducted in order to determine this, focusing on the variability over time of the revenue and costs connected with using a given asset and the parties exposed to the greatest risk. Evolving international standards largely accept this point, but not all national systems do, creating ambiguities as to the conditions under which PPP payment obligations can be treated as off-balance sheet transactions by the public sector.

- *Public acceptance.* A broad public consensus as to the involvement of the private sector in infrastructure is needed, especially for implementing project financing models based on user charges. For example, most attempts to finance the building of new East European transport infrastructure by means of toll revenues have been abandoned or put on hold (von Hirschhausen, 2002), although two exceptions are the M5 highway in Hungary and the A4 (Katowice–Krakow) highway in Poland. The legacy of free infrastructure under state planning has made it difficult to jump immediately to private project financing based on user charges, while a combination of low traffic volumes, low capacity to pay and the availability of free alternative routes means that private concession models based on user tolls are likely for some time to be less profitable in emerging markets than in Western Europe and other industrialized countries.

- *Public administration.* The capacity and skills of public administrations have to be broadened to manage and negotiate successful projects. The difficulties in implementing private financing for transport infrastructure referred to in the previous point, for example, revealed a lack of administrative competence in the development and control of private project financing, as well as a lack of knowledge of future traffic flows, willingness to pay and other determinants of demand-side risk (von Hirschhausen, 2002). There may be the potential to pool the knowledge base. The United Nations (2002) suggests that for PPPs to be promoted and used in the reconstruction of areas like South East Europe, interested government units and departments could be involved in a regional network to improve the governments' capacity to facilitate projects.

SOME POSSIBLE SOLUTIONS

Clearly, a number of significant elements ('enablers') need to be in place to allow PPPs to develop (see Table 9.1). Many of these matters must be tackled at the individual nation level. Others seem likely to require initiatives at an international level. For example, considering the case of European transition

Table 9.1   Key 'drivers' and 'enablers' for PPPs

Drivers	Enablers
• Financial need, e.g. budget deficit • Ageing or poor infrastructure • Growing demands or expectations on public sector services • Search for greater efficiency and creativity • Desire to introduce competition • Shortage of domestic experience or skills • Desire to educate national contractors and remain competitive • Bandwagon effect	• Political framework: stability, explicit political will or commitment, e.g. a dedicated unit, ability to push schemes through, creative and willing local government • Legal framework: no roadblocks, and documentation not excessively complicated • Public acceptance: acceptance of private sector involvement and specific impacts, e.g. environmental impact of new roads • Quality practitioners: good quality, experienced project sponsors and lenders • Readily available finance: including EU and EIB funding in some cases; mature or sophisticated banking sector and capital markets culture

Source: *European PPP Survey 2001* – D&P (2001).

economies, financing support for the accession countries will rely on assistance provided by the European Investment Bank (EIB) and the European Bank for Reconstruction and Development (EBRD). Purely private infrastructure financing may not be a feasible option for many projects in the emerging markets, but that does not exclude expanding private sector participation. Some financing might come from the private sector under different arrangements as the market for PPPs evolves from 'project finance' to 'corporate finance'. D & P (2001) argue that an investor with a portfolio of 20–30 infrastructure projects has an asset or income stream that can be borrowed against or securitized. Project bonds are attractive to pension funds when 'credit wrapped' (that is, when an insurer credit enhances a project to give it a higher credit rating), and may even be sold to retail investors. As high quality infrastructure assets are placed in this way, there might develop an appetite for more risky infrastructure assets in portfolios, bypassing to some extent the reluctance of banks to lend.

Nevertheless, it is not sufficient to design a credible framework to attract funds from the capital markets. Incentives have to be put in place to promote cost containment and economic efficiency, while users of infrastructure services need to accept the validity of the public–private arrangements that draw in the resources for infrastructure projects, and feel that they are paying fair prices for the services received. These three factors – legitimacy, credibility and efficiency – were the ones identified by Berg *et al.* (2002) as needed for sustaining public-private collaboration in infrastructure.

The United Nations (2002) and the American Chamber of Commerce (2002), considering PPPs in the European transition economies, emphasized the following:

- an appropriate legislative framework must be enacted;
- government needs to take a leading role;
- public trust has to be established;
- public acceptance is required at the local political level;
- experienced practitioners are needed;
- financing needs have to be met.

All these are important pre-conditions. Since PPP contracts engage many parties and their resources over a long term, there is a need to have support from suitable legislation, firmly embedded in the legal structure of the country. This relates not only to legal Acts but also to any procedures and administrative rules. Private partners want the elimination of any legal ambiguities and expect clear legal statements; public sector partners want an effective tool for PPP implementation. Establishing a framework for long-term public–private cooperation relies on political support from the public side. Political stability is important when bidding costs are so high. Clear public sector policies about PPPs must exist for resolving contractual issues. A constant dialogue needs to take place between public sector and private sector bodies to create a foundation for true partnering between the two sectors. Many countries may be unable to provide this surety of process.

Such factors relate to the general environment for PPP implementation, and underpin the development of a PPP strategy. But in order for emerging market economies to achieve the benefits that PPPs can bring, considerable detailed preparatory work is required. Evidence presented earlier for developed economies suggests that PPPs can bring efficiency gains and cost savings compared with traditional procurement (some other evidence is examined in Grimsey and Lewis, 2004b). But not all PPPs are successful. Like any other project, PPPs must satisfy their own objectives and meet processes ranging from project initiation to contract management. Factors to be considered include project objectives, contract terms, the scope of activities, contract monitoring, performance measurement, risk management, accounting and tax treatment, resourcing, probity and accountability, political policy and public interest tests. A successful PPP is one in which each of these and other relevant factors, along with the inter-relationships between them, are not just addressed, but also solved.

Because PPPs are a relatively new concept in developing nations, and are certainly so in the transition economies, it is useful to draw on the experiences of other countries in their implementation of PPP schemes, identifying weaknesses in their PPP methodologies and considering whether certain solutions used in other countries can be adapted to suit local circumstances. The idea discussed earlier of locking PPPs into a 'green partnership' agenda is one example. In broad terms, what the experience shows is that PPPs can achieve a wide range of objectives and deliver value for money for the public sector, but that the PPP process is more complex than traditional procurement, and requires all parties to understand the issues shaping it. The public sector procurer, for one, needs to be able to negotiate and manage individual project contracts and access the appropriate financial, legal and technical expertise. Creating a mechanism by which PPP expertise can be captured, retained, shared and used within the public sector is invaluable to work out the PPP model best tailored to the public sector's objectives, local requirements, the enabling environment and public acceptability. It is here that a central PPP unit is valuable.

ESTABLISHING A PPP UNIT

A central policy unit or taskforce has underpinned the successful implementation of PPPs in the UK, the Australian states, Ireland and the Netherlands, for example. Five basic ingredients are necessary for a successful PPP programme, and they will need to be considered when structuring a PPP unit.

1. *Political will.* Political will is fundamental to a successful partnership programme. PPPs represent a significant change to traditional public procurement, and a government needs to build political support before introducing a PPP programme.
2. *The right regulatory environment.* The second factor for successful partnernships is creating the right business environment. One of the major risks in infrastructure investment is regulatory risk – the risk that the rules surrounding the regulation of the business will vary from those that applied at the time of investment. There will inevitably be some risks that the private sector firm will be expected to bear in much the same way as it would under traditional contracting, such as health and safety on

construction sites. But for other risks, such as significant changes in environmental legislation, which the private sector finds difficult to manage and price, the government may be better placed to manage the cost impacts.

3. *Process and skills.* The third ingredient to successful partnerships is consistency and clarity of approach, and the ground rules need to be clear and well documented. Yet procedures in themselves are not enough – there must be people in place with the skills who can deliver the projects. PPPs call on capabilities typically in short supply in public sector organizations in emerging markets, such as proficiency in writing output specifications, experience in negotiating the web of contracts that underpin a private finance deal, and familiarity with the wide range of financing products that investment bankers use to bolt the transactions together. The challenge is to inject these skills into the public sector management team.

4. *Value for money.* Essentially, value for money is generated by a contestable market for PPP projects, and requires an environment that will harness innovation and creativity, and make best use of whole-of-life cycle costing techniques and competitively priced risk management.

5. *Projects.* A government looking to implement a PPP programme must not only invest political capital, create the right investment environment, develop appropriate policies and focus on value, it must also ensure that the programme is a success – measured in terms of the number of projects delivered and the outcomes that result.

With these factors in mind, a PPP unit seem likely to be useful in

- signalling government commitment to the approach;
- establishing or clarifying the legality and powers of public authorities to enter into PPP-style contracts (one of the main challenges faced by government in emerging markets is to identify the agency or ministry that has sole negotiating authority for concession projects);
- defining and developing best practice techniques, structuring policy development and providing guidance to project teams;
- refining public expenditure control regimes to accommodate PPPs;
- removing tax anomalies which can weigh against PPP approaches; and
- selecting the right pilot projects.

This last factor, the selection of pilot PPP programmes, is especially important in emerging markets. Identifying those sectors and projects that should take priority helps to reduce the incidence of unsuccessful procurements and avoid wasted bidding costs that would otherwise be incurred. Providing working examples of PPPs rather than theoretical models as early as possible is desirable if the confidence and trust of public sector procurers and private sector bidders are to be established. Given that relevant expertise will typically be scarce at the outset of a programme, focusing the available resources on a small number of representative projects, so that each is well served, is a sensible way to proceed.[5] One such pilot project is considered in the next section.

Finally, it has to be remembered that a PPP is a partnership, involving the sharing of project objectives, risk and responsibilities in a collaborative framework. A central PPP unit can give leadership and direction to a PPP programme, but the PPP has to work too at the ground level. Rondinelli (2002) argues that the success of PPPs depends on mutual trust between government officials and private sector entities, and on public confidence in the integrity of the partnerships. A cooperative approach is required at each stage of PPP implementation. Discussing each party's interest enables them to reach agreements which are best from both public and private parties' perspective, while not forgetting that the aim is to provide society with highest possible quality of services.

A WATER CONCESSION PROJECT

In Chapter 7 we examined a PPP (effectively a BOOT) project involving the design-build-finance-operate of a wastewater treatment facility in Scotland. Here we consider a water project in a transition economy, in this case based around the French-style concession model. We begin by looking at the various forms of private sector involvement in the water and sanitation industry.

Alternative Approaches

Private capital and private sector managerial abilities can help overcome financial and operational weaknesses that exist in water and sewerage services in developing countries and transition economies. Broadly speaking, a number of problems mark the water sector in these countries. First, revenue collected is low and covers only a small portion of the cost of the water. Second, there is a disregard for commercial operational principles and 'user pays' pricing to conserve water use. Third, water loss due to leakages and other wastages is high. Fourth, the publicly owned water supply utilities suffer from high levels of staffing *vis-à-vis* best practice in developed countries. Fifth, and this is particularly so in many developing countries, coverage is often poor so that less wealthy households do not have access to subsidized, piped water and must rely for their supply on expensive private vendors (Haarmeyer and Mody, 1997).

Sometimes the problem is a lack of capital to extend facilities, upgrade

Table 9.2 Alternative approaches to private sector involvement in water and sewerage

Characteristic	O&M contract	Lease contract	BOT concession	Full-utility concession	Asset sale
Time horizon	2–5 years	10 years	10–20 years	20–30 years	In perpetuity
Ownership of facility	Public	Public	Public	Public	Private
Operational responsibility	Private	Private	Private	Private	Private
Investment responsibility	Public	Public	Private	Private	Private
Nature of customer	Government	Retail customer	Government	Retail customer	Retail customer
Revenue stream	Fixed fee for service	Subject to market risk	Contracted payments due after construction	Subject to market risk	Subject to market risk

Source: Adapted from Haarmeyer and Mody (1997).

operations and replace leaky mains. Injections of capital may also be needed to introduce up-to-date methods of treating wastewater and reduce the risks to public health. In many cases, however, the problem is not only, or not even primarily, a shortage of finance but bad management and inefficient operational practices. These are areas in which private sector participation can help, so long as sufficient revenues can be generated to cover operating costs and meet the financial commitments.

Because the problems are multi-faceted there is no one solution that is best for all countries and circumstances. Table 9.2 lists a number of different ways by which private sector involvement in water can be achieved. At one end there is privatization, whereby a private entity takes over by purchasing the entire utility system (including the production, transmission, distribution of the service and collection of tariffs). Alternatively, the utility's various segments can be split up ('unbundled'), with, perhaps, bulk water supply and water and wastewater treatment separated from the distribution to retail customers, and one or both sold off to private entities.

At the other end of the scale, responsibility for the operations and mainte-nance (O & M) of a treatment facility or an entire water or sanitation system may be transferred to a private company under a fixed-fee contract. With a lease arrangement, a private company is given control over operations and revenue collection, but not capital financing. The principal shortcoming of O & M and lease contracts is that they do not assign full commercial risks to the operator. Consequently, private capital investments are not at risk. BOT or BOO contracts are means of shifting the responsibility for financing, building and operating discrete facilities, such as water or wastewater treatment plants, from the government to the private sector. These contracts are particularly attractive for countries with an urgent need to treat water or sewerage but little capital to finance new projects or upgrade existing ones. This was the situation in the Scottish case considered in Chapter 7 where new facilities were needed quickly to bring wastewater treatment systems up to new European standards. Private capital and management can be brought in to build and operate the new facility, without having to reorganize or privatize the whole of the remainder of the network to accommodate it. The same happened in regional South Australia.

Used in this way, a problem with BOOT/BOO arrangements in emerging markets is that they do not address a utility's fundamental operating deficien-cies – leaks in the water distribution system, overstaffing, and low revenue collection – and thus are not vehicles for transforming financially weak water companies into more efficient organizations. For this reason, some countries have taken the step of awarding concessions for operating an entire utility, so bringing in not only private investment but also private management of the whole system. In contrast to projects under BOO/BOOT contracts that sell specific services to a municipal utility, under a full-utility concession all facets of the system, especially distribution to retail consumers, become the private operator's responsibility.

There are also differences between BOOT-type arrangements and full-utility concessions in terms of the financing methods. The financing of BOOT projects rests on the project financing model, which means that before providing debt finance, lenders appraise the new project's ability to generate cash-flow rather than the strength of the sponsor's balance sheet. In the case of a full-utility concession, existing revenue streams (if adequate) can be used immediately to service debt, thereby reducing some construction financing risk. Over time, the concessionaire can benefit from both a steady flow of revenues from a more diversified customer base and perhaps from a diversified asset base as it expands its operations to other areas. Revenues from creating a more robust balance sheet may permit the utility to obtain financing internally as well as from debt markets. Assigning all the commercial risk to the private sector in this manner heightens performance incentives, but a reliable contractual environment is required to attract the private risk capital. This is the challenge to those involved in designing the concession agreement.

Sofia Water Concession Project[6]

The Sofia Water and Wastewater Concession Project is a major municipal infrastructure concession in Bulgaria and one of the first water concessions to be financed on a limited recourse basis in Eastern Europe. Sofia's water system serves a population of some 1.2 million within a clearly defined metropolitan area and was judged to have strong revenue potential. Yet, at the same time, the system and its operator were characterized by a lack of investment, ageing infrastructure, low operating efficiencies, high staffing levels, outdated management techniques, poor capital structure, low revenue collection, and a high level of unaccounted-for-water (this is the difference between net production of water and paid consumption). High rates of unaccounted-for-water reflect leakages and losses, as well as the inability to bill and collect payments.

In financial terms, the project is bringing in at least US$150 million in capital investment over 15 years. It was led by the municipality of Sofia and its clear objective was to mobilize private sector expertise and capital so as to deliver significantly improved levels of water services, meeting EU standards, to consumers. Strong public sector commitment to the project throughout the PPP transaction process was a key factor.

What we have called the development phase, from the start of preparatory studies to financial close in October 2000, took less than 30 months and this is one indication that the whole process was well prepared and efficiently handled. Another indication is that the project has been supported by the

European Bank of Reconstruction and Development (EBRD). Before the launch of the tender process, a range of studies was undertaken to confirm the feasibility of a concession structure. These studies indicated that the final transaction structure would be sufficiently robust to attract the substantial external finance required to meet projected investment needs while still delivering water and wastewater services at a price that would remain affordable to consumers in Sofia. At that time, the municipality created a dedicated Tender Commission empowered to work with its advisers to develop detailed contract documentation and to steer the tender process through to the selection of a preferred bidder.

A multi-stage procurement process was designed to generate strong interest from leading international water operators. In the initial pre-qualification round eight prospective bidders submitted their credentials, then four consortia were invited to participate in the preparation of detailed bids. The tender evaluation process ensured that the price of water was the key decision variable in the selection of the winning bidder, Sofijska Voda AD (International Water Ltd), with a very competitive bid that required a price increase to consumers of only 15 per cent in real terms with no municipal subsidy or guarantees. Following commercial close, Sofijska Voda, the municipality, the EBRD and their advisers worked closely together to resolve a range of technical, commercial and financial conditions. In line with a partnership agenda, care was taken by the municipality's advisory team to preserve the municipality's negotiating position, while fashioning a balanced contract to the longer term benefit of all parties.

Figure 9.2 sets out the structure of the concession transaction. It is based around an SPV, in which majority shareholding (75 per cent) and management control was passed to the private sector operator, ie International Water UUJ (Sofia). The municipality, through its water utility Vodosnabdajavne I Kanalizatsia EAD (ViK), retained a minority shareholding and representation at director and shareholder level. Such an arrangement offered a pragmatic method of meeting political concerns regarding the outsourcing of public services, without overly impeding the winning operator in achieving its contractual obligations and fulfilling its commercial aspirations. EBRD played a major role in the transaction, as a senior lender to Sofijska Voda AD, the operations of which are regulated by a municipal concession monitoring unit. Financing for the capital investment required over the first five years of the 25 year concession is being provided through a 15 year senior debt facility of up to €32 million from the EBRD, with a further €20 million in equity and quasi-equity to be invested by International Water Ltd.

The project has won a number of plaudits, including Best International PPP of the Year (Public Private Finance Awards 2001), Deal of the Year – Central and Eastern Europe (*Privatization International*, January 2001), and Water

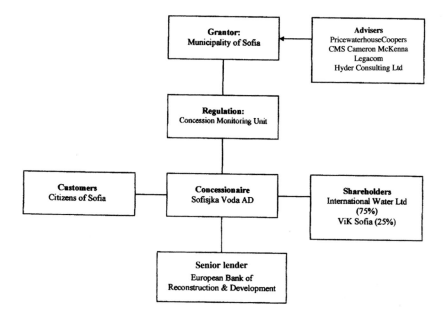

Figure 9.2   Structure of the Sofia water concession

Project of the Year Central and Eastern Europe (*Global Finance*, January 2001). Among the factors that contributed to bringing it to a satisfactory financial closure within a relatively short timespan were clear objectives, municipality commitment to the process, a workable transaction structure, appropriate regulatory framework, a balanced contract, the deal's 'bankability', a transparent procurement process, good data, strong competition between bidders, and structured and phased negotiations.

NOTES

1. Although the conditions are to some degree different in developing countries and transition economies, we will group them together and call them 'emerging markets'.
2. For example Gerrard (1997), Irwin *et al.* (1997), and Asian Development Bank (1998). There is also the World Bank's annual publication *Global Development Finance* (various issues).
3. This section and the next have benefited from Haley (1992), Stewart-Smith (1995), East Asian Analytical Unit (1994, 1998), International Financial Corporation (1999).
4. The rise of institutional investors is examined by the OECD (1998).
5. Developing pilot projects has been part of the successful implementation of PPPs in Ireland (Horner, 1999).
6. The following draws on information supplied by PricewaterhouseCoopers and published in the American Chamber of Commerce (2002).

10. An assessment

CHARACTERISTICS OF PPPS

This volume has examined the role of public private partnerships for infrastructure. Perhaps the most distinctive feature of the partnership mode is its flexibility, and this characteristic can be illustrated in a number of ways. First, the arrangement encompasses a variety of public sector–private sector interactions, such as leasing, franchises, concessions, BOT, BOOT, DBFO, DCMF, and joint ventures. Second, PPPs have been applied to a range of infrastructure categories: 'hard economic' (roads, bridges, railways, telecommunications, etc.); 'hard social' (hospitals, schools, water supply, sewerage, prisons, etc.); 'soft economic' (R & D facilitation, technology transfer); and 'soft social' (community services). Third, partnership-type arrangements operate in countries as diverse as Australia, Bulgaria, Chile, France, Malaysia, the Netherlands, the Philippines, Poland, Portugal, South Africa, the United Kingdom and the United States, to name some examples. PPPs allow for situations where revenues come from tolls and charges on the general public, to ones where the public sector is the customer and procures and pays for the services. The payment schedules build in many service quality and performance incentives. Fifth, if properly structured, a PPP contract is able to take account of new service demands and future monitoring and reporting requirements that may develop over the lifetime of a project.

We have been at pains to argue that while all the different organizational arrangements that come under the rubric 'private public partnership' are ways of engaging the private sector in infrastructure, the degree of 'partnership' involved does differ. A successful partnership is based around commitment, working to common objectives, trust, team building, shared risk, and conflict resolution through openness and problem solving. It is necessarily 'relational' rather than 'transactional'. Nevertheless, there are some common threads through the various approaches, and a PPP tends to have the following characteristics:

- the public sector procurer offers an integrated public project, involving design, construction, maintenance, financing and often operation;
- the public sector focuses on output, that is, the services to be delivered, not the underlying asset;

- services are clearly specified but the method of delivering them is a decision left to the operators;
- alternative methods are appraised to ensure that the best procurement system for a certain project is selected;
- risks are taken by the party which is best equipped to manage such risks;
- transfer of risk is achieved by integrating financing in the agreement; and
- remuneration schedules are based on the quantity and quality of output rather than the delivery of the asset.

One reason for the diversity of partnership forms is that there is not one 'model' of a PPP. Often what is called a PPP is little more than outsourcing. Also, many countries, like France or Spain, have a history of cooperation between the state and private sector, where the government owns assets and private sector utilities operate them under concessions. This may not be a PPP as it is known in the UK or Australia, nevertheless it has worked. Indeed, it is fair to say that the concession is the one enduring PPP model that has stood the test of time. Concession agreements are thus an established model in those countries for drawing private sector managerial skills into infrastructure and these features can be, and have been, exported to other places. One such example was considered as a case study in Chapter 9. Even in the UK, PFI projects can be little more than project finance unless accompanied by imaginative payment mechanisms like those in the prison projects examined in Chapter 5 and the water treatment facility that featured in Chapter 7. A PPP widens the procurement process beyond outsourcing and project finance but there are many grey areas.

In fact, we have argued that, rather than conforming to a model, PPPs should be seen as a process, a systematic way of going about identifying the service needs, defining the outputs expected and the payment mechanism, evaluating and quantifying the financial impacts and the inherent risks, identifying the most appropriate procurement model, developing commercial principles, confirming value for money, overseeing the design process and construction, managing the contract through to handback and monitoring service delivery. If this process is applied rigorously to each contract, then it will inevitably result in a different approach for every project.

INFLUENCES ON PPPs

Another factor creating diversity in the PPP market is that the partnership arrangement has not had a common genesis but the concept has been informed by a number of influences that have operated to varying degrees in different jurisdictions. Among the influences are:

- the 'new public management' agenda that has included the outsourcing, privatization and commercialism of many public services;
- developments in the market for infrastructure as many services regarded as natural monopolies have been opened to market forces by vertical and horizontal 'unbundling'; and
- dissatisfaction with traditional methods of public procurement that have been shown to be marked by extensive cost overruns and revenue shortfalls.

At the same time, there have been a number of developments that have facilitated the evolution of the partnership. Two developments in particular that have been important are:

- the concept of partnering cultivated in the construction industry to overcome the extent of disputes and the adversarial way in which disputes were tackled; and
- the refinement of project financing techniques for 'design and build' and BOT, DBFO approaches to highway construction and similar infrastructure investment by the private sector.

PPPs have been able to draw on, and learn from, these developments so that a fully integrated design, construct, finance and operate approach is now feasible and provides incentives that are desirable. The crucial mind shift is in seeing the PPP as a means of separating the asset from the service it produces. Procurement strategy was driven originally by the need to acquire the asset, but the government really only procured assets in order to get the flow of services from them. Political thinking nowadays places emphasis on the services supplied to the community rather than the asset, and a PPP is about procuring a service. Having available a potential private provider of a capital asset gives public bodies the option to purchase services over time without the need for the prior capital investment.

Historically, large swings have taken place in the involvement of the private sector in infrastructure, which saw private sector initiatives give way to public sector procurement and provision. Private sector provision had a number of problems. Often the sponsors had difficulties in putting together a financial package that would get the venture off the ground. Because of the long time it took to get projects completed, infrastructure investment was vulnerable to changes in technology and regulation. A purely private approach to infrastructure also risked haphazard development of the networks, particularly in transport (duplication of routes, railway 'gauge wars', and different canal widths). Purely public approaches to infrastructure, however, brought their own set of problems: projects bogged down by bureaucracy; political meddling and interference; new and replacement investment starved of funds; and often poor management and maintenance of facilities. A PPP seeks to get the best of both systems, employing private sector innovation and business acumen where appropriate, while allowing overall planning, coordination and regulatory control of the infrastructure networks to reside in public hands.

THE INCENTIVE STRUCTURE

While PPPs are complex arrangements in terms of documentation, financing, taxation, subcontracts, and technical details, the theory underlying them is very simple. It all revolves around incentives. In a world of 'incomplete' contracts, where it is difficult to foresee and contract about uncertain future events, it is important to get the incentive structure right. Any workable incentive scheme is almost certain to be one in which the supplier bears much of the risk, on the grounds that those with money at risk have an incentive to make the best decisions. Shifting risks and responsibilities on to the private contractor under a PPP, while gearing payment only to successful delivery of the services, sends out a powerful message that time and cost overruns and service quality lapses are not to be tolerated and that they put the remuneration system at risk.

Each of the elements of a PPP contract reinforces this message. Shifting the responsibility for design of both the facility and the delivery system on to the private contractor encourages it to choose designs that will work, and to explore innovations that can improve quality and reduce maintenance and operating costs. Giving the responsibility for construction and project management to the private entity creates the incentive for it to keep the project on track and to prevent construction delays and cost overruns. Having the private sector finance the project means that the financiers will look to the security and timeliness of the revenue stream, and put in place controls over the operators that will minimize the risk of project failure. Requiring the private body to operate and maintain the facility, as well as design and construct it, reduces any incentive to skimp on the quality of materials used, while encouraging decisions that maintain services to the desired level and keep costs at a minimum.

As we have said more than once before, it is the fusion of the upfront engineering of the design and the finance with the downstream management of construction and service delivery that gives a PPP its distinctive features from an incentive point of view. Moreover, there is evidence that the private sector does respond to these signals and gets it right more often than not. About 75 per cent of major infrastructure projects in the UK were late and over budget before PPPs came into play. Under PPP/PFI arrangements, 75 per cent of projects are on time and to budget.

SOME CONCERNS ABOUT PPPs

Nevertheless, there are concerns that this return to at least partial private sector financing and operation of infrastructure is, in reality, privatization through the back door. In fact, this is not the case at all. With privatization, the ownership, management, financing, operation, indeed all aspects of the facility, are handed over to the private sector in perpetuity. With a PPP, ownership eventually returns to the public sector, at least in almost all cases. Moreover, the public sector retains a substantial role in the projects, either as the main purchaser of services or as an essential enabler of, and partner in, the project. While the public sector does not own an asset, such as a PPP-built hospital or school, it pays the contractor a stream of committed revenue payments for the use of facilities over the contract period. Once the contract has expired, ownership of the asset either remains with the private sector contractor (under a BOO arrangement), or is returned to the public sector (with almost all other contracts). The public sector monitors the project to ensure that the services specified are delivered to an appropriate standard, and guarantees that the facility to be returned to public sector ownership is properly managed and maintained.

Concerns have also been voiced as to whether private sector participation in infrastructure will dilute accountability and erode the public interest. In reality, we argue that the reverse is true. PPPs offer an opportunity to expand the level of public interest protection. The traditional system of public sector accountability relies on political accountability via a chain of relationships through which authority flows from citizens to MPs, MPs to ministers, ministers to civil servants, and civil servants to service providers. Too often in practice this line was blurred, administrative coordination was flawed, and decisions were made in secret and were not disclosed. The framework of a PPP relies instead on a transparent and open process of consultation with affected parties in which there are many points at which public interest concerns can be aired and resolved.

Partnerships are not, and probably never will be, the dominant method of infrastructure acquisition. They are too complex, and costly, for many small projects, and constitute 'using a sledgehammer to crack a nut'. In some cases, they may be beyond the capacity of the public sector agency to implement and manage. For other projects the tight specification of the outputs required may be difficult to detail for an extended period. Nonetheless, we are confident that PPPs will continue to be an important component of infrastructure policy.

Competition holds the key. As George Stigler (1968) once remarked, 'competition may be the spice of life, but in economics it is more nearly the main dish' (p. 181). Competitive bidding between private enterprises for the financing, construction and operation of infrastructure facilitates the choice of the most efficient solution for market development and project risk. Private financing stimulates development of innovative and incentive-compatible payment mechanisms. Efficient private financing rests on competition between potential operators and keeps a lid on costs. Partnerships provide a framework in which these competitive processes are enacted.

On this basis, partnerships seem likely to be appropriate if:

- service outcomes can be clearly specified and measured;
- there exists the potential, and the incentives to introduce, design innovations and operational changes that can raise efficiency;
- payment mechanisms are devised that give the operators the motivation to maintain service quality;.
- value for money is able to be demonstrated, after allowing for costs of project development and costs of monitoring the contract;
- an integrated service can be provided with close working relationships and good communication between service providers; and
- there are transparent accountability procedures and a due regard for the public interest.

Ironically, perhaps one of the chief benefits of a PPP agenda is to inform conventional procurement policies. Judged by past performance, there would seem to be much to improve. Clearly articulated objectives, better appraisal techniques and the formulation of a more refined business case within the public sector can be seen as 'spin-offs' from a well-developed partnership approach. Whatever the method of procurement, the key objective of an infrastructure programme is to meet the public's social and economic requirements in a cost-effective manner. It is on these grounds that partnerships have a place. A PPP has an in-built incentive system to bring about this objective by injecting the discipline and motivation of the marketplace into infrastructure investment policies.

References

Abdel-Aziz, A. M. and A. D. Russell (2001), 'A Structure for Government Requirements in Public–Private Partnerships', *Canadian Journal of Civil Engineering*, 28, 891–909.

Alchian, A. A. (1965), 'Some Economics of Property Rights', *Il Politico*, 30, 816.

Allen Consulting Group (2003), *Funding Urban Public Infrastructure – Approaches Compared*, Melbourne: The Allen Consulting Group.

Allen, G. (2001), *The Private Finance Initiative (PFI)*, House of Commons Research Paper 01/117, December, London: House of Commons Library.

American Chamber of Commerce (2002), *Public–Private Partnership as a Tool to Develop Infrastructure in Poland*, White Paper, Warsaw: American Chamber of Commerce in Poland.

Andrews, C. (2000), *Contracted and Publicly-managed Prisons: Cost and Staffing Comparisons 1997–98*, London: HM Prison Service.

Argy, F., M. Lindfield, B. Stimson and P. Hollingsworth (1999), *Infrastructure and Economic Development*, CEDA Information Paper No 60, Melbourne: Committee for Economic Development of Australia.

Arndt, R. H. (1998), 'Risk Allocation in the Melbourne City Link Project', *The Journal of Project Finance*, Fall, 11–24.

Arrow, K. J. (1965), *Aspects of the Theory of Risk-bearing*, Helsinki: Yrjo Jahnsson Saatio.

Arrow, K. J. and R. C. Lind (1970), 'Uncertainty and the Evaluation of Public Investment Decisions', *American Economic Review*, 60, 364–78.

Arthur Andersen (2000), *Value for Money Drivers in the Private Finance Initiative*, London: Arthur Andersen and Enterprise LSE.

Aschauer, D. A. (1989), 'Is Public Expenditure Productive?' *Journal of Monetary Economics*, 23(2), 177–200.

Aschauer, D. A. (1995), *Infrastructure and Macro-economic Performance: Direct and Indirect Effects, Investment, Productivity and Employment*, Paris: OECD.

Aschauer, D. A. (2001), 'Output and Employment Effects of Public Capital', in *Public Finance and Management, Symposium on Public Capital*, from http://www.spaef. com/PFM_PUB/v1n2.html.

Ashton, T. S. (1955), *An Economic History of England. The 18th Century*, London: Methuen.

Asian Development Bank (1998), *Governance and Regulatory Regimes for Private Sector Infrastructure Development*, prepared by National Economic Research Associates, Manila.

Audit Commission (2001), *Building for the Future – The Management of Procurement under the Private Finance Initiative*, Audit Commission Management Paper, London: Audit Commission Publications.

Barker, T. (1990), *Moving Millions – A Pictorial History of London Transport*, Aylesbury: BPCC Hazell Books Ltd.

Barnekov, T., R. Boyle and D. Rich (1989), *Privatism and Urban Policy in Britain and the United States*, Oxford: Oxford University Press.

Beauregard, R. A. (1998), 'Public–Private Partnerships as Historical Chameleons: The Case of the United States', in J. Pierre (ed.), *Partnerships in Urban Governance – European and American Experience*, New York: St Martins Press.

Behn, R. D. (2001), *Rethinking Democratic Accountability*, Washington, DC: Brookings Institution.

Bentick, B. L. and M. K. Lewis (2004), 'Real Estate Speculation as a Source of Banking and Currency Instability: Some Different Lessons from the Asian Crisis', *The Economics and Labour Relations Review*, 14(2): 256–75.

Berg, S. V., M. G. Pollitt and M. Tsuji (2002), *Private Initiatives in Infrastructure*, Cheltenham: Edward Elgar.

Bernardo, J. and A. F. M. Smith (2000), *Bayesian Theory*, New York: Wiley.

Blatt, J. M. (1983), *Dynamic Economic Systems*, New York: Sharpe.

Blum, J. M., B. Catton, E. S. Morgan, A. M. Schlesiner Jr, K. M. Stampp and C. V. Woodward (1963), *The American Experience*, London: Rupert Hart-Davis.

Brealey, R., I. A. Cooper and M. A. Habib (1997), 'Investment Appraisal in the Public Sector', *Oxford Review of Economic Policy*, 13(4), 12–78.

Brealey, R. and S. Myers (2003), *Principles of Corporate Finance*, 7th edn, Boston: Irwin McGraw-Hill.

Briggs, A. (1959), *The Age of Improvement 1783–1867*, London: Longmans.

Broadbent, J. and R. Laughlin (2003), 'Public Private Partnerships: An Introduction', *Accounting, Auditing & Accountability Journal*, 16(3), 332–511.

Brown R. (ed.) (1905), *A History of Accounting and Accountants*, Edinburgh: TC and EC Jack.

Brown R. G. (1962), 'Changing Audit Objectives and Techniques', *The Accounting Review*, October, 696–703.

Bruzelius, N., B. Flyvbjerg and W. Rothengatter (1998), 'Big Decisions, Big Risks: Improving Accountability in Mega Projects', *International Review of Administrative Services*, 64, 423–40.

Buchanan, J. M. and G. Tullock (1962), *The Calculus of Consent, Logical Foundations of a Constitutional Democracy*, Ann Arbor: University of Michigan Press.

Campbell, D. and D. Harris (1993), 'Flexibility in Long-term Contractual Relationships: The Role of Co-operation', *Journal of Law and Society*, 20(2), 166–91.

Casson, M. (2000a), *Enterprise and Leadership*, Cheltenham: Edward Elgar.

Casson, M. (2000b), *Economics of International Business – A New Research Agenda*, Cheltenham: Edward Elgar.

Chandler, A. D. Jr (1990), *Scale and Scope – The Dynamics of Industrial Capitalism*, Cambridge, MA. Harvard University Press.

Chapman, C. B. and S. C. Ward (1997), *Project Risk Management – Processes, Techniques and Insights*, Chichester: John Wiley and Sons.

Commission on Public Private Partnerships (2001), *Building Better Partnerships*, London: Institute for Public Policy Research.

Copeland, T. E. and J. F. Weston (1988), *Financial Theory and Corporate Policy*, 3rd edn, New York: Addison Wesley.

Cossons, A. (1934), *The Turnpike Roads of Nottinghamshire*, Historical Association Leaflet, No. 97, London: G. Bell and Sons Ltd.

Court, W. H. B. (1962), *A Concise Economic History of Britain. From 1750 to Recent Times*, Cambridge: Cambridge University Press.

Crowley, L.G. and M. A. Karim (1995), 'Conceptual Model of Partnering', *Journal of Management in Engineering*, Sept/Oct, 33–9.

D & P (2001), *European PPP Survey 2001*, May, Brussels, D & P Secretariat.

Daniels, R. J. and M. J. Trebilcock (1996), 'Private Provision of Public Infrastructure: An Organizational Analysis of the Next Privatization Frontier', *University of Toronto Law Journal*, 46, 375–425.

Demsetz, H. (1968), 'Why Regulate Utilities?', *Journal of Law and Economics*, 11, 55–65.

Department of Treasury and Finance (2003), *Financial Report of the State of Victoria 2002–03*, Melbourne.

Dixit, A. K. and R. S. Pindyck (1995), 'The Options Approach to Capital Investment', *Harvard Business Review*, 73(3), 105–16.

Domberger, S. and P. Jensen (1997), 'Contracting Out by the Public Sector: Theory, Evidence, Prospects', *Oxford Review of Economic Policy*, 13(4), 67–78.

Domberger, S. and S. Rimmer (1994), 'Competitive Tendering and Contracting in the Public Sector: A Survey', *International Journal of the Economics of Business*, 1(3), 439–53.

Drucker, P. (1984), *Innovation and Entrepreneurship*, New York: Harper Collins.

East Asia Analytical Unit (1994), *Tapping into China's Transport*

Infrastructure Market, Working Paper Series No. 4, Canberra: Department of Foreign Affairs and Trade.

East Asia Analytical Unit (1998), *Asia's Infrastructure in the Crisis, Harnessing Private Enterprise*, Canberra: Department of Foreign Affairs and Trade.

Engel, E., R. Fischer and A. Galetovic (1999), 'The Chilean Infrastructure Concessions Program – Evaluation, Lessons and Prospects for the Future', Universidad de Chile, Center for Applied Economics (CEA), Discussion Paper No. 60 (September).

Engel, E., R. Fischer and A. Galetovic (2001), 'Least-Present-Value-of-Revenue Auctions and Highway Franchising', *Journal of Political Economy*, 109(5), 993–1020.

Estache, A., M. Romero and J. Strong (2000), *The Long and Winding Path to Private Financing and Regulation of Toll Roads*, World Bank Institute Policy Research Working Paper 2387, Washington, DC: World Bank.

European Commission (1995), *Structural Funds and Cohesion Fund, 1994–99*, Brussels: European Commission.

European Investment Bank (2004), 'The EIB and PPPs', EIB Information, No 116, 22–34.

Fender, I., M. S. Gibson and P. C. Mosser (2001), 'An International Survey of Stress Tests', *Current Issues in Economics and Finance*, 7(10).

FitzGerald, J. (2003), 'Public Investment and the Irish Economy', *Irish Banking Review*, Spring, 17–31.

Fitzgerald, P. (2004), *Review of Partnerships Victoria Provided Infrastructure*, Melbourne: Review of Partnerships Victoria.

Flemming, J. and C. Mayer (1997), 'The Assessment: Public-sector Investment', *Oxford Review of Economic Policy*, 13(4), 1–11.

Flyvbjerg, B., N. Bruzelius and W. Rothengatter (2003), *Megaprojects and Risk: An Anatomy of Ambition*, Cambridge: Cambridge University Press.

Flyvbjerg, B., M. S. Holm and S. Buhl (2002), 'Underestimating Costs in Public Works Projects – Error or Lie?', *Journal of the American Planning Association*, 68(3), 279–95.

Fouracre, P. R., R. J. Allport and J. M. Thomson (1990), *The Performance and Impact of Rail Mass Transit in Developing Countries* (TRRL Research Report 278), Crowthorne: Transport and Road Research Laboratory.

Friedman, M. (1962), *Capitalism and Freedom*, Chicago: The University of Chicago Press.

Gallagher, D. and M. E. Edwards (1997), 'Prison Industries and the Private Sector', *Atlantic Economic Journal*, 25, 91–8.

Gerrard, M. (1997), *Financing Pakistan's Hub Power Project: A Review of Experience for Future Projects*, Washington: World Bank.

Gilibert, P. L. and A. Steinherr (1994), 'Private Finance for Public Infrastructures: In Search of a New Framework', *EIB Papers*, 23, 77–90.

Girard, J., H. Gruber and C. Hurst (1994), 'A Discussion of the Role of Public Investment in Economic Growth', *EIB Papers*, 23, 13–19.

Goddard, S. (1994), *Getting There: The Epic Struggle Between Road and Rail in the American Century*, New York: Basic Books.

Gramlich, E. M. (1994), 'Infrastructure Investment: A Review Essay', *Journal of Economic Literature*, 32(3), 1176–96.

Gray, J. (1989), *Limited Government: A Positive Agenda*, London: Institute of Economic Affairs.

Grimsey, D. and R. Graham (1997), 'PFI in the NHS', *Engineering, Construction and Architectural Management*, 4(3), 215–31.

Grimsey, D. and M. K. Lewis, (1999), *Risk Analysis in Public Sector/Private Sector Infrastructure Arrangements*, Stockholm: The Third International Stockholm Seminar on Risk Behaviour and Risk Management.

Grimsey, D. and M. K. Lewis (2002a), 'Evaluating the Risks of Public Private Partnerships for Infrastructure Projects', *International Journal of Project Management*, 20(2), 107–18.

Grimsey, D. and M. K. Lewis (2002b), 'Accounting for Public–Private Partnerships', *Accounting Forum*, 26(3), 245–70.

Grimsey, D. and M. K. Lewis (2004a), 'The Governance of Contractual Relationships in Public Private Partnerships', *Journal of Corporate Citizenship*, Issue 15, Autumn, 91–109.

Grimsey, D. and M. K. Lewis (eds) (2004b), *The Economics of Public Private Partnerships*, Cheltenham, Edward Elgar (forthcoming).

Grout, P. (1997), 'The Economics of the Private Finance Initiative', *Oxford Review of Economic Policy*, 13(4), 53–66.

Grout, P. A. (2003), 'Public and Private Sector Discount Rates in Public–Private Partnerships', *Economic Journal*, 113(486), C62–C68.

Gruber, H. (1994), 'A Brief Survey of Growth Theory', *EIB Papers*, 23, 21–37.

Haarmeyer, D. and A. Mody (1997), 'Private Capital in Water and Sanitation', *Finance & Development*, 34(1), 34–7.

Haley, G. (1992), 'Private Finance for Transportation and Infrastructure Projects: A View', *International Journal of Project Management*, 10(2), 63–8.

Harding, A. (1998), 'Public–Private Partnerships in the UK', in J. Pierre (ed.), *Partnerships in Urban Governance – European and American Experience*, New York: St Martins Press.

Hart, O. (2003), 'Incomplete Contracts and Public Ownership: Remarks, and an Application to Public–Private Partnerships', *Economic Journal*, 113(486), C69–C76.

Heald, D. (2003), 'Value for Money Tests and Accounting Treatment in PFI Schemes', *Accounting, Auditing and Accountability Journal*, 16(3), 342–71.

Hellard, R. B. (1995), *Project Partnering Principle and Practice*, London: Thomas Telford.

Hieronymi, O. (1993), 'Decision-making for Infrastructure: Environmental and Planning Issues', in *Infrastructure Policies for the 1990s*, Paris: OECD.

Hirschleifer, J. (1970), *Investment, Interest and Capital*, Englewood Cliffs, NJ: Prentice Hall.

Hirschleifer, J. and J. Riley (1992), *The Analytics of Uncertainty and Information*, Cambridge: Cambridge University Press.

Hirschman, A. O. (1958), *The Strategy of Economic Development*, New Haven: Yale University Press.

HM Treasury (2003a), *The Green Book – Appraisal and Evaluation in Central Government*, London: TSO.

HM Treasury (2003b), *PFI: Meeting the Investment Challenge*, Norwich: HMSO.

Hodgson, G. J. (1995), 'Design and Build – Effects of Contractor Design on Highway Schemes', *Proc Civil Engineers*, 108, 64–76.

Hood, C. (1995), 'The "New Public Management" in the 1980s: Variations on a Theme', *Accounting, Organizations & Society*, 20(2/3), 93–109.

Horner, R. (1999), 'Public Private Partnerships, The Way Forward', *Irish Banking Review*, Summer, 25–34.

Hurdle, D. (1992), 'Does Transport Investment Stimulate Economic Activity?', *The Planner*, 78(9), 7–9.

Hurst, C. (1994), 'Infrastructure and Growth: A Literature Review', *EIB Papers*, 23, 57–76.

International Finance Corporation (1999), *Project Finance in Developing Countries*, Washington: World Bank.

Irwin, T., M. Klein, G. E. Perry and M. Thobani (eds) (1997), *Dealing with Public Risk in Private Infrastructure*, Washington: World Bank.

Jacobs, B. (1997), 'Networks, Partnerships and European Union Regional Economic Development Initiatives in the West Midlands', *Policy and Politics*, 25(1), 39–50.

Kagami, M. (2002), 'The Third Sector's Failure in Japan', in S. V. Berg, M. G. Pollitt and M. Tsuji (eds) *Private Initiatives in Infrastructure – Priorities, Incentives and Performance*, Cheltenham: Edward Elgar.

Karni, E. (1985), *Decision Making Under Uncertainty: The Case of State Dependent Preferences*, Cambridge, MA: Harvard University Press.

Kay, J. (1993), 'Efficiency and Private Capital in the Provision of Infrastructure', in *Infrastructure Policies for the 1990s*, Paris: Organisation for Economic Co-operation and Development, 55–73.

Keating, M. (1998), 'Commentary: Public–Private Partnerships in the United States from a European Perspective', in J. Pierre (ed.), *Partnerships in*

Urban Governance – European and American Experience, New York: St Martins Press.

Kelly, G. (2000), *The New Partnership Agenda*, London: Institute for Public Policy Research.

Kelsey, D. and J. Quiggin (1992), 'Theories of Choice Under Ignorance and Uncertainty', *Journal of Economic Surveys*, 6, 133–53.

Kerzner, H. (1989), *Project Management, A Systems Approach to Planning, Scheduling and Controlling*, 3rd edn, New York: Van Nostrand Reinhold.

Keynes, J. M. (1936), *The General Theory of Employment, Interest and Money*, London: Macmillan.

Kindleberger, C. P. (1974), 'The Formation of Financial Centres: A Study in Comparative Economic History', *Princeton Studies in International Finance*, 36, November.

Kirby, P. (2000), *Report of the Independent Investigation into the Management and Operations of Victoria's Private Prisons*, Melbourne: State of Victoria.

Kirman, A. P. and M. Salmon (eds) (1995), *Learning and Rationality in Economics*, Oxford: Blackwell.

Klein, M. (1997), 'The Risk Premium for Evaluating Public Projects', *Oxford Review of Economic Policy*, 13(4), 29–42.

Knight, F. (1921), *Risk, Uncertainty and Profit*, Boston: Houghton Mifflin.

Lal, Deepak (1999), *Unintended Consequences: The Impact of Factor Endowments, Culture, and Politics on Long-run Economic Performance*, Cambridge, MA: MIT Press.

LeRoy, S. F. and L. D. Singell (1987), 'Knight on Risk and Uncertainty', *Journal of Political Economy*, 95, 394–406.

Lessard, D. and R. Miller (2001), 'Understanding and Managing Risks in Large Engineering Projects', Sloan Working Paper 4214–01, Cambridge, MA: MIT Sloan School of Management.

Levinson, D. (2002), *Financing Transportation Networks*, Cheltenham: Edward Elgar.

Lewis, M. K. (1992), 'Off-the-Balance-Sheet Activities', in P. Newman, M. Milgate, and J. Eatwell (eds), *The New Palgrave Dictionary of Money and Finance*, vol 3, London: Macmillan, pp. 67–72.

Lewis, M. K. (1994), 'Banking on Real Estate', in D. E. Fair and R. Raymond (eds), *The Competitiveness of Financial Institutions and Centres in Europe*, Dordrecht: Kluwer.

Lewis, M. K. (2003), 'Towards the Networked Firm and the End of Geography', in M. Shanahan and G. Treuren (eds), *Globalisation: Australian Regional Perspectives*, Adelaide: Wakefield Press.

Lewis, M. K. and K. T. Davis (1987), *Domestic and International Banking*, Oxford: Philip Allan.

Lewis, M. K. and P. D. Mizen (2000), *Monetary Economics*, Oxford: Oxford University Press.

Lignieres, P. (2002), *Public Private Partnerships: The Other 'French Paradox'*, Paris: Landwell and Associates.

Linder, S. H. (1999), 'Coming to Terms With the Public–Private Partnership', *American Behavioral Scientist*, 43(1), 35–51.

Linder, S. H. (2000), 'Coming to Terms With the Public–Private Partnership – A Grammar of Multiple Meanings', in P. V. Rosenau (ed.), *Public Private Policy Partnerships*, Cambridge, MA: MIT Press.

Linder, S. H. and P. V. Rosenau (2000), 'Mapping the Terrain of the Public–Private Policy Partnership', in P. V. Rosenau (ed.), *Public Private Policy Partnerships*, Cambridge, MA: MIT Press.

Lindley, D. (1985), *Making Decisions*, 2nd edn, London: John Wiley and Sons Ltd.

Linklaters & Alliance (2001), 'PPP in the Netherlands', Linklaters & Alliance, Amsterdam, April.

Lockwood, S. C. (1995), 'Public–Private Partnerships in U.S. Highway Finance: ISTEA and Beyond', *Transportation Quarterly*, 49(1), 5–26.

Lockwood, S. C., R. Verma and M. Schneider (2000), 'Public–Private Partnerships in Toll Road Development: An Overview of Global Practices', *Transportation Quarterly*, 54(2), 77–91.

McDonald, D. C. (1990), 'The Cost of Operating Public and Private Correctional Facilities', in D. C. McDonald (ed.), *Private Prisons and the Public Interest*, New Brunswick, NJ: Rutgers University Press.

Machina, M. (1987), *The Economic Theory of Individual Behaviour Toward Risk: Theory, Evidence and New Directions*, Cambridge: Cambridge University Press.

Mackie, P. and J. Preston (1998), 'Twenty-one Sources of Error and Bias in Transport Project Appraisal', *Transport Policy*, 5, 1–7.

Macniel, I. R. (1974), 'The Many Futures of Contracts', *S Cal Law Rev*, 47, 691–716.

Manning, N. (2002), 'The New Public Management in Developing Countries', in C. Kirkpatrick, R. Clarke and C. Polidano (eds), *Handbook on Development Policy and Management*, Cheltenham: Edward Elgar.

Marglin, S. A. (1967), *Public Investment Criteria*, London: Allen and Unwin.

Martini, C. A. and D. Q. Lee (1996), 'Difficulties in Infrastructure Financing', *Journal of Applied Finance and Investment*, 1(1), 24–7.

Mayston, D. J. (1999), 'The Private Finance Initiative in the National Health Service: An Unhealthy Development in New Public Management?', *Financial Accountability & Management*, 15(3&4), 249–74.

Merna, A. and N. J. Smith (1996), *Privately Financed Concession Contract*, 2nd edn, vols 1 & 2, Hong Kong: Asia Law and Practice.

Milbourne, R., G. Otto and G. Voss (2001), *Public Investment and Economic Growth*, from http://web.uvic.ca/~gvoss.

Miller, R. and D. Lessard (2001), *The Strategic Management of Large Engineering Projects: Shaping Risks, Institutions and Governance*, Cambridge, MA: MIT Press.

Mishan, E. J. (1971), *Cost–Benefit Analysis*, London: Allen and Unwin.

Mott MacDonald (2002), *Review of Large Public Procurement in the UK*, London: HM Treasury.

Mountfield, D. (1976), *The Coaching Age*, London: Robert Hale.

Munnell, A. H. (1992), 'Infrastructure Investment and Economic Growth', *Journal of Economic Perspectives*, 6(4), 189–98.

Musgrave, R. A. (1959), *The Theory of Public Finance – A Study in Public Economy*, New York: McGraw Hill.

National Audit Office (1997), *The PFI Contracts for Bridgend and Fazakerley Prisons*, HC 253 Session 1997–98, 31 October 1997, London: HMSO.

National Audit Office (1998), *The Private Finance Initiative: The First Four, Design, Build, Finance and Operate Roads Contracts*, HC 476, Parliamentary Session 1997–98, London: HMSO.

National Audit Office (2000), *The Refinancing of the Fazakerley PFI*, HC 584 Session, 1999–2000, London: HMSO.

National Audit Office (2001), *Managing the Relationship to Secure a Successful Partnership in PFI Projects*, HC 375 Session 2001/2002, London: HMSO.

National Audit Office (2002), *The PFI Contract for the Redevelopment of West Middlesex University Hospital*, HC 49 Session 2002–03, London: HMSO.

National Audit Office (2003), *PFI: Construction Performance*, Report by the Comptroller and Auditor General, London: HMSO.

North, D. C. (1990), *Institutions, Institutional Change and Economic Performance*, Cambridge, MA: Cambridge University Press.

OECD (1993), 'Foreword', in *Infrastructure Policies for the 1990s*, Paris: OECD.

OECD (1998), *Institutional Investors in the New Financial Landscape*, Paris: Organisation for Economic Co-operation and Development.

Office of Government Commerce (2002a), *Dispute Resolution Guide*, Norwich: OGC.

Office of Government Commerce (2002b), *Green Public Private Partnerships*, Norwich: OGC.

Officer, R. R. (2003), 'The Respective Roles of Government and the Private Sector and Private/Public Partnerships', *Public Private Partnerships Forum*, The Accounting Foundation, The University of Sydney, 8 December.

Parkinson, M. (1981), *The Effect of Road Investment on Economic*

Development in the UK, Government Economic Service Working Paper No. 43, London: Department of Transport.

Partnerships Victoria (2001), *Guidance Material*, Melbourne: Department of Treasury and Finance.

Partnerships Victoria (2003), *Use of Discount Rates in the Partnerships Victoria Process – Technical Note*, Melbourne: Department of Treasury and Finance.

Peters, B. G. (1998), 'With a Little Help from Our Friends: Public–Private Partnerships as Institutions and Instruments', in J. Pierre (ed.), *Partnerships in Urban Governance: European and American Experience*, Basingstoke: MacMillan.

Pickrell, D. H. (1990), *Urban Rail Transit Projects: Forecast versus Actual Ridership and Cost*, Washington, DC: US Department of Transportation.

Pierson, G. and P. McBride (1996), 'Public/Private Sector Infrastructure Arrangements', *CPA Communique*, 73, 1–4.

Pollitt, M. G. (2002), 'The Declining Role of the State in Infrastructure Investments in the UK', in S. V. Berg, M.G. Pollitt and M. Tsuji (eds), *Private Initiatives in Infrastructure – Priorities, Incentives and Performance*, Cheltenham: Edward Elgar.

Pollock A.M. (2000), 'PFI is Bad for your Health', *Public Finance*, 6 October, 30–1.

Pollock, A. M., M. Dunnigan, D. Gaffney, A. Macfarlane and F. Azeem Majeed (1997), 'What Happens when the Private Sector Plans Hospital Services for the NHS: Three Case Studies under the Private Finance Initiative', *British Medical Journal*, 314, 1266–71.

PricewaterhouseCoopers (2002), *Study into Rates of Return Bid on PFI Projects*, London: Office of Government Commerce.

Productivity Commission (2001), *Review of the National Access Regime*, Report No. 17, Canberra: AusInfo.

Quiggin, J. (2003), 'Risk, PPPs and the Public Comparator', *Public Private Partnerships Forum*, The Accounting Foundation, The University of Sydney, 8 December.

Report of the Auditor General (1997), *Report of the Auditor General on the Statement of Financial Operations, 1996–1997*, Melbourne: Auditor General of Victoria.

Ribault, A. (2001), 'Lessons from the French Experience in Public and Private Partnership', *Irish Banking Review*, Spring, 49–60.

Rodrik, D. (2003), 'Institutions, Integration and Geography. In Search of the Deep Determinants of Economic Growth', in D. Rodrik (ed.), *In Search of Prosperity: Analytic Country Studies on Growth*, Princeton, NJ: Princeton University Press.

Rondinelli, D. (2002), 'Public–Private Partnerships', in C. Kirkpatrick, R.

Clarke and C. Polidano, *Handbook on Development Policy and Management*, Cheltenham: Edward Elgar.

Ross, S., R. Thompson, W. Westerfield and B. D. Jordan (2002), *Fundamentals of Corporate Finance*, 6th edn, New York: McGraw-Hill.

Runde, J. (1995), 'Risk, Uncertainty and Bayesian Decision Theory: A Keynesian View', in S. Dow and J. Hillard (eds), *Keynes, Knowledge and Uncertainty*, Aldershot: Edward Elgar.

Sappington, D. E. M. (1991), 'Incentives in Principal–Agent Relationships', *Journal of Economic Perspectives*, 5, 45–66.

Schneider, A. L. (2000), 'Public–Private Partnerships in the US Prison System', in P. V. Rosenau (ed.), *Public–Private Policy Partnerships*, Cambridge, MA: MIT Press.

Seldon, A. (1990), *Capitalism*, Oxford: Basil Blackwell.

Shackle, G. L. S. (1955), *Uncertainty in Economics and other Reflections*, Cambridge: Cambridge University Press.

Small, K. A., C. Winston and C. A. Evans (1989), *Road Work: A New Highway Pricing and Investment Policy*, Washington: Brookings Institution.

Smith, A. J. (1999), *Privatized Infrastructure: The Role of Government*, London: Thomas Telford.

Smith, R. C. and I. Walter (1990), *Global Financial Services*, New York: Harper Business.

Starr, Paul (1988), 'The Meaning of Privatization', *Yale Law and Policy Review*, 6, 6–41.

Stern, N. H. and H. P. Lankes (1998), 'Making the most of markets: The role of IFIs', *EIB Papers*, 3(2), 103–14.

Stewart-Smith, M. (1995), 'Private Financing and Infrastructure Provision in Emerging Markets', *Law and Policy in International Business*, 26(4), 987–1011.

Stigler, G. (1968), 'Competition', *International Encyclopedia of the Social Sciences*, London: Macmillan.

Stoker, G. (1998), 'Public–Private Partnerships and Urban Governance', in J. Pierre (ed.), *Partnerships in Urban Governance: European and American Experience*, Basingstoke: MacMillan.

Stone, W. E. (1969), 'Antecedents of the Accounting Profession', *The Accounting Review*, April, 284–91.

Taylor, R. and S. Blair (2002), 'Public Hospitals – Options for Reform through Public–Private Partnerships', Note Number 241, The World Bank Group Private Sector and Infrastructure Network, Washington, DC.

Taylor, S. (ed.) (2001), *The Moving Metropolis. A History of London's Transport Since 1800*, London: Laurence King Publishing.

Thobani, M. (1998), 'Private Infrastructure, Public Risk', *Finance and Development*, 36(1), 50–3.

Thomas, C. W. (2003), 'Private Adult Correctional Facility Census – A "Real-Time" Statistical Profile', http://www.crim.ufl.edu/pcp/census/2001.

Threadgold, A. (1996), 'Private Financing of Infrastructure and Other Long-term Capital Projects', *Journal of Applied Finance and Investment*, 1(1), 7–12.

Treasury Committee (1996), *The Private Finance Initiative*, HC 146 1995/1996, London: HMSO.

Treasury Taskforce (1998), *Public Sector Comparators and Value for Money*, Policy Statement No. 2 (February), London: HMSO.

Treasury Taskforce (1999), *How to Account for PFI Transactions*, PFI Technical Note No. 1 (June), London: HMSO.

Trujillo, A., R. Cohen, X. Freixas and R. Sheehy (1998), 'Infrastructure Financing with Unbundled Mechanisms', *The Financier*, 5(4), 10–27.

Uher, T. E. and A. R. Toakley (1997), *Risk Management and the Conceptual Phase of the Project Development Cycle*, Sydney: University of New South Wales.

United Nations (2002), 'A Review of Public–Private Partnerships for Infrastructure Development in Europe', Economic Commission for Europe, Working Party on International Legal and Commercial Practice, 11–13 March.

United States Government (1958), *Proposed Practices for Economic Analyses of River Basin Projects (Green Book)*, Federal Inter-Agency River Basin Committee, Subcommittee on Benefits and Costs, Washington.

von Hirschhausen, C. (2002), *Modernizing Infrastructure in Transformation Economies*, Cheltenham: Edward Elgar.

Walker B. and B. C. Walker (2000), *Privatisation: Sell Off or Sell Out? The Australian Experience*, Sydney: ABC Books.

Watson, D. (2003), 'The Rise and Rise of Public Private Partnerships: Challenges for Public Accountability', *Public Private Partnerships Forum*, The Accounting Foundation, The University of Sydney, 8 December.

Whittington, G. (1992), 'Accounting and Finance', in P. Newman, M. Milgate and J. Eatwell (eds), *The New Palgrave Dictionary of Money and Finance*, London: Macmillan, vol 1, pp. 6–10.

Williamson, O. E. (1996), *The Mechanisms of Governance*, Oxford: Oxford University Press.

Wilson, R. A., A. D. Songer and J. Diekmann (1995) 'Partnering: More than a Workshop, a Catalyst for Change', *Journal of Management in Engineering*, Sept/Oct, 40–5.

World Bank (1994), *World Development Report 1994: Infrastructure for Development*, New York: Oxford University Press.

World Bank (1997), *Toolkits for Private Sector Participation in Water and Sanitation*, Washington: World Bank.

Yeaple, S. and S. Golub (2002), *International Productivity Differences, Infrastructure, and Comparative Advantage*, from http://www.econ. yale.edu/seminar/trade/tdw02/yeaple–021216.pdf.

Index